american literary minimalism

american literary minimalism

ROBERT C. CLARK

THE UNIVERSITY OF ALABAMA PRESS
TUSCALOOSA

The University of Alabama Press
Tuscaloosa, Alabama 35487-0380
uapress.ua.edu

Parts of this book were previously published in "Keeping the Reader in the House: American Minimalism, Literary Impressionism, and Raymond Carver's 'Cathedral,'" *Journal of Modern Literature* 36, no. 1 (2012). © Indiana University Press, 2012.
Typeface: Minion Pro and Myriad Pro

Manufactured in the United States of America
Cover photograph: "City traffic" © Alain Lacroix | Dreamstime.com
Cover and interior design: Michele Myatt Quinn

∞
The paper on which this book is printed meets the minimum requirements of American National Standard for Information Sciences—Permanence of Paper for Printed Library Materials, ANSI Z39.48-1984.

Library of Congress Cataloging-in-Publication Data

Clark, Robert C., 1976–
American literary minimalism / Robert C. Clark.—First edition.
pages cm
Includes bibliographical references and index.
ISBN 978-0-8173-1827-7 (hardback)—ISBN 978-0-8173-8750-1 (e book) 1. Minimalism (Literature)—United States. 2. American literature—19th century—History and criticism. 3. American literature—20th century—History and criticism. I. Title.
PS366.M55C53 2015
810.9'11—dc23

2014023607

For Heather

Contents

american
literary
minimalism

Introduction

American literary Minimalism stands as an important yet misunderstood stylistic movement. While Cynthia Whitney Hallett, James Dishon McDermott, and John Barth conclude that it began in earnest after 1950, it is an extension of aesthetics established by a diverse group of authors active in the late nineteenth and early twentieth centuries that includes Hamlin Garland and Ezra Pound. Hallett, Barth, and others generally agree that works within the tradition reflect several qualities: the prose is "spare" and "clean," important plot details are often omitted or left out, practitioners tend to excise material during the editing process, and stories tend to be about "common people" as opposed to the powerful and aristocratic. While these descriptors and the many others that have been posited over the years are in some ways helpful, the mode has not been fully defined.

Defining American Literary Minimalism

The core idea that differentiates American Minimalism from other movements is that prose and poetry should be extremely efficient, allusive, and implicative. The language in this type of fiction tends to be simple and direct. Narrators do not often use ornate adjectives and rarely offer effusive descriptions of scenery or extensive detail about characters' backgrounds. Because authors tend to use few words, each is invested with a heightened sense of interpretive significance. Allusion and implication by omission are often employed as a means to compensate for limited exposition, to add depth to stories that on the surface may seem superficial or incomplete.

Minimalism is best defined on the basis of style rather than generalizations about character types, the perceived role of consumer culture, or domesticity.

The movement is diverse, in part because it is a descendant of rich traditions such as literary Impressionism and Imagism. In some cases, an incomplete understanding of the mode arises from overly narrow temporal parameters. Roland Sodowsky posits that the movement lasted "primarily" from 1975 to 1989, and that stories within the mode are usually set in America.[1] Sodowsky's assertions are overly restrictive because they exclude many important stories and poems, including all of Ernest Hemingway's fiction. Although it may be tempting to generalize about elements such as setting and character demographics, Minimalist fiction does not reflect a predetermined type of content.

Authors working within the Minimalist tradition confront a wide range of themes and subjects, and their fiction is not restricted to a single genre. Despite the fact that most studies of the mode tend to focus on short stories, the movement includes a broad range of poetry and novels. Imagist poems, for example, often share all of the hallmarks of the tendency, as do the short prose pieces that comprise the interchapters of Hemingway's *In Our Time. The Sun Also Rises* is perhaps the quintessential austere novel, and it likely influenced Jay McInerney as he composed *Bright Lights, Big City*. Sandra Cisneros integrates prose-poetic forms into her lengthy novel *Caramelo*.

Minimalist fiction often straddles the boundary between prose and poetry, primarily because it is laconic yet highly implicative. Prose poems, as well as pieces sometimes referred to as "microfiction" and "short-short stories," fit within the category even though they are more condensed than representative tales and novels. Regardless of length, Minimalistic works often achieve a level of profundity generally associated with verse. Both forms necessarily omit relevant information as a means to create a heightened sense of implication. Hallett posits that the style reflects an "aesthetic of exclusion," which is in a sense true, but it is more accurate to say that it employs an aesthetic of suggestiveness.[2] Many authors communicate important information implicitly rather than explicitly, but few use omission to the same degree as Hemingway, Susan Minot, and others.

Current scholarship on Minimalism generally affirms the centrality of efficiency, allusiveness, and suggestiveness, but also tends to become mired in matters of theme and content. Many authors and scholars have at one time or another discussed American Minimalism, but only a few have made a serious attempt at defining it. Extant definitions tend to be lengthy lists that reflect a small cross section of representative works. One of the earliest efforts to describe the mode appears in Frederick R. Karl's *American Fictions, 1940–1980*:

> The two finest examples in modern fiction of minimalism are Camus's *The Stranger* and Beckett's trilogy of *Molloy*, *Malone Dies*, and *The Unnamable*. In such works the reader is aware of the spaces between words, the pauses between breath, the silence between noises. Everything is intermittent. The narrative of these works relies on spurts which barely penetrate as decibels. The author brings us close to boredom, withdrawal, rejection of the work itself. Further, minimalist fiction is nearly always based on a pessimistic view of life, where all the normal goals or controls no longer obtain. It depends heavily on irony, itself a form of negation. In Camus's *The Fall*, depths dominate over heights; narcissism, self-regard, self-indulgence are norms.[3]

While he argues for the centrality of Camus and Beckett, writers who were unquestionably important to the development of the form in a global sense, the majority of Karl's examination focuses on a series of American authors from the 1960s and 1970s. He implies the importance of efficiency but also suggests that the work tends to be fragmentary and disjointed, which it often is. Pessimism, however, is hardly normative and ultimately irrelevant. Karl also affirms the tenet that omission is an important attribute: "The minimalist writer must assure the audience that he, the writer, knows far more about the subject than he is including; that beyond him, in some spatial realm, there is the rest, undefined perhaps, but *there*. Often, the writer makes as his point of reference not the line he develops but the beyond; what is not is as dominant as what is, and possibly more significant."[4] While his position tends to be abstract, it should not be dismissed as representing a separate school.

In his introduction to the *Mississippi Review* special issue devoted to Minimalism, Kim Herzinger distances his own definition from Karl's because he references "another, slightly older, group of writers" that includes authors such as Joan Didion and Jerzy Kosinski, concluding that "we don't want two rooms with the same number in the House of Fiction."[5] Herzinger's assertion results from the assumption that he was dealing with something "new," that what Raymond Carver and Richard Ford were doing was radically different from the work of Didion and Kosinski. While their respective subjects and themes may not have been the same, they shared much in common in technique. The implicit refusal, by Herzinger and others, to acknowledge stylistic continuities among diverse authors has in part contributed to an ongoing discussion over whether the style is even appropriately named.

The fact that the term *Minimalism* does not encompass a specific type of content has not stifled an ongoing desire to invent a name that somehow addresses the subject. Multiple attempts have been made in recent decades to categorize writers in terms of their characters' demographics, but these efforts have often led to fragmentation rather than clarification. Names such as *Dirty realism* and *Kmart Realism* speak to the types of people depicted and matters of plot and tend to include a relatively small number of representative samples. Some authors were unfairly typecast, often leading to a feeling of resentment.[6] In considering the corpus of their work, those who had been categorized had a right to protest. Even within their collections, writers such as Carver and Tobias Wolff write about the working class, college professors, teachers, and a number of other people who do not seem to *do* anything. In considering what to call the movement while drafting a letter to various writers and critics requesting feedback for a special issue of the *Mississippi Review*, Herzinger and his cohorts constructed a lengthy list of possibilities that includes "Dirty Realism (*Granta*); New Realism; Pop Realism; and our own lovable Neo-Domestic Neo-Realism. Interested parties, before or since, suggested White Trash Fiction; Coke Fiction; 'Post-Alcoholic Blue-Collar Minimalist Hyperrealism' (John Barth); 'Around-the house-and-in-the-yard' Fiction (Don DeLillo); Wised Up Realism; TV Fiction; High Tech Fiction; Designer Realism; Extra-Realism; and the svelte Post-Post-Modernism. None seemed to work; they were either prescriptive, baldly inaccurate, aggressively reductive, or blatantly derivative."[7] Herzinger's eventual dismissal of many of these names resulted from the fact that they are narrowly applicable to individual or small groups of writers. Derivations of the term *realism* remain popular, and it is perhaps attributable to the fact that works that fall within the category tend to achieve a high degree of verisimilitude, but again there are noteworthy exceptions. Carver's "Tell the Women We're Going" and "Popular Mechanics" seem strikingly bizarre, similar to Naturalistic works such as Frank Norris's *McTeague* in their extreme violence. Tobias Wolff's "Hunters in the Snow" reflects many of the tendencies of the mode, but the plot is as absurd as it is surreal. At one point Tub, the protagonist, sits inside a diner eating four plates of pancakes while his "friend," a man he shot with his rifle, bleeds to death in the bed of a pickup truck.

Aside from the fact that some Minimalistic works do not achieve verisimilitude, using a derivation of the term *realism* creates a series of other potential conflicts. Scholars such as Tom Quirk and James Nagel view the period from 1865 to 1918 as the era of American Realism and Naturalism. The former denotes fiction that is mimetic, but it also refers to stories that involve characters who find themselves in positions of "ethical crisis."[8] Perhaps the best example of such a scenario is found in chapter 31 of Mark Twain's *Adventures of Huckleberry Finn*, the scene in which Huck makes the existential decision not to turn Jim, a runaway slave, in to the authorities. Few, if any, Minimalist pieces depict moral crises. Narrators either describe experience objectively or, in the case of the first-person narrative, often lack the ability to articulate the ethical or social significance of what is happening around them. From a stylistic perspective, the two movements also differ because Realistic works are not necessarily efficient, allusive, or implicative.

With seemingly no consideration for the historical significance of American Realism, the editors of *Granta* elected to title their issue devoted to Minimalism *Dirty Realism: New Writing from America*. They did so in an effort to group seven works by Carver, Ford, Wolff, Jayne Ann Phillips, Elizabeth Tallent, Bobbie Ann Mason, and Frederick Barthelme. In his introduction, Bill Buford offers a useful list of stylistic attributes:

> This is a curious, dirty realism about the belly-side of contemporary life, but it is realism so stylized and particularized—so insistently informed by a discomforting and sometimes elusive irony—that it makes the more traditional novels of, say, Updike or Styron seem ornate, even baroque in comparison. Many, like Richard Ford, Raymond Carver, or Frederick Barthelme, write in a flat, "unsurprised" language, pared down to the plainest of plain styles. The sentences are stripped of adornment, and maintain complete control on the simple objects and events that they ask us to witness: it is what's not being said—the silences, the elisions, the omissions—that seems to speak most. It is, as Frank Kermode has observed of Raymond Carver in particular, a "fiction so spare in manner that it takes time before one realizes how completely a whole culture and a whole moral condition are being represented by even the most seemingly slight sketch."[9]

Even though the editors at *Granta* elected to use a different title, Buford is talking about American literary Minimalism. Frank Kermode's observation speaks to the centrality of implication and allusiveness to the mode. Buford goes on, however, to make some rather stereotypical, albeit common, remarks focused primarily on how the tales he selects portray working-class people living economically and spiritually depressed lives: "But these are strange stories: unadorned, unfurnished, low-rent tragedies about people who watch day-time television, read cheap romances or listen to country and western music. They are waitresses in roadside cafés, cashiers in supermarkets, construction workers, secretaries and unemployed cowboys. They play bingo, eat cheeseburgers, hunt deer and stay in cheap hotels. They drink a lot and are often in trouble: for stealing a car, breaking a window, pickpocketing a wallet. They are from Kentucky or Alabama or Oregon, but, mainly, they could just about be from anywhere: drifters in a world cluttered with junk food and the oppressive details of modern consumerism."[10] Buford's comments have proven both helpful and harmful in defining the mode. The attributes he identifies do not even describe all of the stories he selected for his own issue: Carver's "The Compartment" is about a father who, during a train ride through Western Europe, grows angry when the watch he purchased for his son is stolen. Buford's list of qualities describes the setting and characterization of some of the works that populate his table of contents but does not adequately apply to works that appeared in the years that followed. Susan Minot's excellent short-story cycle *Monkeys* shares much in technique with the fiction that appears in the issue, but it is about an upper-middle-class family in New England. McInerney's *Bright Lights, Big City* also fits, but it follows a week in the life of a depressed, club-hopping partier in New York City.

Bright Lights, Big City illustrates Buford's final point, however, because the protagonist does indeed drift "in a world cluttered with junk food and the oppressive details of modern consumerism," but these types of references are evidence of the allusiveness common to the style and thus do not support a content-based definition. In an essay on David Foster Wallace, Sven Birkerts succinctly describes the reason for the inclusion of these types of allusions: "These authors [Ann Beattie, Amy Hempel, Frederick Barthelme, and Mary Robison] give us the descriptions of the places, the name brands, the clips of conversation, and we must infer what the innerscape is like."[11] Authors such as McInerney, Hemingway, and Cisneros do not generally write extended passages that describe the historical and cultural context of their stories.

In Minimalistic fiction, allusions to popular culture help provide details about setting that often play an important role in the development of plot, characterization, and theme. McInerney's New York is a collection of facades and fashionable surfaces. The superficiality of consumerism provides the backdrop for a narrator who seeks to reconnect with the things that give his life meaning, such as family and love. Cisneros employs a similar tactic. In

Caramelo, advertisements and brand names provide a means to differentiate between American and Mexican culture. When Lala Reyes and her family cross the border into Mexico, Lala talks about how her senses must adapt to visual and gustatory changes. Buford and others argue that the mention of brands such as Kmart and Jordache is unique to the mode, but numerous writers whose fiction does not fit within the tradition refer to specific places and name brands in their poems, novels, and stories, so it is not ultimately useful to use the practice as a means to separate Minimalist authors from others.

To her credit, Hallett's definition of Minimalism does not refer specifically to the inclusion of brand names as a central attribute, but her description of the movement is so broad its usefulness is limited. While her positions are laudable for their attention to qualities that can be traced to some of the predecessors of the style, she does not make explicit connections among them:

> Collectively, the most identifiable of the varied features of minimalist short fiction include: (1) a blunt, lean, apparently uncomplicated prose; (2) a compact prose that by individual artistic design effects a complex pattern of trope which expands from what first appear to be trivial matters into universal concerns; (3) more dialogue than exposition with no evident auctorial intrusion, and little, if any, narratorial intrusion; (4) non-heroic characters who resemble everyday people doing everyday things; (5) a sense that all "action" either appears to have occurred a while ago, or occurred just moments before the story began, or occurs later "offstage," that is, not within the moments of the story.[12]

Hallett's list is something of a hodgepodge of stylistic and content-based qualities. The first and second tenets speak to the importance of efficiency. The third and fourth are specific to American Realism, and it could be argued that the mimetic dialogue often found in austere fiction descends from the work of the local colorists. In *The Realist Short Story of the Powerful Glimpse: Chekhov to Carver*, Kerry McSweeney refers to Hemingway and Carver only as "realists."[13] Hallet's fifth point could be made about many movements; the same is often true of epic poetry, for example.

Hallett's last four points are perhaps the most contentious, as some have argued that American Minimalism is nothing more than a resurgence of Naturalism within a postmodern paradigm. Hallett echoes some of Stephen

Crane's thematic interests when she posits that stories within the mode examine the "implications of an existential, often absurd, universe in which 'real' communication is impossible and action is useless." She argues that characters are often ineffectual, resigned to the idea that "to protest is to waste one's breath; to fight is to waste one's energies." Her seventh point, however, suggests the influence of postmodern thought. She writes that through their fiction, Minimalist authors demonstrate a paradoxical "recognition that words are useless, for most things are unsayable."[14] Hallett's argument seems out of place. By grouping these attributes, she suggests that deterministic forces suppress verbal expression. Naturalistic authors, however, depend upon the efficacy of words because their works are often powerful arguments in favor of social change.

Hallett's final two observations are exclusive to Minimalism and Naturalism. Characters that populate stories within both movements often succumb to hopelessness because of a pervasive "perception that time passes without resistance" and the feeling that they are helpless members of an "audience rather than . . . participants in their own world and lives" who ultimately conclude that "nothing they do or say can make a difference." Returning again to ideas prominent in Crane's fiction, Hallett argues that in the Minimalistic "universe . . . no one thing appears innately important, so all worth is artificially conferred, decided by individual values."[15] Edward Hoagland asserts that there is a connection between Naturalism and Minimalism while, in no uncertain terms, dismissing the latter: "I am tired of minimalist fiction, or 'dirty realism,' or whatever term the repetition of Anderson-Farrell-Dreiser-Garland-Crane travels under nowadays."[16] Hoagland is not entirely wrong: Carver's and Bobbie Ann Mason's characters often seem to lack agency, their tragic outcomes directed by deterministic forces. Russell Banks wrote an article titled "Raymond Carver: Our Stephen Crane" in which he maintains that "the work of both men is powered by the dramatization of a painful argument with a ferocious, inescapable determinism that, when at last it overpowers their characters, approaches tragedy. Crane's determinism is more Darwinian, perhaps, and his argument with it more romantically male and adolescent, than Carver's, in which fate seems locked on to the life-shaping power of the domestic mundane, the mess and grind of ordinary life, and Carver's argument against it is driven by love."[17] While some of the philosophical leanings found in Naturalistic works seem to appear in Minimalistic fiction, there is an irreconcilable difference in aesthetic concerns.

The fiction of Theodore Dreiser, Frank Norris, and John Steinbeck emphasizes political arguments more than the importance of producing art. In his seminal book *Realism and Naturalism in Nineteenth-Century American Literature*, Donald Pizer writes that the "distinction between realism and naturalism, most critics agree, is the particular philosophical orientation of the naturalists. A traditional and widely accepted concept of American naturalism, therefore, is that it is essentially realism infused with a pessimistic determinism."[18] On the contrary, American Minimalism is comprised of authors who portray beauty in commonplace objects and actions, who accentuate the aesthetic quality of mundane experiences. Their goal is not to diagnose the cause of a social ill such as poverty or racism and then propose a "cure." Carver said in an interview that he tended to write about people who live in fear due to financial desperation because he had "known people like" them throughout his life.[19] McDermott surmises from these comments that Carver was more socially aware than most think.[20] Carver's work, however, does not have a strongly political or activist tone. Some of the most vociferous critics of the movement have posited that its primary problem is a lack of didacticism, that it says virtually nothing about how people should live and act.[21] The same cannot be said of Naturalistic works.

Minimalism is different from Naturalism and other movements in the sense that it is not a traditional "school." But Hemingway, Pound, Yone Noguchi, William Carlos Williams, Minot, and others share the same aesthetic concerns, a core idea of what prose should look like; their work is primarily composed of images, presented without commentary or adornment. The style is often categorized as an extension of postmodernism, as a body of work that implicitly suggests that words resist meaning. Kirk Curnutt, whose *Wise Economies* includes an insightful, fair-minded evaluation of the mode, posits that it is reflective of the ultimate failure of verbal communication, maintaining that "because minimalism, unlike modernism, was never a movement in the sense that its artists shared a general aesthetic agenda, it has been defined more by its detractors than its practitioners. Yet rather than indulge in anomie, much of its fiction concerns a basic theme: the failure of the spoken word."[22] Curnutt's view, similar to Hallett's, is difficult to reconcile with the stylistic emphasis on precision. A perceived emptiness, whether spiritual or otherwise, does not result from loose diction or syntax. Curnutt does not separate the content of the work from the manner of its execution. In other words, the verbal "failure" he sees in the work of Carver and others is not a reflection on the nature of their language but on authorial choices related to characterization. The postmodern nihilistic state of being does not inherently coincide with the practice of writing elliptical works; Curnutt's assertion addresses the content of individual works more than the technical characteristics of the tradition.

The Historical Development of American Literary Minimalism

The stories and novels published in the 1980s were not part of a "new fiction" but represented a continuation of an important, meritorious literary tradition. Chronologically, the first works important to the development of American Minimalism began to appear around 1890. The mode is not as old as the short story itself, the precursors of which date back over six millennia.[23] Barth and Hallet were among the first scholars to attempt a comprehensive history of the movement, but their respective lists of predecessors are excessively broad. Barth's "A Few Words about Minimalism" is a rambling piece, at times playful in tone, in which he lists a series of ancient texts known for brevity as the progenitors of the mode, including "such inherently minimalist genres as oracles (from the Delphic shrine of Apollo to the modern fortune cookie), proverbs, maxims, aphorisms, epigrams, pensées, mottoes, slogans and quips." Not until he mentions Edgar Allan Poe does he begin to address the development of the movement in America. He includes Poe among the forefathers of the style, positing that "the genre of the short story, as Poe distinguished it from the traditional tale in his 1842 review of Hawthorne's first collection of stories, is an early manifesto of modern narrative minimalism: 'In the whole composition there should be no word written, of which the tendency . . . is not to the pre-established design. . . . Undue length is . . . to be avoided.' Poe's codification informs such later 19th-century masters of terseness, selectivity and implicitness (as opposed to leisurely once-upon-a-timelessness, luxuriant abundance, explicit and extended analysis) as Guy de Maupassant and Anton Chekhov."[24] In her description of the origins of the mode, Hallett also includes Poe. She does so, however, because of her position on the development of the short story genre: "The seeds of art and artifice that inform both minimalism and the short story can be traced to such otherwise diverse writers as Edgar Allan Poe, Anton Chekhov, James Joyce, Samuel Beckett, and Ernest Hemingway—all of whose conscious codes of omission were designed to make an audience feel more than they understood."[25] Hallett continues on to mention Poe's emphasis upon a "singleness of effect," a feat that can only be achieved if a work is short enough to be read in a single sitting.

Poe is often included among the forefathers of Minimalism for his insistence on the value of brevity, but he was not part of the tradition and his contribution to the category is slight.[26] While he is often portrayed as an integral figure in the development of the short story, at least in terms of producing a theory about the genre, his work does not include many examples of stylistically austere stories. Hallett's and Barth's arguments that Poe is important to the development of American Minimalism seem more a function of his status as a major figure than the actual brevity of his work. It was not until the turn of the century that fiction became more suggestive and stylistically restrained. Kate Chopin and Hamlin Garland, writers whose fiction was prominent in the 1890s, share more in common stylistically with Hemingway than Poe. Chopin's "Story of an Hour" features many of the central techniques associated with the tendency, although perhaps not to the same degree. This quality is in part due to the influence of an early movement called literary Impressionism, a mode that includes Garland, Joseph Conrad, Stephen Crane, Henry James, André Gide, and Anton Chekhov, among others.

Garland was a student and admirer of the visual Impressionists, invigorated by the vibrant colors he saw on their canvases. Having viewed paintings by European practitioners of the mode at the 1893 World's Columbian Exposition in Chicago, he articulates his conception of the movement in an essay titled "Impressionism": "The fundamental idea of the impressionists, as I understand it, is that a picture should be a unified impression. It should not be a mosaic, but a complete and of course momentary concept of the sense of sight. It should not deal with the concepts of other senses (as touch), nor with judgments; it should be the stayed and reproduced effect of a single section of the world of color upon the eye. It should not be a number of pictures enclosed in one frame, but a single idea impossible of subdivision without loss." In this passage Garland identifies several technical axioms, some of which he later integrates into his fiction. He argues that a work should focus on one object. The image should represent a precise moment in time, and later in his analysis he elaborates on how artists strived to "represent in color an instantaneous effect of light and shade as presented by nature."[27] The immediacy he observes in the art is in part due to an emphasis on the present rather than the past.[28] He is less clear in his appreciation of its painterly qualities, describing it paradoxically as not being photorealistic but simple and "exact"; he suggests that while Impressionist painters may have seemed haphazard, they were still methodical craftsmen.[29]

In his "Chicago Studies," Garland attempts to translate some of his ideas about visual Impressionism into literature. The brief, imagistic pieces were composed in the 1890s but remained unpublished until they appeared in James B. Stronks's essay "A Realist Experiments with Impressionism: Hamlin Garland's 'Chicago Studies'" in 1964. "The City Streets" illustrates how Garland transposes his perceptions of the tradition into fiction:

> The red sun struck across the canon-like thoroughfares, gilding the towering buildings standing like granite crags impassive and sullen.
>
> Far down, the street narrowed till it ran like a tunnel under the gray-black tenuous smoke—and was lost to sight.
>
> In this dim light, beneath this cloud of vapor, teams clamored to and fro, gongs of cars cried out imperiously, angrily, and men rushed back and forth, traversing the jungle of traffic like adroit and fearless insects.[30]

In his description of the light of "the red sun," Garland immediately establishes that he is describing an instant in time, a specific moment in the life of his central object: the city. Both the first and second lines are purely visual, consistent with his observation that Impressionistic art focuses on what is seen. The final image, however, violates this tenet in that it is concurrently auditory and visual: the rapid movement of people combines with the harsh sounds of the "jungle of traffic." The bustling, inexorable metropolitan organism is indifferent to the insect-like people who rush about the streets.

As Garland's prose poem suggests, Minimalism and literary Impressionism share much in common. Authors working within the latter tradition seek "to render in literature the sensory nature of human life, to present to the reader the sensations of a character so graphically that the reader would experience the scene directly, participating in the action on the same epistemological plane as the character."[31] This approach includes an attribute central to both movements: action is reported objectively. Most Impressionistic stories are narrated from a third-person perspective, relayed according to the subjective "lens" of the protagonist's perceptions. The author and narrator are thus self-effacing, and the works lack overt didacticism. This reportorial style borrows from the visual counterpart of the mode, seeking to capture sensory experiences in a series of brief moments: "Impressionistic painting represented a single instant of sensory experience; Impressionistic literature also focused on an intense, abbreviated moment of experience, a Vistazo, and used such moments as either entire works or as units from which to build a larger artistic construct."[32] In an analysis of austere fiction written in the 1970s and 1980s, Sodowsky concludes that "in its most extreme minimalist usage," both first-person and third-person narrators "pass on, without comment, objective narrative 'facts': present-time action, dialogue, and only the most essential exposition."[33] The prose poem, the "short-short story," the vignette, and many short stories employ a similar technique, and in longer pieces it can sometimes lead to a pervasive sense of fragmentation.

Minimalistic stories often require readers to "assemble" images and allusions in order to make a coherent, complete narrative. In a discussion of the brushwork in Impressionistic paintings, James J. Kirschke writes that "the comparative absence of articulation forces the viewer to 'put the painting together' himself."[34] The characterization of protagonists in both traditions reflects the idea that life experiences are disjointed: "Impressionism means instantism. In [Gide's] *Les Nourritures Terrestres* life is reduced to instants. Instants are discontinuous, and life is an instantaneous experience. The self is discontinuous too: each new instant is lived in a new self, not committed to anything, yet always *disponible*."[35] Incongruence is in part the reason that austere fiction should be read with the same level of consideration often reserved for poetry. The reportorial nature of the mode is perhaps the reason some critics find it to be nihilistic or morally neutral. Because authors and narrators tend to be self-effacing, intrusiveness and exposition are rare. Thoughts and emotions are implied rather than told, so there are rarely explanatory passages in which protagonists contemplate what is happening to them.

The fragmentary quality of some Minimalistic works is different from those of Impressionistic stories, however, in that it is not uncommon for authors working in the latter tradition to employ a first-person or even second-person narration. A shift in point of view affects the structure of a work when the narrator's memories and experiences are nonsequential or incomplete. An omniscient third-person narrator, for example, does not black out from drug use or forget important details, both of which happen to the protagonist-narrator in McInerney's *Bright Lights, Big City*. Donald Barthelme and McInerney sometimes employ second-person perspective, perhaps as a means to directly involve readers in their characters' sensory experiences. McInerney's city-street sequences vividly illustrate the effect: "It is still raining. Getting a cab is a long shot. Knots of people on every corner wave their arms at the passing traffic. You walk down Seventh to the bus stop, where some twenty souls huddle in the shelter. A bus packed with grim faces goes by and doesn't stop."[36] The emphasis upon the senses remains, however, because these narrators often lack the ability to articulate their thoughts. In other words, they remain nonintrusive because they cannot comprehend their own feelings and actions to a degree that allows them to communicate a distinct moral or philosophical lesson. The method is different, but the ultimate effect is essentially the same.

Imagism is in some ways the poetic equivalent of Impressionism because authors identified with the group crystallized sensory experience into suggestive, highly efficient poems.[37] Because of the kinship in their stylistic programs, Imagism is a part of Minimalism. The leader of the former, Ezra Pound, was an exacting editor who encouraged fellow writers to move away from excessive prose and abstraction. While the tradition includes a number of writers, its American contingent has proven important to the development of Minimalism. Amy Lowell, William Carlos Williams, and John Gould Fletcher, among others, preserved the tenets of the mode once Pound moved on to Vorticism. And even though they separated from Pound, who is one of the most dynamic literary figures of the twentieth century, they continued to experiment and expand the stylistic parameters of the movement.

The emphasis on efficiency in American Minimalism is in many ways attributable to Pound, a figure rarely discussed in scholarship on the movement. In his brief essay "Imagisme," he lays out three important axioms. The first two speak to the importance of avoiding abstraction and writing with precision: "1. Direct treatment of the 'thing,' whether subjective or objective. 2. To use absolutely no word that did not contribute to the presentation."[38] Following Pound's dictate, Minimalist stories are seldom abstract. The material items that appear in them are often invested with intense emotion but carry no symbolic significance. Objects tend to work in concert within a fully developed image, thus they function together as an objective correlative. The emotionally paralyzing sense of "menace" induced by unexpected telephone calls in Carver's "A Small, Good Thing," for example, is developed using this technique. Carver said in an interview that he respected Pound's commitment to cutting any material that was vague or could not be understood.[39] He stated that he kept a three-by-five-inch index card near his desk on which was written one of Pound's dictums: "Fundamental accuracy of statement is the ONE sole morality of writing."[40] His goal to write with a "fundamental accuracy" is a means to avoid, not create, postmodern obfuscation. In *The ABC of Reading*, Pound reiterated that "good writers are those who keep the language efficient.

That is to say, keep it accurate, keep it clear."[41] This assertion suggests a degree of authorial self-effacement. Pound implied that the author should step out of the way as a means to allow readers to assemble their own interpretation of what has been shown. Pound's editorial work for the young Hemingway is well documented, but less examined is his influence on Carver.[42] Given the connection between him and two of the most important figures in the category, Pound's call for directness should be a central element in any definition of the style.

Following the lead of British philosopher T. E. Hulme, Pound fashions the central axioms of Imagism as a rebellion "against the rhetoric and sloppy technique of much nineteenth-century poetry."[43] J. B. Harmer divides the mode into three stages, describing it as a "succession of small groups. In all there were three: one fostered by T. E. Hulme in 1909; a second led by Ezra Pound from 1912 to 1914; a third organized by Amy Lowell from 1914 to 1917."[44] The first "version" included poets such as Edward Storer, F. S. Flint, Joseph Campbell, and Hulme.[45] Pound became involved around 1909 but did not assume leadership until he joined with Flint, H. D., Richard Aldington, Allen Upward, and William Carlos Williams in the second manifestation of the group. Amy Lowell was a late addition to the assemblage in 1914, and her inclusion was in part due to her wealth; Pound and his cohorts needed money in order to publish their work.[46] After Pound's departure, many of the same members stayed on, but John Gould Fletcher and D. H. Lawrence also began to participate. Hulme provided the intellectual basis for the tendency by calling for precision. He argued for control, brevity, and the centrality of the image when he wrote that "each *word* must be an image *seen*, not a counter. That dreadful feeling of cheapness when we contemplate the profusion of words of modern prose. The true ideal—the little statue in Paris."[47] Hulme argues not for the miniaturization of thought but of verbal expression. He suggests the importance of the concrete over the abstract, an increased emphasis upon the image. Edmund S. de Chasca says that the Imagists sought to write with a "hardness," focusing "on concrete objects and small pieces of reality which they then visually rendered." Perhaps more importantly, they emphasize "*precision* and *economy*."[48] The result is poetry that tends to be elliptical yet implicative. While they are self-contained, they also constitute the building blocks of longer Minimalist pieces written in prose.

The Imagist movement changed somewhat when it was left in the hands of Lowell, migrating to the stylistic "borderlands" of prose and poetry. The schism with Pound in 1914, caused primarily by his dislike of Lowell, allowed for increased experimentation. The group became more "democratic": "The Imagists were to publish quietly as a group of friends with similar tendencies rather than with dogmatic principles."[49] Along with Fletcher, Lowell developed an important form of writing they termed "Polyphonic Prose." Fiction written in this mode is close to the heart of Minimalism because it is written using poetic devices such as internal rhyme and alliteration. Many of Lowell's finest pieces are synesthetic, not in the sense that they depict characters who "taste sounds" or "hear colors," but because they focus upon intense, diverse sensory experiences in an instant of time, much like the work of literary Impressionists. They are image driven and offer little in the way of exposition or intrusiveness. Lowell was never able to fully abandon some of her Romantic tendencies, one example being her proclivity to become effusive in poems involving natural imagery, but she was a talented storyteller who was able to communicate much in a relatively efficient manner.[50]

Lowell's and Pound's interests in Asian poetics also proved formative. American Minimalism does not begin with seventeenth-century Japanese and Chinese poets, but each tradition draws from the same pool of philosophical ideas. Pound was an inventive man, but he is also famous for being a borrower. His 1915 collection *Cathay* is in part a series of poems "translated" from the Chinese, a "collaboration" with sinologist Ernest Fenollosa and the poet Rihaku.[51] His most well known Imagistic poems are in the tradition of haiku. To *Des Imagistes*, the original anthology published by the Imagist school and the only one to which he gave his blessing, he contributed, among other pieces, "Liu Ch'e" and "Fan Piece for Her Imperial Lord."[52] Both feature an imagistic delicacy suggestive of purity and romance. While he was no doubt influenced by a number of writers, arguably one of the most important is the relatively obscure Yone Noguchi.[53]

Scholar Yoshinobu Hakutani describes Noguchi as having "played the most vital role in disseminating Japanese poetics and haiku, in particular, to the west." An acquaintance of W. B. Yeats, Noguchi wrote several important books on his homeland's aesthetic philosophies. He was acquainted with Pound "as early as 1911," and it is quite possible that Pound was aware of Noguchi's excellent books about haiku.[54] He was a bilingual poet whose works had garnered the appreciation of a broad range of authors.[55] Many of the ideas he shared in his books and lectures suggest a continuation of traditions important to both Imagism and American Minimalism. While it is a rather obvious step to compare Pound's "In a Station of the Metro" and a traditional seventeen-syllable poem, the aesthetic principles that inform each mode are not as apparent. Noguchi played a vital role in "explaining" the verse of his homeland to a receptive modernist audience. Perhaps the most prominent parallel, one that he wrote about frequently, is the stylistic decision to write implicative and efficient verse. He maintains that "'hokku' (seventeen syllable poem) in Japanese mind might be compared with a tiny star, I dare say, carrying the whole sky at its back. It is like a slightly open door, where you may steal into the realm of poesy. It is simply a guiding lamp. Its value depends on how much it suggests. The Hokku poet's chief aim is to impress the reader with the high atmosphere in which he is living."[56] It is important, however, that this last line does not suggest a need for authorial intrusion. All is subtle and suggestive, the author a meager presence in his text.

The adage "less is more" has been relegated to the realm of cliché, which is lamentable because it is a succinct phrase that implies a type of self-denial. According to Noguchi, the haiku poet published little as an extension of artistic and spiritual humility. Minimalistic stories and poems operate in much the same way because they are written by authors who want the focus to be on their art and not on the act of writing: omission and brevity force readers into a deeper engagement with what is before them. In *The Pound Era*, Hugh Kenner identifies William Carlos Williams's statement "no ideas but in things" as "an epistemology (what you can know is in front of you)."[57] The implication of this axiom is that authorial and narrative intrusion draws emphasis away from the images themselves. Noguchi argues that this principle was a part of his homeland's aesthetic philosophy when he wrote that "explanation is forbidden in the House of Poesy for Japanese."[58] This technique necessitates a limiting of the ego. De Chasca states that one of the tenets Pound and his cohorts shared was that "the poet should desist from making running comments in his proper person, that he should avoid being an interpretive presence in the poem."[59] Contrary to postmodern works, Minimalistic fiction is not self-referential; Williams, Carver, Cisneros, and Minot were not composing fiction about the act of composition or wrestling with the nature of genre. Their stories eschew abstraction yet demand imagination.

Haiku, like well-wrought Minimalistic pieces, suggest but do not explicitly offer visual or narrative totality. In his description of the form, Hakutani writes that "because of their brevity and condensation, haiku seldom provides [*sic*] the picture with detail. The haiku poet delineates only an outline or highly selective parts, and the reader must complete the vision."[60] In other words, they are Impressionistic. The poems are often fragmentary, seemingly composed of objects and images in need of interpretive repositioning. The relationship among the "pieces" is not always clear, but a good haiku should evoke intellectual and spiritual sublimation. Noguchi's English poetry reflects these attributes, but he tended to write more expanded works that did not fit into one of the many syllabic patterns of traditional haiku.[61]

Noguchi's work, particularly the pieces that comprise his two-volume collection *The Pilgrimage*, illustrates the movement away from traditional haiku into Imagist poetics. His poem "Tragedy" employs some imagery typical of ancient forms, such as the willow, but evokes a rich imagistic atmosphere:

> The shadow of the lonely willow
> Swings
> Ghastly, ghastly;
> The roads are lost
> In the hoary-aired mists of eve;
> A strange green light in the distance
> Drifts
> As a wandering fay;
> I hear a wild cry
> In the dark air,
> In the stream,
> In the stars.[62]

The sense of menace present in the scene grows from sensorial confusion. The only certainty is the tree, but it seems predatory rather than comforting. The vision of the "strange green light in the distance" and the sound of the "wild cry" combine to enhance the speaker's sense of fear and hopelessness, but there is little in the way of narrative. Noguchi does not talk about where the protagonist is or why he is there, only that fear shapes his perceptions. In this way, "Tragedy" is similar to the eleventh part of Wallace Stevens's "Thirteen Ways of Looking at a Blackbird," in that it is about the way a person's mental state influences his interpretation of the objects surrounding him.

Stevens was not an Imagist per se, but the fact that "Thirteen Ways" is essentially a collection of haiku speaks to the broad influence Asian poetry asserted on American literature in the early twentieth century. Given its context, Mark Helprin's statement that authors of austere fiction "took their stylistic cue from the haiku" is derisive, but that does not mean he was wrong.[63] On the other hand, traditional haiku is not in itself Minimalistic. One difference is that Japanese poets used a specific set of images, objects, and concepts that were supposed to appear in their poetry. Cherry blossoms, which are frequently mentioned, are distinctly symbolic. Haiku traditionally contain a reference to one of the four seasons.[64] In other words, there were rules that governed content. The same cannot be said of Minimalism.

The brevity and suggestiveness of the haiku and Imagist poem do not have clear analogues in the realm of visual art, a fact that has not stopped some scholars and critics from arguing for a connection between literary and sculptural Minimalism. The relationship, however, is tenuous. The "broken" brushwork of an Impressionist painting has more resonance with the style than do the large, industrial shapes artists such as Ronald Bladen and Robert Morris weld.[65] Hallett seems generous in her appraisal of any shared attributes, stating that "the similarities between visual and literary minimalism are obvious but perhaps superficial, especially since both involve apparently simple means and forms that prove to be not so simple upon close scrutiny." Her conclusion is helpful, however, because she differentiates the sculpture from the literature by saying that the former presents itself as being representative of only itself, whereas the latter can employ allusions and tropes as a means to expand interpretive significance.[66] Regardless, the connection between the two modes is in name alone.

Although sculptural Minimalism lost momentum at the end of the 1970s, the 1980s were a pivotal time in the history of American literary Minimalism. Carver's *What We Talk About When We Talk About Love* and *Cathedral,* Minot's *Monkeys,* and McInerney's *Bright Lights, Big City* and *Ransom* continue the stylistic tradition Noguchi, Pound, Hemingway, and various other literary Impressionists and Imagists founded. Kosinski and Ford wrote *Steps* and *Rock Springs,* respectively, according to the tenets of the form but later returned to a more expansive prose style. Ford's Frank Bascombe novels, one of which, *Independence Day,* won the Pulitzer Prize, are rather "maximalist." Tobias Wolff's early fiction, such as his collection *In the Garden of the North American Martyrs,* is Minimalistic, but the same cannot be said of later works such as *Old School.* It seems that when the mode was at the height of its popularity, perhaps around 1986, the critical reception turned from acclamatory to scornful.

Critics in the 1980s whose tastes were more attuned to avant-garde work published by smaller presses attempted to make sense of the popularity of brief, elliptical works that appeared with regularity in a variety of magazines and journals.[67] John W. Aldridge and Carol Ianonne lament a perceived lack of philosophical and moral direction, suggesting that this "fresh" material was reflective of an empty, nihilistic era in American life.[68] The mode attracted considerable mass appeal. McInerney's *Bright Lights, Big City*, for example, earned instantaneous suspicion after selling over 300,000 copies.[69] Brief, highly implicative short stories published in periodicals such as the *New Yorker* led to outcries from maximalists (including John Updike) who desired a continuation of a tradition that favored a "fuller" prose style in the vein of the one practiced by writers like Philip Roth and J. D. Salinger.[70]

Although it is in many respects difficult to identify a reason, the movement proved a controversial subject during the second half of the 1980s. The ranks of naysayers grew as the decade progressed. In 1987, Joe David Bellamy wrote that "some of the so-called minimalists have sacrificed stylistic richness or sophistication in search of other values. Of course, pure styles can be conceived and delivered in six-word sentences and in fiction that more or less eliminates exposition, as Hemingway sometimes tried to do. But it isn't easy. It isn't the sort of feat everyone should be trying for at once. So, whatever else the newest American fiction might try to do in the years ahead, my hope is that, stylistically and imagistically, it will strive for more robust, more muscular, more ambitious performances—a swing of the pendulum back in the direction of Faulkner and Flannery O'Connor."[71] Bellamy echoes the sentiments of Updike and the maximalists, although in a somewhat more ambassadorial manner. T. Coraghessan Boyle's complaint was different in that he thought the tendency was repetitious, contending that "actually, contemporary North American fiction is too much of one thing—the safe, minimalist/realist story purveyed by a group I like to call the 'Catatonic Realists.' (You know the story, you've read it a thousand times: Three characters are sitting around the kitchen of a trailer, saying folksy things to one another. Finally one of them gets up to go to the bathroom and the author steps in to end it with a line like, 'It was all feathers.')"[72] Boyle's final quip may have been a reference to a story by Carver called "Feathers," which does indeed involve characters "sitting around." Lee. K. Abbott seems not only opposed to the "new fiction" but also infuriated by it. In response to a query from Kim Herzinger of the *Mississippi Review* requesting an opinion about it, Abbott replied that "this is an issue I take seriously enough to fist-fight about."[73] Although less outwardly aggressive, Carver, who is perhaps the most important minimalist author from the 1980s, seems exasperated: "'Minimalism' vs. 'Maximalism.' Who cares finally what they want to call the stories we write? (And who isn't tired to death by now of that stale debate?)."[74] Carver's irritation over names and titles is understandable given the many appellations circulating at the time.

Lost in the debate, however, is a sense of history. Garland, Pound, Hemingway, and others who were important to the development of the style seemed to fall subservient to fellow modernists such as Faulkner. In an absurdly arrogant and censorious gesture, Stephen Koch, Tom Jenks, Madison Smartt Bell, Mary Gaitskill, and Meg Wolitzer gathered at Columbia University for a roundtable discussion of the tradition titled "Throwing Dirt on the Grave of Minimalism." Bell boldly declared that "what we are doing here is composing the epitaph of this movement described as minimalism, which is now effectively over. I think the fad has ended, it's not likely to be revived at any significant level of intensity."[75] Fortunately, many talented authors rejected the premise of Bell's ceremony.

The basic tenets of the style remain intact in twenty-first-century American literature. Minimalism continues to show vitality in "microfiction" such as Robert Olen Butler's *Severance* and *Intercourse*; recent anthologies of prose poems and "short-short stories" such as *Models of the Universe* and *Great American Prose Poems: From Poe to the Present*; short story collections such as Lydia Davis's *Collected Stories* and Dagoberto Gilb's *Before the End, After the Beginning*; and novels such as Cisneros's *Caramelo*, Cormac McCarthy's *No Country for Old Men*, and Peter Heller's *The Dog Stars*. Minimalist fiction has not been buried, and it will not be unless people lose interest in the basic acts of reading and telling stories. It reflects daily experience, artistically mimicking what is for many a common mental activity. A doctor trying to diagnose the reason for his patient's ailment or a person reading a newspaper often engage in the same investigative and imaginative process of synthesizing fragments of information in order to construct a coherent, complete narrative.

1

L'Ancienne

Ernest Hemingway's *In Our Time*

Ernest Hemingway is a dominant figure in American Minimalism. From the brief interchapters of *In Our Time* to his late short story "I Guess Everything Reminds You of Something," Hemingway affirms many of the principles of his one-time mentor Ezra Pound, stressing the importance of authorial self-effacement and direct treatment of subject. His narrators are nonintrusive, telling stories without drawing attention to themselves. In chapter 16 of *Death in the Afternoon*, Hemingway writes that "prose is architecture, not interior decoration, and the Baroque is over. For a writer to put his own intellectual musings . . . into the mouths of artificially constructed characters which are more remunerative when issued as people in a novel is good economics, perhaps, but does not make literature."[1] Hemingway is commenting on the monetary benefit of publishing fiction versus collections of less lucrative nonfiction essays, but he is also talking about removing reference to himself. The magnitude of his devotion to craft, the precision with which he approaches his technique, cannot be overstated.

In addition to his considerable contribution to American literature, Hemingway articulates some of the theoretical concepts that inform Minimalism. In *Death in the Afternoon*, he discusses his iceberg theory in detail, explaining that important ideas and events can be left out of a story but maintain an intellectual presence if the author has a concrete idea of what has been withheld.[2] Twenty-six years later, Hemingway reiterated his original stance, maintaining that "anything you can omit that you know you still have in the writing and its quality will show. When a writer omits things he does not know, they show like holes in his writing."[3] Imagists had already employed this approach in their poetry, striving to suggest the importance of events and concepts not explicitly described. Following the Impressionists, they composed verse that displayed an adherence to the principles of "compression, to the direct presentation of a scene," and "sharp restrictions in length,"[4] qualities that are essential to the development of suggestiveness. Linda Welshimer Wagner observes the "montage effect" used in *In Our Time*, the unrelenting juxtaposition of concrete images that gives the collection a rapid pace, as Hemingway's "most obvious tribute to Imagism."[5] The iceberg theory is a rudimentary concept at work in *In Our Time* and in much of the austere fiction written over the last century.

Hemingway's Minimalist novel *The Sun Also Rises* is replete with examples of how the iceberg theory operates. A particularly good instance occurs in chapter 7 when Jake Barnes, the protagonist-narrator, and Lady Brett Ashley enter a popular Montmartre cabaret in 1920s Paris called Zelli's.[6] After the couple dances for a time, the "nigger drummer" waves "at Brett" and the two engage in a brief exchange:

> "Hahre you?"
> "Great."
> "Thaats good."
> He was all teeth and lips.
> "He's a great friend of mine," Brett said. "Damn good drummer."[7]

Although this conversation does not seem important, Hemingway implies much. Brett acknowledges that she is friends with the man, and given her sexual promiscuity throughout the novel, Hemingway is suggesting that they have at one point been romantically involved. The details of the relationship are omitted: Hemingway does not explain how long ago the two were together or the depth of their commitment. In the context of the iceberg theory, the conversation represents what resides above the surface, the facts of Brett's relationship represent part of what lies below. Additionally, there are broader implications given that Brett and the drummer are not of the same race. While Paris was less divided than America in the 1920s, the hint of miscegenation would have achieved some level of controversy. It is also interesting that Jake does not offer much in the way of an answer to or acknowledgment of Brett's revelation. His lack of response to Brett's statement, along with his derisive recollection that the drummer was "all teeth and lips," implies that he either has no interest in the man or that he is silenced by jealousy.

Also part of the submerged portion of the iceberg is the fact that the drummer was based on an important figure. The little information Hemingway reveals about him carries considerable significance. In his essay "Who Was That Black Man? A Note on Eugene Bullard and *The Sun Also Rises*," Frederic J. Svoboda identifies the real-life model for the unnamed drummer as Eugene Jacques Bullard, a former infantryman and pilot in World War I. He played drums for the "Zig Zag Band at Joe Zelli's Jazz Club" from 1922 to 1924. Svoboda documents many of the similarities between Jake and Bullard, how each man was in love with a noblewoman and wounded in the Great War.[8] Like Hemingway, Bullard was a boxer. His injuries were such that he was not able to continue fighting after he was discharged, so he learned to play the drums.[9]

Soon after Brett's exchange with the drummer, Barnes returns to the theme of miscegenation. The drummer reappears, singing a song as Brett and Jake dance:

> "Oh, darling," Brett said, "I'm so miserable."
>
> I had that feeling of going through something that has all happened before. "You were happy a minute ago."
>
> The drummer shouted: "You can't two time—." (70)

As Brett shares her misery with Jake, and he considers the volatile nature of his romance with her, Hemingway adds another layer of meaning to the scene through an allusion to Ida Cox's "Cherry Picking Blues." Although *The Sun Also Rises* was published in 1926, it was not until 2007 that H. R. Stoneback correctly identified the song.[10] He mentions several possible implications and biographical parallels for the number, the fact that both Bullard and Cox were from Georgia and that she completed her major recordings in Chicago, but does not discuss Cox's lyrics in detail.

The implied narrative in "Cherry Picking Blues" parallels the plot of *The Sun Also Rises*. The speaker is a woman who says her lover has "mistreated" her, likely a white man who has been surreptitiously visiting her. In the first line, she calls him by a name that, perhaps coincidentally, Hemingway preferred as his own nickname: "Come here pretty papa, sit down on your mama's knee."[11] The song is an airing of grievances; the four words Hemingway quotes in *The Sun Also Rises* come from the emotional apogee:

> You can't slip back to your brownskin, I mean your used to be
> I know you're crazy 'bout your cherry pie but you can't two-time me
> I've got my trunk all packed and I'm going to leave this town.

On one level, the drummer shouting "you can't two-time—" could be construed as an angry warning to Brett that she needs to be faithful to him or perhaps less promiscuous in general. The central theme in the ballad, however, that disloyalty is emotionally painful, applies equally to Jake and Brett's situation. Throughout the novel, he expresses profound grief over the fact that he cannot consummate his relationship with her because of his wounded genitals. The final line of "Cherry Picking Blues" is a crude allusion to what happened to Jake during the war and how his injury has affected his life with Brett: "goodbye little papa, another man has cut your cherry tree down." It is remarkable how much depth Hemingway achieves through four seemingly unimportant words.

The evolution of Hemingway's Minimalist aesthetic was an intricate process that began in his youth. From the time he was a teenager in Oak Park, Illinois, he was an active writer. While his early work was influenced by Ring Lardner, so much so that the young Hemingway referred to himself as "Ring Lardner Jr." in his school's newspaper,[12] he was already drafting stories with complex allusions. His early tendencies were reinforced during the period he spent as a reporter for the *Kansas City Star* and the *Toronto Star*, working for editors who expected concision. The introductory rules on the style sheet at the *Kansas City Star* demanded that its reporters write with precision and brevity, directives that Hemingway applied throughout his artistic life.[13] After his service in the American Red Cross during World War I, he continued to refine his methods by attempting to create fiction he could sell to the *Saturday Evening Post*. Upon moving to Paris, the final phase of his "apprenticeship" commenced, and he began to compose the aggressive, declarative prose for which he is known. Amy Lowell, Ezra Pound, and their fellow Imagists were significant to Hemingway's development, directly and indirectly encouraging him to focus on images and objects rather than literary abstractions. Lowell's polyphonic prose was also important because it provided a clear illustration of how prose could be merged with poetry, a fusing of genres evident in the interchapters that comprise "IN OUR TIME" (1923) and *in our time* (1924). Synthesizing lessons and techniques learned from a diverse assemblage of stylistic masters, Hemingway wrote *In Our Time* (1925), a seminal work in American literary Minimalism.

Hemingway's earliest extant fiction indicates that his style was developing while he was still a student in the western Chicago suburbs. Unsurprisingly, Hemingway's juvenilia does not reflect the craftsmanship demonstrated in the work he produced seven years later, but it shows his promise. He did not think highly of the pieces printed in Oak Park High School's *Tabula*, namely "Judgment of Manitou," "A Matter of Colour," and "Sepi Jingan." He wrote to one of his early biographers, Charles A. Fenton, that his high school poems and stories were "shit."[14] Constance Cappel Montgomery disagrees with Hemingway's assessment, however, maintaining that the tales "show that he had formed the basis of his style," and that he "had chosen his subject matter of violence and manliness before his World War I experiences."[15] The narratives also demonstrate a degree of self-effacement; the narrator does not moralize or explain "the point." David Marut observes that the pieces include "relatively little of the intrusive authorial commentary that might mark a novice writer" and notes that Hemingway's characters "speak for themselves through localized dialogue."[16] The narratives reflect an indebtedness to Lardner and Mark Twain,[17] but they also intimate that Hemingway was perhaps exposed to a variety of storytelling traditions as well. The dialogue in "Judgment" is often contrived and Hemingway's distrust of adjectives had not yet developed, but his plot reflects an interest in the life and death themes that run throughout the oral and written histories of the Lake Superior region.

The Hemingway family spent much of their summers in northern Michigan, and they were close with the Native American population that lived nearby. While all three high school stories contain violent subject matter, "Sepi Jingan" and "Judgment of Manitou" suggest that Hemingway may have been familiar with Great Lakes mythology. In *Legends of the Land of Lakes*, George Francis Thomas relays tales of murder, betrayal, and romance. In one episode, he describes how in 1722 a trader had left his wife and offspring behind at an "old French fort" on the shores of Lake Superior in order to "make his annual purchases," placing his family in the care of a "native." In the father's absence, the caretaker makes "unholy advances" on the wife and, having been rebuffed, murders both her and the children. The killer "escaped and went to another country," eventually settling with a different tribe. When he drunkenly admits what he has done, "several of his indignant comrades held their guns to his head. One fired; and that was the end of the villain."[18] In both Thomas's and Hemingway's narratives, punishment results from a transcendent obligation to justice.

Hemingway's "Judgment of Manitou" illustrates a similar, seemingly supernatural cycle of crime and retribution. Suspecting that his trapping partner, Dick Haywood, has stolen his wallet, Pierre, a Cree Indian, enacts a violent plan for retribution. While out checking his line, Haywood is caught in Pierre's snare and eaten by timber wolves. While his victim is being devoured, Pierre realizes that the "tief" is in fact a red squirrel. He races out to save his erstwhile friend but is caught in the bear trap Haywood "had come to tend." Instead of suffering the same fate as his cohort, he reaches for his rifle, implying that he has elected to kill himself rather than be eaten. Before he dies, he attributes his demise to the "judgment of Manitou," the supreme being of the Cree.[19] "Judgment" demonstrates that Hemingway was a precocious Minimalist, well versed in the technique of using allusions and historical references as a means to add depth.

Meaningful, suggestive imagery is almost entirely absent from Hemingway's high school prose, but his poems are a different matter. During their senior year, Hemingway and a classmate named Fred Wilcoxen coauthored three pieces that reflect the attributes of Imagism and Impressionism. In the first, titled "Athletic Verse: The Tackle," a self-effacing speaker synesthetically and kinetically describes the momentary sensations of making a football tackle: "A heaving, gasping chest, / Alert, shifting mud-stained legs. / A quick pull, a thrust, a headlong dive at a / Group of rushing legs."[20] Hemingway's grouping of fragmentary sensations, held together only by the progression of the player's physical movement, is reminiscent of Hamlin Garland's and Amy Lowell's prose poems. The point of view Hemingway and Wilcoxen employed is also interesting because it draws the audience into the experience, creating and sustaining the emotion that fuels the intensity of the act. Hemingway frequently uses this technique in *In Our Time*.

In the two years after he graduated from high school, Hemingway experienced life-changing events that shaped both the content and style of his fiction. In October 1917, he left for Kansas City and began a six-month tenure as a cub reporter for the *Kansas City Star*. The editors emphasized the importance of concision and, as Carlos Baker explains, "to work on the paper was to learn how 'to write declarative sentences,' how to 'avoid hackneyed adjectives,' and how 'to tell an interesting narrative.' There was also a stylebook which the young reporters were supposed to study. It said that the key to fine reporting was to 'use short sentences. Use short first paragraphs. Use vigorous English, not forgetting to strive for smoothness. Be positive, not negative.'"[21] Hemingway did not receive bylines for his articles at the *Star*, so it is unknown to what degree he absorbed these axioms.

Perhaps inspired by a coworker at the *Star* named Theodore "Ted" Brumback, Hemingway ended his tenure at the Kansas City newspaper in late April 1918 and joined the Red Cross ambulance corps. He returned to Oak Park for a short time and then began his journey to Europe on May 11.[22] One of his primary duties was to deliver chocolate and cigarettes to men at the front as a means to maintain their morale. While responsible for a canteen in

Fossalta di Piave on July 8, 1918, Hemingway sustained multiple injuries to his legs from Austrian mortar and machine-gun fire. Despite his wounds, it is reported that he attempted to assist one of his fellow comrades during the attack. Hemingway was sent to Milan and was falsely thought to have been the first American wounded during the war. During his convalescence, he began a romance with a nurse named Agnes von Kurowsky, a relationship that would heavily influence his fiction. Once he had adequately healed enough to travel, Hemingway sailed for New York on January 4, 1919.[23] When he returned home, he resumed his commitment to becoming a writer.

Hemingway's first postwar prose efforts were about as successful as his high school material, but in 1919 he authored a series of sketches titled "Crossroads—An Anthology." Begun in November, the pieces are based on figures Hemingway observed in the area of Horton Bay, Michigan.[24] Perhaps the most noteworthy of the group is the first, "Pauline Snow." The plot is relatively simple. Pauline Snow, "the only beautiful girl we ever had out at the bay," has her reputation ruined because she likes to take evening walks with a man named Art Simons. Some of the townsmen spot them and make "a complaint." In the end, Pauline is sent away to the "correction school" and Art marries "one of the Jenkins girls." As Michael Reynolds observes, the vignette seems heavily influenced by Stephen Crane's *Maggie: A Girl of the Streets*.[25] Pauline is said to be "like an Easter Lily coming up straight and lithe and beautiful out of a dung heap," reminiscent of Crane's description of Maggie as a girl who "blossomed in a mud puddle."[26] Maggie's seducer, Pete, is paralleled by Art, a callous and brutish man interested in Pauline only for her body. The direct, declarative sentences, as well as some of the details Hemingway employs, suggest that he had read Sherwood Anderson's *Winesburg, Ohio*, published earlier in 1919.[27] Art appears similar to Wing Biddlebaum, the protagonist in Anderson's "Hands," in that he "couldn't come to most places at the Bay" and has "thick blunt fingers . . . always touching" Pauline "when he talked."[28] Hemingway's prose is highly implicative: Art has done something ignominious, probably of a sexual nature, to earn the ire of the town. Like so many of Hemingway's later stories, the plot of "Pauline Snow" is in part shaped by omitted events that are implied to have happened before the action begins. Although Hemingway had also written trite, florid tales such as "The Mercenaries—A Story" in 1919, he was beginning to embrace the central tendencies of Minimalism, particularly in his continued use of allusion.

The two years following Hemingway's return from the war were aesthetically and experientially transitional. Between the time he returned to Oak

Park in 1919 and left for Paris in December 1921, he sold features to the *Toronto Star*, including a clever story about receiving a free shave,[29] and married his first wife, Hadley Richardson. He quarreled with his mother, Grace, who told Ernest in a July 1920 missive that he needed to "come to yourself, cease your lazy loafing, and pleasure seeking."[30] Once he and Hadley had moved into their first Paris apartment on January 9, 1922, Ernest began to write what Carlos Baker called "short, impressionistic pieces, where every word must count both for itself and for its effect on all the others."[31] Hemingway had composed brief, sensorial verse in high school but was moving toward a more reportorial approach.

In March 1922, Hemingway introduced himself to Gertrude Stein, commencing a complex relationship that helped determine his approach to the epistemic parameters of his stories. Richard Hasbany writes that Stein introduced the young writer to her "technique of rendering subjective states of characters through repetition." The resulting effect is that "the repetitious phrase of Stein captures a rhythm of imprecise thought and perception, of the mind hitting and missing and hitting again what it really sees and truly feels."[32] Hemingway's exposure to Impressionist art and literature may also have planted some of these same ideas within his aesthetic consciousness. In addition to the pieces he viewed at the Art Institute of Chicago and in the major Paris museums, Hemingway was familiar with the work of Hamlin Garland, Ambrose Bierce, and Stephen Crane.[33] Using techniques found in their fiction, Hemingway exploits the fundamental difference between experiencing and understanding in many of the pieces that comprise *In Our Time*.

Hemingway's opinion of Stein changed in the decades after he lived in Paris, but he consistently expressed admiration for Ezra Pound.[34] Along with the central Imagist principles of precision and suggestiveness, Pound's primary contribution to Hemingway's development was in his emphasis on the importance of linking images with specific emotions. Scott Donaldson asserts that "Pound taught both Eliot and Hemingway how to recreate emotions, not through a general ooze of feeling, but through specific concrete images." Eliot formulated this concept as the "objective correlative."[35] In Hemingway's fiction, narrators rarely supply direct information about feeling. Images and actions are reported objectively, as "truly" as possible, but Hemingway still generates emotional depth through implication. Experience and sensations rarely have a distinct unity, however, because they are innately volatile.

Although it achieves unity because of its thematic and stylistic continuity, *In Our Time* is essentially an arrangement of fragments. Harry Levin maintains that "editors rejected" many of Hemingway's early pieces because they were "nothing but sketches and anecdotes," but Levin concludes that "fragments of truth, after all, are the best that a writer can offer; and, as Hemingway has said, '. . . Any part you make will represent the whole if it's made truly.'"[36] *In Our Time* has a varied and somewhat convoluted publication history, and it is a fitting illustration of the accretive nature of Hemingway's image-centered prose. The first pieces were six vignettes that originally appeared in the spring 1923 edition of the *Little Review* under the heading "IN OUR TIME."[37] These later served as chapters I, II, III, IV, V, and IX of the 1925 and 1930 editions of *In Our Time*. Hemingway combined them with twelve others in assembling the 1924 collection titled *in our time*. In 1925, he released *In Our Time* using two tales that had previously been in print in his first book, *Three Stories and Ten Poems*, "Out of Season" and "My Old Man," and added them to ten narratives primarily written in 1924.

Since 1930, *In Our Time* has begun with a harrowing, prose-poetic vignette called "On the Quai at Smyrna."[38] In many ways a nontraditional story, it has no discernible plot. A man is speaking to the narrator, recalling a scene from the burning of Smyrna during the Greek and Turkish War, a conflict Hemingway observed and wrote about in 1922.[39] The narrative technique is somewhat complex, as it is a third-person narrator who is conveying the events described by another man who, given his diction, is likely British. The vignette is Minimalistic, a recounting of visual and auditory details seemingly remembered in fragments. "On the Quai" is as much about the nature of memory as it is about the horrors of civilian life during a war. In an interview with George Plimpton published in the *Paris Review*, Hemingway included Hieronymus Bosch among his influences, and the opening image of "On the Quai" is reminiscent of the Dutch painter's nightmarish scenes of hell.[40] In an emotionally deadened and reportorial manner, the protagonist recalls that "the strange thing was . . . how they screamed every night at midnight. I do not know why they screamed at that time. We were in the harbor and they were all on the pier and at midnight they started screaming. We used to turn the searchlight on them to quiet them. That always did the trick."[41] The speaker seems cavalier about what he is describing, a perspective Louis H. Leiter describes as a "factual, businesslike, apparently unfeeling tone, playing over the horror and grotesque."[42] The seeming flippancy of the last sentence does not result from indifference. "On the Quai" is essentially a first-person retrospective narration relayed in third person, and the implication is not that the man is cruel and uncaring but that he has not yet emotionally come to terms with what he has witnessed.

The deadpan, detached voice of "On the Quai" is one that Hemingway uses frequently in *In Our Time*. The two prose poems dealing with Mons, interchapters III and IV, are narrated in the same tone. Charles A. Fenton identifies the inspiration for the voice as Hemingway's friend Eric Edward "Chink" Dorman-Smith, who served in the Royal Northumberland Fusiliers during World War I,[43] and this connection likely explains the use of British terms such as "topping" and "potted." Beyond the careless attitude with which the speaker approaches the efficient killing of German combatants, these images of easy success, the "perfect barricade," later a "perfect obstacle" (37), serve as an ironic reminder that the "glorious" gains won at Mons were unusual in the course of what turned out to be a terrible war.[44] The historical context illustrates a theme that runs throughout the collection: human experience is entropic.

The Mons vignettes point to orderly beginnings whereas the other interchapters, particularly those based on the Greco-Turkish conflict, tend to focus on chaotic events. Hemingway reported on the evacuation of the Greeks from Adrianople, and Fenton provides an extensive account of how Hemingway trimmed away the extraneous, emotive language of his journalism in order to form the grim images in chapter II.[45] Fenton also articulates one of the primary effects that Minimalist authors achieve by relaying sensory details through a nonintrusive narrator: the intensity of the "horror was far greater" because the audience was required to reach their "own conclusions."[46] The final four sentences are the most provocative: "Women and kids were in the carts crouched with mattresses, mirrors, sewing machines, bundles. There was a woman having a kid with a young girl holding a blanket over her and crying. Scared sick looking at it. It rained all through the evacuation" (21). Like his counterpart in Ivan Turgenev's *Sportsman's Sketches*, the narrator objectively renders a circumstance that demands a moral response but offers little or no direction as to what it should be.[47] The closest the narrator comes to making himself a part of the image is when he says "scared sick looking at it." The referent is ambiguous and could be the speaker or the young girl. Hemingway wrote about his personal response to the scenes he saw on the Karagatch road outside of Adrianople. After marveling at the ease with which his acquaintance Shorty Wornall, an American cameraman, was able to fall asleep after filming a burning village, Hemingway wrote that "I couldn't get the horror of that twenty mile long procession out of my mind, and I had seen some dreadful things that day."[48] Perhaps as a means to achieve a type of closure, at least within the parameters of the collection, Hemingway wrote two more pieces based on his observations of central Europe.

Chapter V and the final vignette in *In Our Time*, "L'Envoi," are vivid illustrations of retribution and punishment deferred. In the first, the horrors of the Karagatch road have consequences for six Greek ministers who are lined up and shot. Hemingway did not witness the execution but likely derived the piece from a story published in the Paris *Tribune*.[49] After the Turks had destroyed his army, King Constantine of Greece fled to England, abdicating in favor of his son George, and left his cabinet ministers to defend themselves against the new military leadership. England and America, whose governments and citizens had considerable economic interests in Greece, did little to stop the violence against the former regime.[50] Hemingway dramatizes the execution using images reminiscent of Pound's "In a Station of the Metro," his narrator recalling that "there were pools of water in the courtyard. There were wet dead leaves on the paving of the courtyard. It rained hard. All the shutters of the hospital were nailed shut."[51] The falling, pooling rain and the sealed hospital serve as imagistic correlatives, juxtaposed with a minister who is "sick with typhoid" and "sitting in the water with his head on his knees" when he is shot (51). The scene generates moral and emotional complexity, the pathetic end of the ministers placed against King Constantine's blithe new life in an English garden. Hemingway wrote in a letter to Pound that "L'Envoi" was based on an account from Wornall and that it brought an end to the Greco-Turkish war material: "The refugees leave Thrace, due to the Greek ministers, who are shot. The whole thing closes with the talk with the King of Greece and his Queen in their garden, (just written), which shows the king all right. The last sentence in it is ——— Like all Greeks what he really wanted was to get to America. ——— My pal Shorty, movie operator with me in Thrace, just brings the dope on the King. Edifying."[52] Constantine's sentiments about the deceased ministers display an ironic emotional detachment, a state Hemingway repeatedly describes in the collection, telling the narrator, "I think he [Plastiras] did right though shooting those chaps. If Kerensky had shot a few men things might have been altogether different. Of course the great thing in this sort of an affair is not to be shot oneself!" (157). Hemingway shows remarkable control in this sketch, allowing the repugnance of the king's figurative myopia to speak for itself.

The precision with which Hemingway molds his narrative voices allows him to communicate emotional depth in even the most compressed sketches. Fear is ubiquitous in *In Our Time*, and Hemingway deftly conveys it through the manipulation of perspective. As the Mons interchapters show, the implications of Hemingway's fiction depend upon the way an image is described. Recalling an evening moving along the road on the way to Champagne, the speaker in chapter I bluntly reveals that "everybody was drunk" (13). The result of the men's overimbibing seems to have been a mix of hunger, paranoia, and unease. Nick Adams, perhaps Hemingway's most well known protagonist, says in "A Way You'll Never Be" that he "was stinking in every attack," an admission that he was afraid.[53] The narrator in chapter I says that he was "kitchen corporal" and remembers being told by an adjutant to put out his kitchen fire lest the enemy see the light. His drunkenness has affected the quality of his memory as the only reaction he can summon to what happened is that it was "funny going along that road" (13). The suggestion is that it was "funny" in the sense that the men were on edge, but it is also a bland adjective that shows the speaker lacks commitment. He is, in other words, being cautiously imprecise. Without light, they are moving through the night without certainty or direction. The implication is that they have been drinking in order to combat a sense of foreboding. Hemingway omits the term "afraid" but implies it is the mental state that governs the scene.[54]

In some cases, an important yet omitted term can be derived from manuscript evidence: "Soldier's Home" provides such an example. In the version that appears in *In Our Time*, Harold Krebs arrives in Oklahoma to find "a world that is corrupt, artificial, and hypocritical and in which he no longer feels at home."[55] The title "Soldier's Home" is ironic; Krebs's home now inspires unease.[56] The "hysteria" with which the town had at first responded to the returning men has faded, and when he feels the need to talk about what has happened, "no one wanted to hear about it" (69).

In the first draft of "Soldier's Home," Hemingway wrote two sentences that use terms that are crucial to the intellectual core of the tale. Upon returning home, the narrator says that "the war was well over. The reaction to the war time ~~hysteria~~ feelings had set in." He goes on to describe how "Krebs knew he was a hero. At least he had done for a long time what the other ~~men~~ soldiers from his town had done a little."[57] "Hysteria" and "heroism" are important concepts in the story of Harold Krebs, but the latter does not appear. His feelings of loss and purposelessness, despite the excellence of his service, are exacerbated by the zealousness of his family and home town. He has sacrificed something of himself in the war, perhaps experienced a significant "psychic shock," but he receives no recognition and no empathy. In the end he seems disgusted by his lack of fortitude, paradoxically illustrating that home-life can sometimes be more emotionally harrowing than a battlefield. Most troubling, however, is his admitted inability to love.

Hemingway seldom presents love as a positive, or even mildly curative, emotion; it more often leads to feelings of disaffection, confusion, and resentment. "A Very Short Story" is typical of Minimalism because it is an admixture of the imagined and the autobiographical. Scott Donaldson maintained that writing "A Very Short Story" was essentially a "therapeutic" act, a tale that resulted from Hemingway's desire to punish Agnes von Kurowsky for her infidelity.[58] While it is impossible to know Hemingway's exact emotional response to the end of the relationship, it is telling that he used some of the circumstances and language from Agnes's "break-up" letter in his fictional account. The narrator says that "on the train from Padua to Milan they quarrelled about her not being willing to come home at once" (66). The narrative provides a detail omitted from the letter, as Agnes says only that "I tried hard to make you understand a bit of what I was thinking on that trip from Padua to Milan, but, you acted like a spoiled child, & I couldn't keep on hurting you."[59] Hemingway's narrator says that the letter Luz sends to the protagonist declares that "she loved him as always, but she realized now it was only a boy and girl love" (66). Agnes was seven years older than Hemingway, a fact that formed part of her rationalization for her actions: "But, I am now & always will be too old, & that's the truth, & I can't get away from the fact that you're just a boy—a kid."[60] Hemingway does not reveal that his protagonist was acting like a "spoiled child" or that there was a significant age difference between the lovers, instead changing the terms to "boy and girl love." The main character in "A Very Short Story" is repeatedly victimized by women, never the transgressor.

In his tales dealing with marriage, Hemingway presents equally bitter situations but tends to be more subtle in his method. Biographical information is less important, but much meaning can be derived from a single word or action. "Mr. and Mrs. Elliot" is somewhat unusual, a cruel polemic about a sexually incompatible couple that ends with the wife contentedly embracing lesbianism. Originally titled "Mr. and Mrs. Smith," the story was an attack on the poets Chard Powers Smith and T. S. Eliot; the former wrote an angry letter in response and was in turn threatened by Hemingway.[61] Less salacious and more successful works of fiction than "Mr. and Mrs. Elliot," "Out of Season" and "Cat in the Rain" are closely related as both explore the destructive nature of capriciousness. In "Out of Season," a husband insists that his wife accompany him on an illegal fishing trip. Hemingway does not indicate the motivation for the expedition, and the venture in many ways defies logic. The couple is in Italy, and their guide, Peduzzi, speaks poor English, in part because he is drunk. The journey to the fishing spot is, unsurprisingly, fraught with tension. Peduzzi insists they stop for Marsala, and he finds that the Specialty of Domestic and Foreign Wines shop is closed, information that "someone passing" delivers to Peduzzi "scornfully" (98). The expedition seems cursed from its inception, a darkly humorous account of failure.

Peduzzi's incompetence exacerbates the friction between the young man and his wife. The protagonist asks the elder man about fishing before lunch, but during the meal the couple quarrels. The subject of their disagreement is ambiguous, although Kenneth G. Johnston argues that they are having a dispute over whether the wife, Tiny, should have an abortion. Shortly after the couple arrives at the Concordia for Marsala, the husband apologizes, telling his wife,

> "I'm sorry you feel so rotten, Tiny," he said. "I'm sorry I talked the way I did at lunch. We were both getting at the same thing from different angles."
>
> "It doesn't make any difference," she said. "None of it makes any difference." (99)

Johnston interprets "her lagging behind, her sullenness, her leaving her drink untouched" as signs that she is in opposition to her husband's desire that she terminate the pregnancy. The key to Johnston's position, however, is Tiny's misunderstanding of the drunken Peduzzi's English. Johnston argues that when the guide says "daughter" and Tiny hears "doctor," it is a type of Freudian slip.[62] The more likely cause of the couple's disagreement is that she is frustrated with her husband's lack of empathy: she does not want to go fishing. When he introduces the idea at lunch, she says as much and he does not listen to her. She does not feel well, what they are doing is illegal, and Tiny does not like being involved in one of her husband's improprieties. The man eventually regrets his decision, admitting that

> "everybody in the town saw us going through with these rods. We're probably being followed by the game police now. I wish we weren't in on this damn thing. This damned old fool is so drunk, too."
>
> "Of course you haven't got the guts to just go back," said the wife. "Of course you have to go on."

> "Why don't you go back? Go on back, Tiny."
>
> "I'm going to stay with you. If you go to jail we might as well both go." (100)

Before the trip becomes a resolute failure because the men have no *piombo*, or lead, for sinkers, Tiny heads back to the hotel. Not yet completely defeated, the young man gives Peduzzi four lire and halfheartedly commits to another attempt at fishing the next day.

Well after he had written "Out of Season," Hemingway made a series of provocative comments about it in a letter to F. Scott Fitzgerald. He admitted that the piece is strongly autobiographical, and that it "was an almost literal transcription of what happened. Your ear is always more acute when you have been upset by a row of any sort, mine I mean, and when I came in from the unproductive fishing trip I wrote that story right off on the typewriter without punctuation."[63] Hemingway also revealed that the plot was to focus on Peduzzi, that "Out of Season" was intended "to be a tragic [*sic*] about the drunk of a guide because I reported him to the hotel owner—the one who appears in Cat in the Rain—and he fired him and as that was the last job he had in town and he was quite drunk and very desperate, hanged himself in the stable. At that time I was writing the In Our Time chapters and I wanted to write a tragic story *without* violence. So I didn't put in the hanging. Maybe that sounds silly. I didn't think the story needed it."[64] Peduzzi seems an ancillary figure in the narrative, so it is somewhat surprising that Hemingway meant to cast him in the central role of a tragedy.

In the years since Hemingway's death, scholars have dismissed Peduzzi's supposed suicide, but it deserves careful consideration. While external, after-the-fact revelations and biographical information do not form part of a work's figurative iceberg, they can serve to illuminate what resides below the surface. In *A Moveable Feast*, Hemingway attributed his decision to withhold information about the guide's death to his desire to put the iceberg theory into practice, arguing that, "I had omitted the real end of it which was that the old man hanged himself. This was omitted on my new theory that you could omit anything if you knew that you omitted and the omitted part would strengthen the story and make people feel something more than they understood."[65] Carlos Baker, Joseph Flora, and James Steinke roundly dismiss Hemingway's purported experiment.[66]

While there is no textual evidence to support Hemingway's assertion, and the usefulness of what "people feel" is diminished by the inherent subjectivity of emotions, it is a feasible argument if "Out of Season" is read in the context of "A Clean, Well-Lighted Place." Peduzzi has been rejected by his town and stripped of his dignity. When he points out his daughter to the young couple, she turns away from him and disappears inside her home (100). He is, Hemingway implies, a lonely outcast. Given his age, penchant for alcohol, and unwanted social solitude, he is in many ways comparable to the old man in "Well-Lighted Place." The latter has lost his wife and is estranged from his family, perhaps because he too has lost his sense of purpose. Both Peduzzi and the old man have been disconnected from their respective communities, and within the economy of Hemingway's fiction, extreme isolation is a state that leads to depression and death. After spending time with Tiny and her husband, perhaps Peduzzi has been reminded of his own failed relationships and concludes that there is little hope for reconciliation.

In "Cat in the Rain," Hemingway uses a series of precisely wrought images in his portrayal of similar relational dysfunction. Composed in the early spring months of 1923, "Cat in the Rain" is a remarkable narrative in that, on its surface, it is rather mundane.[67] Like "Out of Season," the narrative is essentially about the destructiveness of capriciousness. The young woman is impulsive, craving attention regardless of whether it is positive or negative. When she decides she wants a pet, she does not think about her immediate circumstances. The wife's unspoken desire that her husband capture, or perhaps steal, something that belongs to someone else is absurd.

Constructed of a series of fragmentary images, it is appropriate that Hemingway begins "Cat in the Rain" with a painterly description of the scene outside of the hotel. Rendering the war monument in the square, the narrator says that "it was made of bronze and glistened in the rain. It was raining. The rain dripped from the palm trees. Water stood in pools in the gravel paths. The sea broke in a long line in the rain and slipped back down the beach to come up and break again in a long line in the rain" (91). The repetition of "rain" and "long line" represents a melding of poetic language with sensory detail, the sound of the rain falling in puddles and the breaking of the waves implying a soft sonic consistency. Hemingway frequently commented on his indebtedness to the French artist Paul Cézanne, first in the excised section of "Big Two-Hearted River" and again in *A Moveable Feast*. Hemingway's precise, direct sentences are metaphorically reminiscent of the painter's brushstrokes, which art historian John Walford describes as a "repeated series of short gestures" laid "on the surface of the canvas so as to register individually on the eye." In *Hemingway and the Arts*, Emily Stipes Watts compares the suggestive nature of Hemingway's sentences with the technique of both Cézanne and Francisco José de Goya, positing that they "emphasized economy and demanded that each brush stroke function as completely as possible. For them, a brush stroke was intensive and essential."[68] Each painter's devotion to craft was broadly inspirational to Hemingway, reaching beyond technique alone.

While Hemingway's prose style was in part shaped by Cézanne, the content found in interchapters IX through XIV, all of which deal with the Spanish bullfight, was influenced by Goya. The tragedy of the ritual is depicted as a confluence of sensorial stimulation in fragmentary images. In his review of *in our time*, Edmund Wilson maintains that Hemingway's "bull-fight sketches have the dry sharpness and elegance of the bull-fight lithographs of Goya. And, like Goya, he is concerned first of all with making a fine picture. Too proud an artist to simplify in the interests of conventional pretenses, he is showing you what life is like."[69] E. R. Hagemann observes that "grouped together as they are, these six Chapters comprise a miniature *tauromaquia* derived ultimately from Francisco Goya's thirty-three etchings of 1816."[70] While the poignancy of the prose poems is generally derived from narrative style and austerely described physical motion, a single image tends to stand out in each. In IX, for example, the exhausted *torero*, who has had to kill five bulls, "sat down in the sand and puked and they held a cape over him while the crowd hollered and threw things down into the bullring" (83). The pageantry of the cape is oddly juxtaposed with the implied tastes and smells associated with the matador's action. Hemingway occasionally incorporates scatological references into the interchapters as a means of adding sensorial power. In chapter XV, the soon-to-be-executed Sam Cardinella "lost control of his sphincter muscle," and the guards who had been carrying him "were both disgusted" (143). The images in the other chapters on the *torero* are a similar mixture of the beautiful and the grotesque: the confident movements of a picador alongside the hanging entrails of his horse (89); the vigor of Villalta and his bull charging at each other, man and beast becoming "one"; and "the red hilt of the sword sticking out dully between the bull's shoulders" (105). Goya and Hemingway continually tested the boundary between allure and repugnance, perhaps leading Wilson to draw a comparison between painter and writer.

Hemingway repeatedly suggests that life is replete with moments of beauty and brutality. His varied narrative voices offer no mitigating reassurances or reasons for optimism, but they communicate wonder alongside ugliness.

Sheldon Norman Grebstein maintains that Hemingway's fiction differs from that of his peers because he "almost always avoids direct exposition of theme, didactic description or discussion of character, and authorial commentary upon action and motive."[71] The closest he comes to offering a type of guidance is the occasional mention of a rule or law. In chapter VIII, another scene derived from a newspaper article that involves a pointless act of violence, a policeman named Drevitts asks his partner, Jimmy Boyle, if they are going to get in trouble for shooting a Hungarian pair of cigar-store robbers without first attempting to apprehend them.[72] With disturbing simplicity, Boyle points out that the perpetrators were "crooks" and "Wops," and therefore expendable. The implication is that there is no way to rationalize an irrational act, so by default there is nothing for the speaker to ponder. Joe Butler, the boy in "My Old Man," attempts to maintain the dignity of his father's legacy but overhears two men refer to his dad as a "crook." Their irreverence leads him to nihilistically conclude that it "seems like when they get started they don't leave a guy nothing" (129). Perhaps influenced by the work written in the American literary Naturalist tradition, Hemingway often depicts negative forces as unrelenting and indifferent. Even though the protagonist in "The Revolutionist" is described as a resolute idealist, in the end he must accept the cruel irony of a Sion jail cell.[73] Hemingway's narrators, however, do not always seem completely unsympathetic. In the Nick Adams stories, the speaker seems most closely attuned to the protagonist, implying an uncommon sense of empathy and understanding.

"Indian Camp" is told by a third-person narrator who seems to have a special affinity or sensitivity toward the experience of the young protagonist, Nick Adams. The subtlety of the narration, the absence of important details, and the numerous implications that can be drawn from the narrative are in part what make it one of the finest tales in the American Minimalist tradition. Scholars such as Philip Young, Robert M. Slabey, Joseph Flora, and Clinton S. Burhans focus their criticism on Nick as an innocent figure who has been initiated into, or victimized by, a vicious world. Nick Adams's life is marked by a series of events that have the potential to cause long-lasting and substantial psychological harm, so part of what motivates the ongoing conversation about "Indian Camp" is the degree to which this experience has been damaging.[74] The Nick Adams stories are often interpreted in the context of one another despite the fact that they were not written according to a linear chronology; Nick's presence at the camp has deep implications for all of the narratives in which he is involved.

The younger Adams's interactions with his father and uncle, and the way they respond to him, raise a number of interpretative possibilities. One of the more obscure arguments to arise about "Indian Camp" is over whether Uncle George is in fact the father of the child.[75] The case for Uncle George's paternity is predicated on seemingly minor plot details. He arrives at the camp before Nick and Dr. Adams, and the narrator says that Uncle George is smoking and "gave both the Indians cigars" (15). His vulgar attitude toward the mother, who he calls a "damn squaw bitch" for biting him (17), may suggest his irritation is due to nerves. When the unusually excited Dr. Adams tells his younger brother that the impromptu surgery is "one for the medical journal," George acidly replies, "Oh, you're a great man, all right" (18). At the end of the narrative, George stays behind, and the reason for his remaining in the camp is not given.

In the original manuscript of "Indian Camp," dated November 4, 1923, Hemingway presents a different set of possibilities and shows that the iceberg for this tale is rather complex. The first eight pages of "Indian Camp" were excised, an editorial decision that in retrospect was wise. Philip Young published the omitted material in *The Nick Adams Stories* in 1970, calling it "Three Shots." Uncle George's attitude about the journey to the camp has largely been shaped by his irritation with Nick. The manuscript reveals that during a bout of cowardice inspired by Fanny J. Crosby's hymn "Some Day the Silver Cord Will Break," a song centered on a consideration of the inevitability of death, Nick disrupted Uncle George during a fishing expedition.[76] Nick was instructed to fire his rifle three times if there was trouble at the camp, and when his uncle hears the shots he complains,

> "Damn that kid," Uncle George said as they rowed back. "What did you tell him to call us in for? He's probably got the Heeby Jeebies about something."
>
> Uncle George was an enthusiastic fisherman and his father's younger brother.
>
> "Oh well. He's pretty small." His father said.
>
> "That's no reason to bring him into the woods with us."
>
> "I know he's an awful coward," his father said. "but ~~this is the~~ we're all yellow at that age."
>
> "I can't stand him," George said, "He's such an awful liar."

Hemingway deleted several telling lines from the exchange, cuts that Young honored when he published "Three Shots." Trying to assuage his angered brother, Dr. Adams continues by saying,

> "Oh well forget it. You'll get plenty of fishing ((anyway)). ~~Besides jacklighting isn't much of a sport~~."
> ~~"Anything that's worth doing is worth not being interrupted in."~~
> ~~"Forget it."~~[77]

In the deleted dialogue, Dr. Adams subtly insults his brother by insinuating that George's irritation is unwarranted because he himself is engaged in something that is improper. George is not fishing the "right way," just as Nick is not exercising an expected degree of courage and self-sufficiency. When George later tells his brother that he is a "great man," the implication is that the younger Adams has not forgotten the original slight. By gloating in the aftermath of what seems to have been a general success, Dr. Adams has also committed a violation of decorum. In the context of the material Hemingway withheld, George is not a new father but rather an angered sportsman who is finally given the opportunity to retaliate by pointing out his brother's imperfections.

Subtle questions of propriety often cause friction in the Nick Adams stories. True to the Imagist axiom that no word be wasted, the language in Hemingway's narrations often seems extraordinarily momentous. In tales such as "The Doctor and the Doctor's Wife" or "The End of Something," actions cannot be disregarded as unreasonable or impulsive. Perceived slights are at times indicative of self-righteousness. In "The Doctor," Henry Adams is insulted by Dick Boulton, a man he has hired to help saw logs. The wood has washed up on the beach in front of the Adamses' cabin, lost by a boat from the logging company. Dr. Adams considers it "driftwood"; Dick feels it is stolen property. Henry threatens Boulton but the bigger man backs him down, forcing him to accept his own cowardice.[78] Dr. Adams tells his wife that his adversary "wanted a row" so he would not have to repay a debt. Mrs. Adams, a Christian Scientist and in Sheridan Baker's terms an "exacting hypochondriac,"[79] condescendingly tells her husband that she hopes he did not lose his temper and that "he who ruleth his spirit is greater than he that taketh a city" (25). The only relief the doctor receives comes when he finds Nick, who may or may not have witnessed the scene on the beach, and they disappear into the woods in search of black squirrels.

Nick rarely seems to have a curative effect on others; he spends much of his time coming to terms emotionally with his own difficult experiences. Even with his dad, his presence is positive, but he does not say anything particularly profound or helpful. On the other hand, a young boy is not necessarily expected to perform such a role in his father's life. As Nick's story progresses, he begins to face more mature matters. "The End of Something" and "The Three-Day Blow," both of which were inspired by Hemingway's "brief romance" with Marjorie Bump, are about his painful breakup with a young woman.[00] The narratives are Minimalistic: actions are more meaningful than dialogue or exposition. Adams is in his early to mid-teens in these stories, no longer the young innocent who appears in "Indian Camp" and "The Doctor." In "The End," he employs tactics similar to those of Dick Boulton by engineering an argument with Marjorie so it will be easier to part with her. The couple goes out fishing together, and Nick grows irritated with Marjorie because she repeatedly shows that she is in many ways the young man's intellectual equal. She sees through his ruse and asks him to explain the true problem; all he can articulate is that "it isn't fun anymore. Not any of it" (34). The one indication that the breakup was planned is that Nick's friend Bill arrives in the end and asks if there was a "scene" (35). Bill offers little consolation, unable to interpret his comrade's body language.

In "The End of Something," Nick Adams is not a particularly sympathetic figure, and "The Three-Day Blow" accomplishes little in recasting him as such. "The End" opens with exposition about the final days of "Hortons Bay" as "a lumbering town," now ruined and vacated. While there are obvious imagistic parallels between the collapse of the town and the dissolution of the young couple's relationship, the opening paragraphs speak directly to Nick's own emotional arc. The implication is that he and Marjorie did have "fun" at some point, that she aroused his senses, and that the problem is that her presence no longer elicits an emotional reaction. Nick is not yet old enough to break up with Marjorie in a manner that shows he is empathetic; everything about his methods reflects profound self-absorption. Nick shows even less tact in the first draft of the story, which Hemingway wrote in March 1924. In the published version, Marjorie sees the ruins of a mill and romantically opines that it "seems more like a castle." In the manuscript, Nick's girlfriend is less confident and he more negative:

> "What's that ruin Nick?" Marjorie asked.
> "It's Stroud's old mill."

> "It looks like a castle."
> "Not much."[81]

Hemingway achieves a stronger balance in the final draft in terms of characterization. Given the circumstances, Marjorie acquits herself rather well. The equanimity she shows as she rows away from the picnic site contrasts with the carousing that takes place in the narrative that follows "The End." Seeking a means to quell his feelings of loss, Nick drinks with Bill in "The Three-Day Blow," numbing himself with talk of books and baseball.

Similar to Harold Krebs, Nick Adams does not achieve a sense of peace in matters of love, at least not within *In Our Time*. In "Cross-Country Snow," he shows ambivalence about the prospect of returning home to his wife and becoming a father. The implication is that the emotional high Nick feels from skiing cannot be matched by the faded joys, and responsibilities, of domestic life.[82] As he settles into a warm inn after taking a run, Nick proclaims that "there's nothing really can touch skiing, is there? . . . The way it feels when you first drop off on a long run" (109). His sentiments are reminiscent of those he expresses to Marjorie, implying that his home life "isn't fun anymore." With his anticlimactic wedding out of the way, he knows that "there isn't any good in promising" because of the vicissitudes of life. Circumstances can change quickly, which he knows because he has been to war.

While much of the fiction in *In Our Time* involves physical conflict, only one interchapter (chapter VI) and one short story ("The Battler") are specifically about Nick's fighting experiences. In "The Battler," Nick is knocked from a moving railcar in northern Michigan and meets a former boxer named Ad Francis. A third man, Bugs, a figure who is almost certainly modeled after Bildad Johnson from Sherwood Anderson's "I Want to Know Why," is Ad's caretaker.[83] The focus of "The Battler" is on the fragility of the human psyche, and it becomes clear early on that Ad and Bugs are mentally frail. Early in their conversation, Ad says,

> "I'm crazy. Listen, you ever been crazy?"
> "No," Nick said. "How does it get to you?"
> "I don't know," Ad said. "When you got it you don't know about it. You know me, don't you?" (56)

Ad's paradoxical self-awareness seems strange until Bugs is required to knock him out with a blackjack. In his deft control over the broken-down fighter, the caretaker's complexity is demonstrated through his actions more than his words. Bugs's deliberate, ritualistic treatment of the food he cooks adumbrates Nick's careful preparation in "Big Two-Hearted River."[84] Francis's instability implies that unlike his companion, he has not found routines that grant him the ability to function in a somewhat sound manner.

Ad Francis has been wounded mentally and physically during his career as a fighter. Bugs tells Nick that Ad was accused of marrying his own sister and that the publicity caused her to leave him. His ear is missing, suggesting that he has taken many beatings inside and outside of the ring. By comparison, however, Nick's medical history is more complicated. In chapter VI, the next piece after "The Battler," he is shown sitting with his back to a church. His "legs stuck out awkwardly," and the narrator reveals that he is injured because he has "been hit in the spine" (63). Nick tells his wounded friend, Rinaldi, that they have "made a separate peace," having essentially paid whatever nationalistic debts they may have owed. Philip Young argues that chapter VI is central not only to *In Our Time* but also to much of Hemingway's oeuvre, maintaining that "it would be quite impossible to exaggerate the importance of this short scene" and that Nick's injury "culminates, climaxes and epitomizes the wounds he has been getting as a growing boy."[85] The extent of Nick's spinal wound is difficult to gauge, however, because he is able to hike, ski, and fish after he is demobilized. In a later work, "A Way You'll Never Be," he admits that he has suffered from a serious head injury for which he should have been trepanned.[86] In "Cross-Country Snow," he tells George that he cannot telemark because of his leg wound, a detail that indicates Nick may have been hurt in the same way Hemingway was during his service with the Red Cross.

The emotional and physical toll of Nick's experiences motivate his actions in "Big Two-Hearted River," so the tale is in some ways a "culmination." However, the narrative is about a young man going through the process of healing, not an "end" to anything but rather an illustration of a single step in a long phase of recovery. In *A Moveable Feast*, Hemingway recounts a day he spent working on the story, probably in August 1924, and how it "was about coming back from the war but there was no mention of the war in it."[87] Read in the context of the vignette about Nick, as well as all of the other accounts of his time in World War I, the centrality of the omitted war becomes apparent. Nick's every word and movement suggest that he is on the verge of something and that his mental stability is at stake.

Similar to the opening passages of "Cat in the Rain" and "The End of Something," the first paragraph of "Big Two-Hearted River" contains meaningful images that establish the plot in a concrete time and place. Nick arrives in Seney, Michigan, by train and finds a charred landscape, a scene that Kenneth G. Johnston describes as being "like a Cézanne watercolor created from touches of blacks and grays and patches of white."[88] The narrator explains that "there was no town, nothing but the rails and the burned over country. The thirteen saloons that had lined the one street of Seney had not left a trace. The foundations of the Mansion House hotel stuck up above the ground. The stone was chipped and split by the fire. It was all that was left of the town of Seney. Even the surface had been burned off the ground" (133). The logging town had been destroyed by a forest fire in 1891.[89] The implication is that what Nick sees reminds him of the war, and that his movement toward river country that is fertile represents regeneration. The scene may be allusive to T. S. Eliot's *The Waste Land*, and many scholars have posited that the poem plays a role in several of the stories in *In Our Time*. Wendolyn E. Tetlow and Linda Welshimer Wagner, for example, maintain that Hemingway mimicked some of the techniques found in Eliot's verse.[90] William Adair detects a reference to the "Game of Chess" section of *The Waste Land* in "Cat in the Rain."[91] Carlos Baker writes that Hemingway "was unable to take it [*The Waste Land*] seriously," however, at least when beginning to write "Cat in the Rain."[92] Given his war experiences, Hemingway had other material to draw from. In his journalistic pieces on the Greco-Turkish conflict, he describes Constantinople as a city in which "the dust is so thick that a dog trotting along the road that parallels the Pera hillside kicks up a puff like a bullet striking every time his paws hit the ground. It is almost ankle deep on a man and the wind swirls it in clouds. If it rains this is all mud. The sidewalks are so narrow that everyone has to walk in the street and the streets are like rivers."[93] When he arrived in Adrianople, the scene was equally dire, and he reported that he "found the station a mud-hole crowded with soldiers, bundles, bed-springs, bedding, sewing machines, babies, broken carts, all in the mud and the drizzling rain. Kerosene flares lit up the scene."[94] In light of his own knowledge and memories, it seems unlikely that Hemingway drew imagistic inspiration from a cryptic poem written by a poet he did not seem to admire.[95]

In *The Waste Land*, Eliot makes frequent reference to the past, to literary and historical traditions belonging to defunct civilizations. Conversely, Nick Adams spends most of his time focusing on the present in "Big Two-Hearted River." The narrator is methodical in his descriptions, concentrating on sensorial details rather than Nick's contemplative moments. Early in part I, the speaker says that Nick's "muscles ached and the day was hot, but Nick felt happy. He felt he had left everything behind, the need for thinking, the need to write, other needs. It was all back of him" (134). Hemingway engages the senses throughout the story, particularly with his use of light and color. In a letter to Gertrude Stein, he says that in "Big Two-Hearted River" he was attempting "to do the country like Cézanne,"[96] a goal he at times accomplishes through sharp, clear images of the landscape: "Nick kept his direction by the sun. He knew where he wanted to strike the river and he kept on through the pine plain, mounting small rises to see other rises ahead of him and sometimes from the top of a rise a great solid island of pines off to his right or his left. He broke off some sprigs of the heathery sweet fern, and put them under his pack straps. The chafing crushed it and he smelled it as he walked" (136). Hemingway creates a layered effect by subtly shifting visual perspective. Like the Impressionists, he begins by communicating the position of the light. As Nick progressively ascends and descends, his view of the landscape is gradually elongated and he is able to progressively see farther into the distance until he views "a great solid island of pines" rather than more rises. In the last two sentences, Hemingway brings the focus back in close to Nick, describing what he smells as the "heathery sweet fern" crushed against his shoulder. Working his way toward the area he will fish, Nick favors experience over synthesis.

When Nick is inactive, the narrator's sentences reflect the protagonist's agitation by becoming clipped, or more staccato. At the end of the first day, Nick climbs into his tent and grows uneasy: "He had not been unhappy all day. This was different though. Now things were done. There had been this to do. Now it was done. It had been a hard trip. He was very tired. That was done. He had made his camp. He was settled. Nothing could touch him. It was a good place to camp. He was there, in the good place. He was in his home where he had made it. Now he was hungry" (139). His thoughts unwinding in an odd series of brief rationalizations, Nick finally relaxes when he realizes that there is more work to do, more for him to accomplish. Passages such as these demonstrate a musicality reminiscent of Amy Lowell's polyphonic prose in that the length of the "phrases" matches the emotional tenor of the content. The pace of Nick's thoughts implies a sense of paranoia, an increase in his heart rate that finally leads to a decrescendo of more elongated sentences.

The methodical fishing sequence in part II implies that Nick is safe when he focuses on the present but feels threatened when recalling the past. The rigorous hike into the forest from Seney, along with the current of the river, likely causes pain in his back and knee. His moments of agitation are probably related to his head wound as well as all of the brutality he has witnessed during his life. The war is nowhere more present than when Nick contemplates fishing in "the swamp," a place that in the context of "Big Two-Hearted River" serves as an objective correlative for the murky darkness of Nick's memories. Conveying the protagonist's thoughts, the narrator says that "in the swamp the banks were bare, the big cedars came together overhead, the sun did not come through, except in patches; in the fast deep water, in the half light, the fishing would be tragic. In the swamp fishing was a tragic adventure" (155). Without the distraction of the river's movement and the comfort of daylight, Nick would have no option but to confront his memories. As Nick heads back to camp after catching two sizeable trout, the narrator, again conveying Nick's thoughts, says that "there were plenty of days coming when he could fish the swamp" (156). In that moment, however, Nick is not ready.

The story did not originally end with the narrator admitting that Nick is still psychologically fragile but with a lengthy contemplation of fishing and writing that Pound would likely have dismissed as "licherary." The omitted passages are useful because they speak to Hemingway's aesthetic but would have weakened the tone and unity of "Big Two-Hearted River." For example, Nick opines that "talking about anything was bad. Writing about anything actual was bad. It always killed it. The only writing that was any good was what you made up, what you imagined, what made everything come true."[97] Hemingway did not share his character's view. In his own writing, Hemingway often begins with autobiography and imaginatively transforms it into fiction, an approach Minimalists such as Jay McInerney later practiced. "Big Two-Hearted River" is loosely based on a fishing trip Hemingway took with friends in 1919.[98] He seems to be attempting to fashion Nick into a separate writer with his own credo, but it does not work. In fact, Nick thinks of his spouse at one point and she happens to have the same name as Hemingway's first wife: "They were all married to fishing. Ezra thought fishing was a joke. So did most every body. He'd been married to it before he married Hadley. Really married to it. It wasn't any joke. So he lost them all. Hadley thought it was because they didn't like her."[99] The mood and method of this portion of the tale is inconsistent with the parts that precede it. The excised section of "Big Two-Hearted River" was later published in Philip Young's *The Nick Adams Stories* as "On Writing," an appropriate title because it is more of an essay than a narrative.[100] It is a series of what Gertrude Stein would have termed "meditations," and she famously told Hemingway that such "remarks are not literature."[101] Stein's advice is an important axiom for all writers, but it is crucial to Minimalists.

Hemingway's role in the development of American literary Minimalism cannot be overemphasized. Perhaps more than any other book, *In Our Time* models the aesthetic tenets of the mode. By alluding to historical events and creating precisely wrought objective correlatives, Hemingway wrote compressed tales that achieve the interpretive depth of poetry. While not all of his attempts at generating implication through omission are unqualified successes, narratives such as "Indian Camp" and "Big Two-Hearted River" stand among the finest stories in the tradition. Hemingway did not singlehandedly invent the central techniques found in austere fiction, but he showed what was possible: sparely written fiction, spoken by a self-effacing, nonintrusive narrator, can achieve emotional and intellectual depth. Perhaps the greatest testament to the magnitude of his achievement, however, is his enduring legacy. Although Hemingway's work has fallen in and out of favor since his death, it has influenced a number of important authors. In 1963, a young, ambitious writer named Raymond Carver admitted to a friend that after the deaths of Hemingway and William Carlos Williams, he felt a burgeoning pressure to act as their successor.[102]

2

A Chekhov-Hemingway Amalgamation

Raymond Carver's *Cathedral*

Raymond Carver was, as Michael Gorra asserts, the "chief practitioner of what's been called 'American minimalism'" during the 1970s and 1980s and an important figure in the development of the mode.[1] Carver's aesthetic began to take shape early in his life. His first wife, Maryann Burk Carver, said in her memoir that when he was seventeen, Raymond told her that, "I'm going to be a writer, Maryann. A writer like Ernest Hemingway."[2] His statement was prescient, perhaps an expression of his desire to achieve Papa's fame as much as an insight into the foundation of his future style. When asked about his early influences, Carver replied in an interview that after reading *In Our Time*, he considered Hemingway "marvelous" and concluded that "this is *it*; if you can write prose like this, you've done something."[3] Despite his admiration for Hemingway and Anton Chekhov, the debate continues over whether Carver was a devotee of austere fiction throughout his career.

Adam Meyer argues that "Carver's membership in the minimalist fraternity has never been fully established" and that his second collection of stories, *What We Talk About When We Talk About Love*, is sparser than *Will You Please Be Quiet, Please?* and *Cathedral*.[4] In other words, Meyer maintains that Carver was only briefly a Minimalist. Recent revelations have complicated Meyer's analysis, however. William L. Stull and Maureen P. Carroll, editors of a collection of Carver's work for the Library of America, assert that the author's long-time editor, Gordon Lish, was primarily responsible for the elliptical quality of *What We Talk About*.[5] Their implicit claim seems to be that Carver was not a Minimalist but has been cast as such because of Lish's penchant for cutting material. Lish's influence faded, however. Biographer Carol Sklenicka describes how Carver was more protective of *Cathedral* and did not allow his editor free rein.[6] Stull and Carroll write that "Carver's trust in Lish had been eroded,"[7] so Carver was more assertive about upholding the integrity of his narratives as they were edited for inclusion in *Cathedral*. For this reason, the tales that comprise the book are presumably more reflective of Carver's "true" aesthetic. Although the tales in the collection are more "generous" than many of Carver's other works, particularly those over which Lish asserted editorial dominance, each story in *Cathedral* nonetheless reflects the central attributes of American Minimalist fiction.[8]

Throughout his career, Carver's tendencies were consistent with the Minimalist mode. He was by many accounts inclined to cut words rather than add and to imply significant information rather than write expository passages. His early mentor, John Gardner, was an exacting editor who "deleted words, phrases, and sentences" with the understanding that his changes were not to be opposed.[9] Carver maintained Gardner's standards when guiding his own students. Jay McInerney, who was one of Carver's pupils at Syracuse University, remembers that "manuscripts came back thoroughly ventilated with Carver deletions, substitutions, question marks, and chicken-scratch queries. I took one story back to him seven times; he must have spent fifteen or twenty hours on it. He was a meticulous, obsessive line editor."[10] Like Hemingway and Cormac McCarthy, Carver was adept at removing unnecessary material. Maryann Burk Carver recalls that "he was a crack self-editor, objective and detached. If a story could be made better by cutting a scene he really liked or had enjoyed writing, he cut it. The effect of the whole story was more important, period."[11] A comparison of the *Esquire* variant of "Vitamins" with the version published in *Cathedral*, for example, illustrates Carver's inclinations: numerous sentences were deleted and many others changed.[12]

Carver omits, and in some cases withholds, key information from each tale in *Cathedral*, makes frequent allusions, and implies more than he explicitly reveals about his characters. His fiction also shows a profound debt to literary Impressionism, likely attributable to his admiration for Chekhov.[13] The narratives in *Cathedral* are not, however, as efficient as Carver's previous works. In his discussion of the collection, Marc Oxoby maintains that "the stark minimalism of his [Carver's] early work gives way, by the time we get to *Cathedral*, to a richer, more detailed style. Although they can still be considered minimalist, the stories are not pared down to the level of those in *What We Talk About When We Talk About Love*. Instead, as Bruce Weber has noted, they are 'fuller, more generous and more optimistic.'"[14] Carver said in an interview that he had experienced an "opening up" while writing "Cathedral," implying that his fresh approach was in part a response to being defined in a manner he disliked: "In a review of the last book, somebody called me a 'minimalist' writer. The reviewer meant it as a compliment. But I didn't like it. There's something about 'minimalist' that smacks of smallness of vision and execution that I don't like."[15] However, concepts such as pessimism, optimism, and "smallness of vision" are irrelevant to a definition of Carver's *style*.

The narratives in *Cathedral* are "fuller" in that they are more developed and imagistically complex. They represent the peak of Carver's abilities as a craftsman. "The Bath," now thought to be Lish's version of "A Small, Good Thing," is shorter than the versions that followed but is not as implicative. Much material has been omitted, but this does not necessarily mean that "The Bath" is more Minimalistic. In his best fiction, Carver's extreme efficiency is made possible by his frequent use of poetic techniques that imbue stark images with depth. For example, he often employs devices such as objective and imagistic correlatives. Like many authors working in the tradition, he was an accomplished poet, so his work often reflects the attributes of prose poetry.[16] Carver also adds layers of meaning to his fiction by subtly referring to autobiographical events; multiple works about Carver suggest that he often alluded to occurrences from his own life in his fiction. These facts provide crucial information about the implications of his work. "Cathedral," for example, is based on the time Tess Gallagher's blind friend, Jerry Carriveau, visited. Carver often constructs narrow epistemic parameters, focusing with extreme precision on the few essential details revealed. His fiction seems more accessible, however, when placed within biographical context.

Carver's characters are a reflection of the kind of people he knew best. While some of them seem firmly middle class, such as the Weisses from "The Bath" and "A Small, Good Thing," many of the people who populate his narratives struggle financially. Carver was born to lower-middle-class parents in Clatskanie, Oregon, in 1938. His father was a drinker with "a penchant for wandering" who labored in a sawmill, a place where Carver also worked as a young man.[17] He was told during an interview that the people who populate his stories are "basically inarticulate" and cannot "verbalize their plights" or "grasp what is happening to them." He responded that the reason this is so is because they are the types with whom he relates: "The things that have made an indelible impression on me are the things I saw in lives I witnessed being lived around me, and in the life I myself lived. These were lives where people really *were* scared when someone knocked on their door, day or night, or when the telephone rang; they didn't know how they were going to pay the rent or what they could do if their refrigerator went out."[18] Many of his figures drink their days away, unable to see a way out of cycles of alcoholism and depression. *Cathedral* does not tell of heroes and adventures but of common men and women searching for meaningful relationships. *Cathedral* breaks from *What We Talk About* and *Will You Please Be Quiet, Please?*, however, in that some of the tales that comprise the collection suggest the possibility of profound interaction, redemption, and hope.

The intimate moments that take place at the end of stories such as "Cathedral" and "A Small, Good Thing" are sometimes catalyzed by a material belonging. Carver often invests mundane objects with emotional force in order to shape his primary themes, a technique common in Minimalist fiction. In his essay "On Writing," he writes about the way an everyday item can create emotional force: "It's possible, in a poem or a short story, to write about commonplace things and objects using commonplace language and to endow those things—a chair, a window curtain, a fork, a stone, a woman's earring—with immense, even startling power."[19] In every tale in *Cathedral*, characters invest themselves in things that populate their daily lives, often attempting to use them as a way of connecting with others. It is a realistic artistic effect: commonplaces such as telephones and wristwatches are familiar and thus serve as the grounds for a range of actions and emotions.

A Carver character's response to individual objects and images often intimates what resides below surface actions, evidence that the author was an adherent to Hemingway's iceberg theory. While he maintained that other writers did not have a direct influence on his fiction, Carver said in an interview that he admired Hemingway's work and referred to the theory: "Hemingway is an author whose work I admire greatly. I still go back and read his work with pleasure. You're probably familiar with his comment comparing a literary work to an iceberg: nine-tenths of the iceberg is under water. But as long as the writer knows what he's leaving out, that's okay. If he's just writing and doesn't know that he's leaving out crucial things, then that's not so good. If you read Hemingway's stories, you get just enough and no more."[20] Each narrative in *Cathedral* was first published independently, and the majority of the earlier versions contain information that was later omitted.[21] "Cathedral," "Chef's House," and "Vitamins" originally appeared in September, October, and November 1981, and "A Small, Good Thing" was composed between 1979 and 1980.[22] A considerable amount of text was deleted from "Vitamins" and "Where I'm Calling From," and as a result they rely more on implication. In some instances, little was changed: "Preservation," "The Train," and

"Feathers" appear much as they did in their earlier states. Some of the adjustments made from the journal and magazine publications to those that appear in *Cathedral* were ostensibly made to guard against confusion or overlap.[23] The final narrative in the book, "Cathedral," was not radically changed. The fact that it provides the title for the entire collection is fitting given that it explicitly deals with a central, unifying concept: blindness.

"Cathedral" is based on an interaction Carver had with a blind man, although there are conflicting accounts of what specifically transpired between them. Citing what the author told him, Tom Jenks maintains that Carver had experienced the same basic events that occur in the story: a jealous husband is unsettled by the upcoming visit of his wife's blind friend, Robert, but the husband comes to understand the man better by drawing a cathedral with him while watching a late-night television program.[24] Jerry Carriveau recalled visiting Carver and Tess Gallagher in Syracuse but contradicted some of Jenks's assertions. While Carver uses some of Carriveau's characteristics in shaping his fictional counterpart, the events that occur at the end were fabricated. He said that he did not draw anything with Carver during the visit and maintained that he was "not good at following pen scratchings or hand movements and would not have been able to do so on a paper bag with a subject as complicated as a cathedral."[25] Carver said that his inclination was to use things that have "really happened" or that he "overheard" as material for his stories but that he would also incorporate imagined scenarios: "Cathedral" seems to be no exception.[26]

The story illustrates many of the technical similarities between Minimalism and Impressionism, primarily the relationship between perception and epistemic limitation. The oft-anthologized tale is a first-person retrospective narration, a crucial fact that scholars tend to either miss or ignore.[27] The scholarship generally focuses on whether the narrator undergoes a clear epiphany in the end. The most fundamental, and perhaps important, fact about "Cathedral," however, is that the present action of the piece is the act of the telling. The narrator's temporal relationship with past events in part addresses why he is talking about them at all.

The most likely reason for the telling of the story is that the protagonist is recalling an occurrence that was personally and emotionally transformative; "Cathedral" chronicles the unnamed narrator's metamorphosis from prejudice to understanding. He recalls having a negative attitude about the entire idea of the visit, an event complicated by his own feelings of jealousy and inadequacy. He resents blindness, although he does not seem able to clearly express why. He is also fixated on the fact that his wife and Robert recorded tapes for each other and exchanged them through the mail and shared intimate details about their lives. The implication is that the man's marriage is fragile.

Carver conveys the narrator's perturbation by making him sound terse and reportorial, a technique Hemingway uses in "The End of Something" and that Cormac McCarthy employs in *No Country for Old Men*. One of the most tension filled moments in the latter occurs during a conversation between the murderous Anton Chigurh and a well-meaning convenience store clerk:

> Will there be somethin else? the man said.
> I dont know. Will there?
> Is there somethin wrong?
> With what?
> With anything.
> Is that what you're asking me? Is there something wrong with anything?[28]

The less that is said, the more pointed the statement and the more menacing the tone. The two sections in "Cathedral" in which the narrator recalls the recordings, paradoxically, seem emotionless: "She wanted to talk. They talked. He asked her to send him a tape and tell him about her life. She did this. She sent the tape." The more he talks about the content of the conversations, the more reluctant he is to ponder the subject: "The blind man made a tape. He sent her the tape. She made a tape. This went on for years."[29] The anger that resides below the surface of the narration is driven by jealousy: the speaker has not achieved a meaningful connection with his wife the way Robert has. The tense atmosphere begins to dissipate, however, as the group eats and settles in for an evening by the television. Once Robert arrives at the house, the narrator relates how they quickly ate a big dinner then followed up by eating dessert, smoking dope, drinking, and watching a television program about cathedrals. Robert has no conception of what the churches looked like, so he asks the narrator if he would draw one with him. The two men draw the picture together, and it is this intimate action that has reshaped the protagonist's attitude.

The narrator's epiphany is rooted in the evolution of his perception. Mark A. R. Facknitz observes that "Carver redeems the narrator by releasing him from the figurative blindness that results in a lack of insight into his own condition and which leads him to trivialize human feelings and needs."[30] Carver said in an interview that he did not like to employ irony in his stories, but he does so in "Cathedral."[31] The protagonist describes himself as a person who was in the past emotionally disconnected from others, particularly his wife. He talks about her suicide attempt and previous marriage in a coldly analytical way, as if he can barely believe that it truly happened. His problem is that he does not "see" his wife in the sense that he does not seek to understand who she is. The apparent difference between the men is that Robert, despite his physical lack of vision, is open to new experiences. When the narrator apologizes because there is nothing good on television except for a program about cathedrals, Robert's reply illustrates the epistemic gap between the men: "'Bub, it's all right,' the blind man said. 'It's fine with me. Whatever you want to watch is okay. I'm always learning something. Learning never ends. It won't hurt me to learn something tonight. I got ears,' he said" (222). Carver here alludes to Deuteronomy 29:4, "But to this day the Lord has not given you a mind that understands or eyes that see or ears that hear," accentuating the fundamental difference between the two men. The narrator lacks empathy because of his acute interpersonal limitations. He did not have "ears" or "eyes," and this is the reason he does not "have *any* friends" (212). At no time during the narrative does the speaker explicitly acknowledge that he is in fact the "blind" person, but his willingness to talk about his experience with Robert suggests that he has become someone who is open, someone who finally has "eyes" and "ears."

While spare prose is not central to Impressionism and serves as a means to differentiate it from Minimalism, epiphanic moments result from a shared stylistic tendency. Both modes emphasize the immediacy of sensory experience; narrators report occurrences and eschew explaining their moral or philosophical importance. The scene in which Robert and the narrator draw a cathedral together is sensorial: "I put in windows with arches. I drew flying buttresses. I hung great doors. I couldn't stop. The TV station went off the air. I put down the pen and closed and opened my fingers. The blind man felt around over the paper. He moved the tips of his fingers over the paper, all over what I had drawn, and he nodded" (227). The sensory intensity of the moment erases all concerns about time; raw sensation drives the action more than the external significance of the channel going off the air, which marks the passing of time. Removing any semblance of an intellectual explanation for what it all meant, the narrator at no point says anything coherent or specific about the meaning of his experience; all he can reveal is that "it was like nothing else in my life up to now" (228). The protagonist does not articulate this experience because in Minimalistic stories perception, or the reporting of raw sensory experience, supersedes the communication of a larger moral or philosophical lesson. In "Literary Impressionism and *In Our Time*," James Nagel explains the connection between sensation and thematic development: "The themes of Impressionism dealt with a character coming to terms with the world, coming to understand it better through epiphanies, and struggling constantly with problems of truth and illusion."[32] The narrator in "Cathedral" is only able to note a vague perceptual change. He does not completely comprehend why, but it is implied that for perhaps the first time he has wrestled with matters of "truth and illusion" and become more aware of a world outside of himself.

Despite integrating a subtle message about the consequences of emotional blindness, Carver was like one of the literary Impressionists who influenced him, Anton Chekhov, in that he did not want to use his fiction to force a political or moral lesson upon his audience. "Cathedral" is not, after all, a story about why individuals, or perhaps society in general, should be kinder and more sensitive to people who are blind. In *Literary Impressionism: James and Chekhov*, H. Peter Stowell describes the technical stance of the Impressionist author, a description that applies equally well to Minimalist writers: "The impressionists' belief in the primacy of perception forced the pose of the omniscient, didactic, and discursive author out of the work. He was replaced by an elusive presence who allowed all characters to perceive for themselves the ambiguous and ultimately unknowable surfaces of sensory reality."[33] The narrator's epiphany in "Cathedral" is only possible because he treats the person he was in the past as a separate entity. His position is one of remembrance; he is thinking back to a previous state of "self." Time and distance have not, however, granted him the capacity to explain in specific detail why he is different.

Because the fiction in both modes tends to feature epiphanic moments, the interplay of rejection and acceptance frequently appears in Impressionistic and Minimalistic works, particularly in those of Chekhov. Chekhov's "The Grasshopper" is thematically similar to "Cathedral," as both are about perceptual and epistemic limitation. In each piece the narrator recounts the experiences of an emotionally estranged married couple, and each ends with one of the spouses coming to a moment of profound realization. "The Grasshopper" is about the marriage of Olga Ivanovna, a vivacious art lover, and her dry, cerebral husband, Osip Stepanovich Dymov. While Olga flits around with her artist friends, her steady, unemotional husband time and again proves his love and devotion. He advances in his career, becoming a well-respected doctor. Craving passion and spontaneity, Olga has an affair with a painter, Ryabovsky, who ultimately tires of her and leaves. As do so many of Chekhov's fictions, it ends tragically.

Chekhov subtly develops a sense of irony as it becomes more apparent that for all the pleasure she takes in artists, clothing, and paintings, Olga, like the narrator in "Cathedral," is figuratively blind. She does not "see" the artistry and beauty in her husband's scientific pursuits. Dymov eventually dies of diphtheria, which he develops after foolishly sucking the pus from a diseased boy's throat, but his actions can be interpreted as self-sacrificial. Only after his death is Olga able to comprehend her husband's value, and her blindness is such that she is only able to have her epiphany after a family friend, Korostelev, delivers an impassioned appreciation of Dymov: "'Dying,' he repeated in a high voice and again sobbed. 'Dying, because he sacrificed himself. What a loss to science!' he said with bitter emphasis. 'In comparison with all the rest of us he was a great man, a remarkable man. What a gift! What hopes he inspired in us all!' went on Korostelev, wringing his hands. 'My God, my God, he would have been such a scientist, such a rare scientist! Osip Dymov, Osip Dymov, what have you done? Oh. God!'"[34] Olga's epiphany is not as subtle as that of the protagonist in "Cathedral," but it is a moment in which she recognizes that her perception of him was limited: "Olga Ivanovna went back in memory over her whole life with him, from beginning to end, in the utmost detail, and suddenly realized that he really had been a remarkable man, an unusual man, a great man, in comparison with all the others she had known. And remembering the attitude to him of her late father, and of all his colleagues, she realized that they had all seen in him a future celebrity. The walls, the ceiling, the lamp and the carpet on the floor winked mockingly at her, as if trying to say: 'You've missed your chance!'" (89). Olga's thoughts shape her sensory experience in the epiphanic moment; in her mind she personifies the mundane objects in the room, perceiving them as derisive of her misperception. This is not, however, a moral issue; Chekhov does not indicate that Olga has done something *wrong*. She has instead missed an opportunity to live a life that could have been fuller and more expansive. The narrator does not, for example, imply that it is Olga's infidelity that has caused Dymov's death. If anything, "Cathedral" and "The Grasshopper" suggest that a lack of vision results in an isolation that leads to a poverty of the senses: life is not as rich as it *could* be. Chekhov implies that there is hope, however, because not everyone in Olga's world has shared her fate. Others who saw Dymov's ability differed from her by refusing to see beauty only in common mediums such as painting and sculpture. Carver and his fellow American Minimalists developed an aesthetic focused upon broadening ideas about what constitutes a suitable artistic subject.

"Cathedral" in many ways serves as the thematic model for the rest of the stories in the collection in that each involves figurative blindness. Kirk Nesset posits that the narratives that comprise *Cathedral* are linked by common themes of "insularity."[35] While this is fundamentally true, it is attributable to the stylistic influence of Chekhov and literary Impressionism rather than thematic development alone. Sensory experience is limited, and it restricts the epistemic parameters of Carver's characters. "Feathers" is essentially about the emotional expansions and constrictions visual stimulus causes. Jack and Fran's decision to become parents turns out to be a disaster, primarily because neither is able to assess objectively whether, given their divergent mindsets, the idea of having a child is feasible or rational. Fran's idealized vision of motherhood trumps the fact that their baby is an object that repels her partner.

The dramatic irony in "Feathers" is generated by Jack and Fran's inability to see beyond the surface of their immediate experience. Because it is a retrospective narration, Jack can now talk about the past with a modicum of clarity. The couple's decisions are driven by visceral reactions rather than careful thought, perhaps best expressed by Fran's insipid request for her spouse to "fill me up with your seed" (25). Jack and Fran's discontent stems from the pervasiveness of "ugliness," the term that Carver uses to articulate the end of their one-time intimacy. Fran's mind churns over what has become of her dreams and ambitions. In one of the most subtly harrowing scenes in the story, the husband describes how his wife rants at odd moments: "'Goddamn those people and their ugly baby,' Fran will say, for no apparent reason, while we're watching TV late at night. 'And that smelly bird,' she'll say. 'Christ, who needs it!' Fran will say. She says this kind of stuff a lot, even though she hasn't seen Bud and Olla since that one time" (25–26). Fran has difficulty acknowledging her own culpability in what her life and marriage have become while Jack is unable to interpret the true problem, implying that the couple will remain in a common state of blindness.

Married couples with a limited, pessimistic view of their future are not rare in *Cathedral*. "Chef's House" is similar to "Feathers" as it too ends with failure and isolation. The narrative is based on an episode between Raymond and Maryann Burk Carver that took place while their marriage was slowly dissolving, during which they shared a home in McKinleyville, California, in the early weeks of Raymond's sobriety.[36] Wes, a recovering alcoholic, has been given the use of a home near the ocean in the Pacific Northwest by his friend Chef. He calls Edna, who was once his wife, and asks her to join him. She leaves a male friend behind and she and her former husband share an idyllic time. Being in the house together brings order to Wes and Edna's lives: "Wes had a little money, so I didn't have to work. And it turned out Chef was letting us have the house for almost nothing. We didn't have a telephone. We paid the gas and light and shopped for specials at the Safeway. One Sunday afternoon Wes went out to get a sprinkler and came back with something for me. He came back with a nice bunch of daisies and a straw hat. Tuesday evenings we'd go to a movie. Other nights Wes would go to what he called his Don't Drink meetings" (28). This new life abruptly ends when Chef comes by to tell Wes that his sister, Linda, needs to move in. Edna tries to console Wes, but he is beyond hope. When she suggests that he could resume a relationship with their grown children, he replies that "it won't matter." The version of "Chef's House" that appeared in the *New Yorker* suggests that Wes feels time has gotten away from him: "But it won't matter then (because I'll be so damned old it won't make any difference)" (43).[37] Unable to assuage her husband, Edna concludes her narration by saying, "There wasn't much else. We'll clean it up tonight, I thought, and that will be the end of it" (33). Leaving will conclude Wes and Edna's revival as a couple.

Wes's problem is depicted as a lack of both optimism and vision. The narrator pays attention to Wes's eyes, and what the forlorn man sees is particularly meaningful. Geoffrey Wolff praises Carver for his deft use of this device, maintaining that "he knew better than anyone where his characters should look. I don't mean point of view. I mean where their eyes fall—what they see and what they don't see."[38] Once Wes determines that his sobriety is over, "he leaned back in the sofa, folded his hands in his lap, and closed his eyes." Edna continues her attempts to gain his attention, and finally "he opened his eyes. But he didn't look at me" (32). He gazes "toward the window," an interesting detail in that Edna does not speculate about what he is focusing upon, although she says earlier that the "clouds . . . were building up" over the ocean (31). Her reportorial mode of telling continues as she describes how he "got up and pulled the drapes and the ocean was gone just like that" (33). Wes's decision to close off his physical view of the world outside, a "clouded" and uncertain "horizon," serves as an imagistic correlative that represents the cessation of his hope. His actions also reflect a measure of theatricality: he has effectively ended the "act," signifying that another, less fulfilling experience awaits.

The couple in "Preservation" is perhaps the most dysfunctional portrayed in *Cathedral*, far less genial than Wes and Edna, and their inability to communicate with each other is acute. The narrative is relatively simple in terms of plot, but the underlying tension is communicated by implication. Sandy's husband feels powerless and directionless, and purchasing a refrigerator provides an unusual opportunity for him and his wife to interact. Finding a replacement becomes a potential point of connection but does not ultimately provide one. The dialogue accentuates the idea that Sandy and her husband reside in two separate worlds:

> She glanced down at the paper, then at the food that had thawed. "I've got to fry pork chops tonight," she said. "And I have to cook up that hamburger. And those sandwich steaks and the fish sticks. Don't forget the TV dinners, either."
>
> "That goddamned Freon," he said. "You can smell it." (42)

The couple's inability to listen and respond to each other suggests that it is unlikely the marriage will last. Her husband does not see the grief she continues to feel over the tragic death of her father, nor does he wish to participate in actions that will perhaps help Sandy to resolve long-buried emotions.

Carver's use of non sequiturs suggests that the couple do not have the imagination necessary to empathize. Sandy does not recognize that her husband, an unemployed roofer, is suffering from a debilitated ego and that he does not comprehend that his wife wants to form a meaningful emotional connection. Carver illustrates the man's figurative blindness early in the tale when the narrator describes how he was reading "something called *Mysteries of the Past*. He held the book in front of him with both hands, his head inclined over the pages, as if he were being drawn in by what he was reading. But after a while she noticed that he didn't seem to be making any progress in it; he still seemed to be at about the same place—somewhere around chapter two, she guessed" (36). While it would seem that his lack of progress would be an apt metaphor for his life, that he is essentially bogged down and trapped on his couch, the implication is that his mind is overactive. He is fixating on something else, unable to expand the range of his thoughts to the degree that would allow him to discern a proper course of action. The book title alludes to the mysteries of his wife's past, events that he is unable to understand due to his lack of interest in anything outside of his own, limited purview.

Carver's manipulation of biographical events in the story that follows "Preservation," "The Compartment," suggests that he was at times blind to the emotional needs of his family. The tale is based on Raymond's trip to Europe in the summer of 1982, during which he visited his son, Vance, who was living in Paris. Raymond marred his son's childhood with his alcoholism, but they began a period of reconciliation in the late 1970s and early 1980s. The bitterness and negativity that Myers feels for his son in "The Compartment" caught Vance off guard when he first read the story, and he questioned why his father would take "an experience that ultimately cemented our reconciliation and, instead, turned it into such a dark, unsettling story."[39] Vance's observations about the narrative are insightful, and its disquieting qualities largely result from the complexity of the protagonist.

Myers craves insularity on a level that surpasses Sandy's husband, a type of sensory deprivation that will shield him from the unfamiliar. While on a train trip to see his estranged son, he thinks about his divorce and an altercation he had with his boy. Some of Myers's thoughts suggest that he prefers being by himself. For example, out of the window, he sees "a farmhouse and its outbuildings, everything surrounded by a wall" and determines that it "might be a good way to live—in an old house surrounded by a wall" (48).[40] The narrator also says, however, that Myers is "sorry he hadn't arranged to be with a group. He was lonely" (51). His active thought-life is disrupted when he leaves his compartment to visit the bathroom. He returns to find that the gift he purchased for his son, an "expensive Japanese wristwatch," has been stolen (52). The theft is the emotional turning point and indicates that the watch has become an important object in the fragile relationship between father and son. Myers grows angry with the other people on the train, derisively thinking of them as criminals and "foreigners" (54). Because of his lack of vision, he does not comprehend that *he* is the foreigner; he does not demonstrate a knowledge of local languages or customs.

Unlike "The Compartment," "A Small, Good Thing" ends with a moment of redemption, the first story in *Cathedral* to end with a tincture of optimism. The long-held belief about the tale is that it is an expansion of "The Bath," which first appeared in *What We Talk About*.[41] A new thesis has emerged, however, that suggests that "A Small, Good Thing" was in fact the "true" first version and that Lish whittled it down into what was released as "The Bath." Stull and Carroll published the initial version in *Beginners*, which they maintain is how it would have appeared in *What We Talk About* if not for Lish.[42] Removing Carver's editor from the process by comparing the three published renderings, however, reveals that Carver's tendency was to cut, rather than add, material. Most importantly, each version is Minimalistic.

In all three renderings of "A Small, Good Thing," the basic plot is the same. The focus of the first part of the version printed in *Cathedral* is upon the interaction between Ann and Howard Weiss, but the primary action takes place in the last third when the Weisses confront the baker, the man who has been making the frightening and untimely calls. Ann initiates the trip to the bakery and shapes what happens when she and her husband arrive:

> "I know bakers work at night," Ann said. "They make phone calls at night, too. You bastard," she said.
>
> The baker continued to tap the rolling pin against his hand. He glanced at Howard. "Careful, careful," he said to Howard.
>
> "My son's dead," she said with a cold, even finality. "He was hit by a car Monday morning. We've been waiting with him until he died. But, of course, you couldn't be expected to know that, could you? Bakers can't know everything—can they, Mr. Baker? But he's dead. He's dead, you bastard!" (86)

Ann's raw emotions serve as the catalyst for the baker's apology and his eventual redemption. Carver deleted a line that reinforces the religious overtones of the scene when preparing "A Small, Good Thing" for publication in *Cathedral*: "'But I'm deeply sorry. I'm sorry for your son, and I'm sorry for my part in this. (Sweet, sweet Jesus,)' the baker said. He spread his hands out on the table and turned them over to reveal his palms."[43] Even though the Weisses will grieve the loss of their son for many years, their ability to forgive provides reason for hope. The baker is not the only person who needs to be forgiven. Ann and Howard will at some time have to offer their forgiveness to Scotty's unknown murderer if they are to move beyond the tragedy emotionally.

The *Beginners* version of "A Small, Good Thing" is the "fullest" in terms of length, but word count is irrelevant in determining whether a work is Minimalistic. Carver deleted many lines or made changes that resulted in more concise, mellifluous prose. Some adjustments also suggest that Carver became more reportorial, focusing more on images and actions than on intellectual synthesis. A paragraph about Howard Weiss illustrates Carver's shift in approach. In the initial rendering, "Howard drove home from the hospital. He took the wet, dark streets faster than he should have, then caught himself and slowed down." The second sentence is reformulated in *Ploughshares* and *Cathedral*: "He took the wet, dark streets very fast, then caught himself and slowed down" (62). The phrase "than he should have" is a judgment from the narrator rather than a projection of Howard's thoughts, a reproach leveled at a man who is acting recklessly shortly after his son has been injured by a careless driver. By removing the line, the narrator becomes more self-effacing and maintains an objective stance. The focus remains on Howard, who by catching himself implies that he is thinking about his son's circumstances with a heightened level of sensitivity. Later in the same paragraph, Carver originally wrote, "he shouldn't have left the hospital, he shouldn't have, he cursed himself."[44] In the later forms, he writes, "he shouldn't have left the hospital, he shouldn't have. 'Goddamn it!' he said" (62). Carver elects to show rather than tell, again lessening the "presence" of the narrator.

Carver was similarly vigilant in his editing of "Vitamins." Narrated by a protagonist whose actions are consistently self-serving and reprehensible, the central character seems an unrepentant version of the redeemed baker. The protagonist's girlfriend, Patti, sells vitamins, and he works nights cleaning floors at a hospital. The details about their respective occupations are biographical: Carver worked as a night janitor at Mercy Hospital in Sacramento, California, while his wife, Maryann, was building a successful career in sales with Parents Magazine Cultural Institute.[45] Maryann's fictional counterpart grows overly attached to her product, and it becomes apparent as the plot progresses that her addictions, coupled with the narrator's indifference to her, are damaging her life:

> "I'm my only customer," she said. "I think taking all these vitamins is doing something to my skin. Does my skin look okay to you? Can a person get overdosed on vitamins? I'm getting to where I can't even take a crap like a normal person."
>
> "Honey," I said.
>
> Patti said, "You don't care if I take vitamins. That's the point. You don't care about anything. The windshield wiper quit this afternoon in the rain. I almost had a wreck. I came this close." (98)

Because of her limited perception, Patti abuses something that is supposed to make her healthier. After this exchange, the narrator proves Patti's statements about him to be true as he continues on his own pathetic downward spiral. While on a date with Patti's coworker, Donna, he drinks RC Cola and whiskey at a bar called the Off-Broadway and barely avoids a physical confrontation with a drunk Vietnam veteran named Nelson (99, 107). The former soldier at one point reveals that he has kept an enemy ear as a memento, an object that has become desiccated and shriveled. Nesset describes it as an "emblem" of a "general deafness" that affects other characters in *Cathedral*.[46] After returning home, the protagonist completes his descent. In the final paragraph he fumbles around in the medicine chest and recalls that he "knocked down some more things. I didn't care. Things kept falling" (109). The narrator's final words presumably describe the trajectory of his future.

Unable to help himself or accept help from the equally apathetic Patti, the protagonist in "Vitamins" seems hopeless. Like "Cathedral," however, the tale is a retrospective. The speaker's admission that he "didn't care" suggests that he is looking back on past events having learned something from his experiences. The same cannot be said for Lloyd, the central figure in the narrative that follows "Vitamins." A darkly humorous story, "Careful" is about Lloyd, a man who suffers from some of the same feelings of worthlessness as Wes and Patti. Inez, Lloyd's wife, has initiated a separation and asked her husband to move out. He has found a makeshift apartment with low, slanted ceilings. He drinks champagne throughout the narrative—ironic because it is something generally associated with luxury and celebration. He is living alone because Inez asked him to assess his condition and begin a recovery. Douglas Unger, Carver's brother-in-law, said in an interview that "Careful" is based on actual events: "Ray had rented a small apartment on Castro Street in San Francisco. Just like in 'Careful,' which describes that apartment exactly, Ray had somehow convinced himself that if he only drank champagne, he'd be able to taper off and quit. He'd go out in the morning and buy bottles of the cheapest Andre, but this wasn't working and he knew it. At that point, everyone had given up hope."[47] Lloyd is under many illusions, and Unger's recollection suggests that Carver's fictional counterpart drinks champagne under the mistaken notion that it will help him wean himself off of alcohol.

As the narrative progresses, Carver suggests that Lloyd's central problem is his metaphorical blindness, a state resulting from his inability to listen. Inez apparently remains supportive, a fact her willingness to visit him in the first place suggests. Even though he is disheveled, he is comforted to have her near him, likely because "she knew everything there was to know about him" (115). Despite Inez's caring and attention, the end of "Careful" does not offer evidence of a bright future for the couple. Even though Lloyd can hear, he is not in any better position to communicate with his spouse. Although it is only around three o'clock in the afternoon, he is petrified of going to sleep, so he pops the cork off of a fresh bottle to help suppress his fears. The object of Inez's ire provides Lloyd temporary relief from overwhelming emotions.

Markedly different from "Careful" and "Vitamins," "Where I'm Calling From" is told from the perspective of a man trying to rejuvenate himself by achieving sobriety. The relationships depicted are not in the process of ending; they have already been damaged, though not irreversibly. "Where I'm Calling From" is narrated in first person by an unnamed speaker in present tense. Because Carver does not give him a name, the story seems to primarily be about Joe Penny, referred to as "J. P." The two men are in "Frank Martin's drying-out facility" somewhere in the mountains across the valley from where "Jack London used to have a big place" (137). On two different occasions in 1977, Carver was a resident in a similar facility called Duffy's, located in Calistoga, California.[48]

"Where I'm Calling From" is a powerful testament to the disruptive nature of alcohol addiction, and it suggests that healing in part depends upon an expansion of vision. J. P. and the narrator's common need to rid themselves of it brings them closer together. Nesset asserts that it is "listening, and the imagination required for close listening" that allows the narrator to approach "the heart of his own problems."[49] Frank Martin's is a voluntary facility; the two men are free to leave at any time. The optimistic mood is linked to the idea that J. P. and the narrator have recognized their failures and taken a step toward rehabilitation and reconnection with their loved ones. Carver cut part of Frank Martin's "sermon" before publishing the story in *Cathedral*. The speech implies the tenuous nature of the two men's prospects: "(But we could have helped Jack London, if we'd been here in those days. And if he'd let us. If he'd asked for our help. Hear me? Like we can help you. *If. If* you ask for it and *if* you listen.) End of sermon."[50] Even without the excised section, J. P. and the narrator appear to have the option to choose sobriety and a place in society. The thematic emphasis in "Where I'm Calling From" is upon the possibility of redemption, a product of grace only obtained by those who have "ears to hear."

Many of the figures that populate Carver's stories seem to lack the capacity to comprehend the perspectives of others or empathize with those they have hurt. "The Train" features a character, Miss Dent, who is unlike the men in "Where I'm Calling From" in that she violently acts out as a means to be seen, heard, and, perhaps most importantly, understood. Used and forgotten, she can no longer abide her state of figurative invisibility. The content of the narrative is different from the others in *Cathedral*; Carver wrote it as a "sequel" to a tale by John Cheever called "The Five-Forty-Eight." For this reason, it is one of Carver's most literarily allusive pieces. The confrontation between Miss Dent and her former boss, Mr. Blake, occurs in Cheever's tale, so it takes place "off stage" within the context of "The Train."

Although Blake is mentioned only as "a man" in "The Train," he is in many ways similar to Carver's other isolated, misanthropic personae. In Cheever's narrative, Blake's narcissism contributes to his profoundly impoverished imagination, which in turn causes him to lack any semblance of empathy. Three darkly humorous scenes illustrate his lack of caring. In the first, the smitten Miss Dent places a rose on Blake's desk, but "he had dropped it into the wastebasket. 'I don't like roses,' he told her."[51] Shortly after he has had a one-night stand with Miss Dent, "he called personnel and asked them to fire her," opting not to confront her himself.[52] Blake's blindness to the emotions of others is perhaps best illustrated, however, in his treatment of his own wife, Louise. The narrator recounts how "Blake had come home one night, overworked and tired, and had found that Louise had done nothing about getting supper. He had gone into the kitchen, followed by Louise, and had pointed out to her that the date was the fifth. He had drawn a circle around the date on the kitchen calendar. 'One week is the twelfth,' he had said. 'Two weeks will be the nineteenth.' He drew a circle around the nineteenth. 'I'm not going to speak to you for two weeks,' he had said. 'That will be the nineteenth.' She had wept, she had protested, but it had been eight or ten years since she had been able to touch him with her entreaties."[53] The final sentence suggests that Blake has for many years closed himself off from others, hearing but not listening and watching without seeing. Carver's Miss Dent is a menacing figure who has attempted to break through Blake's sensorial barricade: "she tried to make him see that he couldn't keep trampling on people's feelings" (147). Cheever offers no indication, however, that Blake's experience with Miss Dent has done anything to reshape his perspective.

The raw confidence Miss Dent displays is uncommon in Carver's stories. Many of his figures, such as Wes and Lloyd, tend to resign themselves to living lives marked by defeat and faded potential. In "Fever," a high school art teacher and father of two named Carlyle proves similar to Miss Dent in that he must summon the courage necessary to confront an antagonistic figure. His former spouse, Eileen, is nothing like Mr. Blake, however, as she is not coldly misanthropic.

"The Bridle" does not conclude with the same level of certainty as "Fever." The tale begins and ends with a family attempting to flee from self-imposed hardships. The story is an illustration of the proverb "no matter where you go, there you are." Holits and his wife, Betty, have moved to Arizona from Minnesota to start over. They rent an apartment, and the complex manager's wife,

Marge, is the narrator. The family's deterioration was set into motion when Holits became involved in horse racing; he purchased a horse and named it "Fast Betty." The implication is that he lost his family's farm through a series of bad bets and neglect. In the version of the "The Bridle" that appeared in the July 1982 edition of the *New Yorker*, Betty tells the narrator that "at the time, it didn't seem like he was letting any of the other things go."[54] This line was deleted from the version that appears in *Cathedral*, and it is an important omission. The suggestion is that the farm was squandered, in part, because Holits was not fulfilling his duties.

The Holitses' marriage is marred by unresolved tension; it becomes apparent early in the tale when she remarks to the narrator that "he knows everything there is about horses" (189). Her resentment toward him is complex, stemming from his inability to acknowledge the sacrifices she has made in an attempt to salvage their relationship. Carver offered additional reasons for marital tension in his first rendering. Betty tells the narrator that "Holits and I have been married for eight years, going on nine. We couldn't have any children. We tried. It must be my fault." She goes on to add, "but that's the way it goes. Those that want to can't. And, sometimes, them that can shouldn't."[55] Carver's omission is significant, but he includes lines that imply Betty maintains a conciliatory maternal drive. Holits has two sons from a previous marriage, and Betty insists that "I love them like they were my own" (198). She is willing to compromise and adapt to make their relationship work, but he is rigid in his approach to his wife, a state suggested by the fact that he has kept Fast Betty's bridle.

Despite Betty's deference to her wayward husband, the Holitses' marital problems deepen. Betty works long hours as a waitress while he sits at home, presumably doing nothing. Reminiscent of Sandy's husband in "Preservation," he has lost his sense of purpose. He begins to drink. During an impromptu pool party, he tries to jump from the top of a pool house into the water. It is ambiguous whether he is trying to kill himself or miscalculates, but he lands on his head and suffers a serious injury. Shortly after the incident, the family moves out of the apartment. When the narrator goes up to clean the place, she finds the bridle has been left behind: "It must have been passed over in their hurry. But maybe it wasn't. Maybe the man left it on purpose." She also thinks of the object's relationship to Betty: "But I know that one part fits in the mouth. That part's called the bit. . . . The bit's heavy and cold. If you had to wear this thing between your teeth, I guess you'd catch on in a hurry.

When you felt it pull, you'd know it was time. You'd know you were going somewhere" (208). It is ambiguous whether the end signifies that Betty will now be able to live life on her own terms.

Uncertainty is prominent in Carver's work, and it often results from limited vision. Because of its sparse, implicative prose and acutely defined epistemic parameters, Carver's fiction reflects the convergence of Hemingway's and Chekhov's styles. He was not the "father" of the Minimalist tradition, but his contribution to its development is significant. Carver's legacy as an important stylist has nothing to do with his choice of subject matter or the length of his narratives. Much has been written about whether his works are optimistic, pessimistic, dark, or hopeful, and what that means in terms of how his oeuvre is categorized, but Carver's legacy illustrates that a specific type of content does not define American literary Minimalism. He had a unique ability to examine profound themes through simple plots and seemingly superficial characters. His language is spare but precise, evidence of his devotion to craft. Identifying beauty in the mundane, Carver demonstrated that everyday experiences can be unexpectedly meaningful.

3

Popular Minimalism

Jay McInerney's *Bright Lights, Big City*

Raymond Carver and Ernest Hemingway deeply influenced many of the young writers who achieved prominence in America during the 1980s. Spare, implicative fiction was near the height of its popularity, and it marked the reemergence of a tradition that had, to borrow a phrase from Amy Lowell, "fallen into desuetude." In *Bright Lights, Big City*, Jay McInerney, who was at one time Carver's student, uses efficient prose, allusion, and omission to explore some of the same themes Hemingway wrote about during the 1920s, but in the context of a tempestuous, narcissistic social scene unmatched in even *The Sun Also Rises*. Under the artificial glare of the New York City lights, McInerney's nameless protagonist navigates an internal wasteland, trying to find meaning in the wake of a failed marriage and unrewarding career. He is particularly noteworthy because he is a radical departure from what is considered to be the stock Minimalist figure: he is neither blue collar nor unsophisticated. He is typical, however, because he withholds much about himself, although at the end of the novel he becomes more generous in his revelations.

The drug-filled, materialistic world found in McInerney's fiction often seems governed by an unwritten but well-understood hedonistic code. Luke McGavock, in McInerney's *The Good Life*, articulates it best when he ponders that many people in his rarified Manhattan universe believe the tenets "live to spend, dress to kill, shop and fuck your way to happiness."[1] Virtually all of the characters in McInerney's five novels wrestle with consumerist "ideals," which is perhaps why they often seem shallow and helpless. They know that there are more important things in life, but it is painful and unsettling to pursue them. Even worse, seeking them is not pleasurable. The central theme in McInerney's fiction is that human experience is a constant battle to find a balance between self-control and excess. In his behavioral economy a person can casually snort a line of cocaine at a party, but anyone who uses it every day is damned. Ironically, McInerney wrote moralistic literature in an era when absolutes seemingly became irrelevant. Judging by the thematic consistency of his work, little has changed in his aesthetic during the last two and a half decades. *Bright Lights, Big City*, his first book, deals with many of the same issues examined in *The Good Life*: both are about rediscovering moderation. *Bright Lights, Big City* is markedly different from McInerney's other contributions, however, in that it was written using techniques central to American literary Minimalism.

Even though it is in many ways Minimalistic, McInerney did not write *Bright Lights* with the same degree of sparseness often found in the work of two of his greatest influences, Carver and Hemingway. While *Bright Lights, Big City* is efficient, it is not, for example, as lean as Carver's *What We Talk About When We Talk About Love*. Günter Leypoldt's assertion that McInerney "favors a traditional neorealism with only minimal realist leanings" carries substantial validity.[2] But the fact that the book is highly allusive, and important information is implied rather than directly stated, outweighs an occasional lack of economy. McInerney's use of parataxis in passages reminiscent of Impressionistic works concretizes his connection with his stylistic predecessors.

Much of the scholarship on *Bright Lights, Big City* is devoted to matters of technique and philosophical paradigm. Philip E. Simmons asserts that McInerney was "one of a generation of younger writers influenced by Carver" and that Minimalism is a "highly self-conscious response to the postmodern critique of representation, one which knowingly simulates a 'return' to plain style while remaining properly ironic about the discredited representational conventions on which plain style rests."[3] While McInerney does at times write spare, direct sentences, or in what Simmons refers to as "plain style," his writing is most Minimalistic when it is paratactic and sensorial: "It's ten-fifty when you get to Times Square. You come up on Seventh Avenue blinking. The sunlight is excessive. You grope for your shades. Down Forty-second Street, through the meat district. Every day the same spiel from the same old man: 'Girls, girls, girls—check 'em out, check 'em out. Take a free look, gentlemen. Check it out, check it out.' The words and rhythm never vary. Kinky Karla, Naughty Lola, Sexsational Live Revue—girls, girls, girls" (13). Using a technique literary Impressionists often employ, McInerney composes precise, declarative sentences that directly address sensory experience in a moment of time. Like Hamlin Garland's prose poem "The City Streets," McInerney's passage begins by describing the position and intensity of the light. It is similarly fragmentary, transitioning from visual stimulation and then to sound while maintaining unity. The narrator offers the time of day as a means of establishing the temporal parameters of the moment, that it is a *vistazo*, as well as the position of the sun. The tone in this sequence suggests that the protagonist is suffering from sensory overload, as he must "grope for" his "shades" while he copes with the auditory monotony of a sex peddler. His movement is subtly implied, as he only says "down Forty-second Street," a comment that implies a moral as well as physical direction. David Kaufmann includes McInerney among "a number of highly successful young writers" whose work is marked by "the remarkable prevalence of paratactic constructions," but Kaufmann's insight would be more complete if he had acknowledged that the use of parataxis establishes an important connection between Minimalism and the work of literary Impressionists such as Garland and Stephen Crane.[4]

McInerney himself has defined Minimalism in two different ways. In an essay titled "Writers of Wrong," published in 1989, he contends that

> Raymond Carver and Ann Beattie are the literary godfather and godmother of the largest brood of young writers of the Eighties—the deadpan domestic realists. While both to some extent dodged the critical bullet, their influence has been much decried; millions of words have been fired at a straw man called minimalism. Carver's career as a story writer and prose stylist had several distinct phases; only his second collection, *What We Talk About When We Talk About Love*, can really be called minimalist—a conscious attempt to leave almost everything out. (Among the descendants, I would be tempted to call the admirable Amy Hempel a minimalist.) These writers did seem stripped down and laconic after the sprawling novels of the Sixties and early Seventies, their concerns narrowly domestic after the political and apocalyptic noises of immediate predecessors like Pynchon, Gaddis, Barth, and Vonnegut. They seemed artless and naïve to the metafictionalists who were all wrapped up in epistemology, the status of storytelling and fictional discourse, how to go on.[5]

Given McInerney's affinity to Hemingway and Carver, this definition displays a surprising absence of self-awareness. McInerney almost completely dissociated his own work with that of his important influence and mentor, Carver, and is unclear whether he includes himself among "the deadpan domestic realists."[6] His preferred label suggests a specific type of content, that Carver, Hempel, and others wrote exclusively about various forms of domesticity, an assertion that does not bear scrutiny. He also repeats what is a standard explanation for why Minimalism first came into being: it was a response to the ornate, sprawling novels of "metafictionalists." He is also slightly off in his statement that practitioners of the mode want to "leave almost everything out" because what is left out must be implied. Fortunately, he later adopted a more sophisticated view of the mode. His more recent definition of the style suggests a connection between Impressionism and Minimalism.

In his 2006 collection of essays, *A Hedonist in the Cellar*, McInerney offers a definition of the mode that takes into account the influence of Impressionism; he describes winemaker Greg Brewer as a "minimalist" due to the fact that he "wants to let the grapes and the vineyard express themselves without interference." McInerney emphasizes that he uses the term as a means to connect a literary philosophy with enology: "Whether consciously or unconsciously, the former professor [Brewer] seems to be echoing Flaubert when he says, 'I want to be invisible, I want to get out of the way, I don't want a stylistic stamp.'"[7] This marks a shift for McInerney because he makes a distinct connection between nonintrusiveness and the tenets of Hemingway's iceberg theory. The concept of self-effacement is important to American Minimalism because of its roots in Impressionism and Asian poetry. This formulation of the style applies to *Bright Lights, Big City*. McInerney's narrator often describes his sensory experiences without elaborating on their moral or philosophical meaning. Zoltán Abádi Nagy observes that this type of narration is a common feature within the mode, although he does not establish a connection with earlier traditions: "The minimalist agent . . . is consequential, anaesthetized, perhaps inarticulate, partially presented, but one who *observes*, *registers*, and is *reactive* (rather than proactive) most of the time."[8] McInerney's narrator lacks the self-awareness necessary to articulate the reasons for his loneliness. He tells his story in a series of concentrated, sensorial images.

In light of McInerney's Minimalist tendencies, the compositional origins of *Bright Lights, Big City* are remarkably appropriate: it originated as a piece of "flash fiction." In the introduction to *How It Ended: New and Collected Stories*, McInerney reveals that *Bright Lights, Big City* began as a single paragraph he composed "after a disastrous night on the town."[9] He spoke about that evening in more detail during an interview earlier in his career, saying that he was at "a club called Berlin" feeling as though he was "out of brain cells," pondering whether he should ask a woman to dance when he began to wonder if he was "the kind of guy who would be in a place like this."[10] At the behest of editor George Plimpton, he extended the Impressionistic blurb into a short story that was eventually published in the *Paris Review* under the title "It's Six A.M. Do You Know Where You Are?"[11] The tale relates two sequences of events that serve as the beginning and ending of *Bright Lights, Big City*; McInerney essentially divides "It's Six A.M." and creates a new center. Michael Schumacher writes that McInerney finished the first draft of the work "in six weeks."[12] The final version is a sincere tale about a lost young man enamored with facades. McInerney shows remarkable control, particularly in terms of tone. While critics such as John Duka and Peter Bricklebank praise the novel for its deft portrayal of the zeitgeist, Michiko Kakutani fails to see anything profound in terms of plot and characterization.[13]

One of Kakutani's criticisms is that *Bright Lights, Big City* is "autobiographical," something that is not universally viewed as a literary weakness. The novel contains several biographical parallels, many of which have been addressed in various publications. McInerney's first wife, Linda Rossiter, was a model, and she left him in much the same way that the protagonist's model wife, Amanda, does. He worked as a fact checker for the *New Yorker* for nine months until in 1981 he was tacitly encouraged to either "quit or be fired"[14]; the protagonist has a similar job at a prestigious (though unnamed) magazine. Given the reference to a song by Talking Heads titled "Crosseyed and Painless," the second number on their seminal album *Remain in Light*, which was released in October 1980, the novel is likely set in late 1980 or 1981.[15] McInerney was a self-described roisterer who "had a taste for alcohol and 'Bolivian Marching Powder,'" the latter term a euphemism for cocaine employed throughout his debut novel.[16] McInerney said in an interview that his "mother died of cancer and the character in the book's mother died of cancer," but he goes on to state that he did not grieve in the same way. His use of biographical details is a conscious element of his aesthetic. He told Joyce Wadler of the *Washington Post* that he thought "most good fiction begins in autobiography and ends somewhere else altogether."[17] The second-person point of view used in *Bright Lights, Big City* seems a good fit for a consideration of personal history because the narrative is essentially a lengthy internal monologue.

Narrated entirely in second person and present tense, *Bright Lights, Big City* is a somewhat unusual novel. The protagonist never offers his name, addressing himself throughout as "you." This choice of perspective is at times off-putting, but it is not entirely uncommon in Minimalistic stories and novels. Ernest Hemingway at times shifts into second person, and Frederick Barthelme uses it in his short story "Shop Girls." In a comprehensive study of the use of second person in literature, Monika Fludernik mentions Nathaniel Hawthorne's "The Haunted Mind" as one of the earliest examples of an American work that uses the perspective exclusively.[18] The practice is perhaps attributable to the movement's kinship with literary Impressionism. Many of the most poignant sequences in *Bright Lights, Big City* are purely sensory, and the narrator's use of second person suggests that he wants his audience to actively "share" his experiences.

The narrator is similar to his counterpart in Carver's "Cathedral" in that he wants to communicate objectively what is happening but he has difficulty articulating his thoughts and feelings. In emphasizing the immediacy of his experience, he closes off important information about his past. Like Carver, McInerney uses non sequiturs as a means of hinting at tensions that fester below surface actions. Perhaps the best example occurs early in the plot when the narrator stops by a local deli for lunch. As the man behind the counter prepares a sandwich, he says, "and now for a little mustard—just how your mom used to make it." For reasons that are at this point unclear, the protagonist replies, "what do you know about it." Shortly after he receives his lunch, he offers a seemingly incomplete, random excuse for his behavior: "All of this, the dead meat on ice behind glass, everything, puts you off your meal" (27). While it is possible to discern the implications of the narrator's actions through a close reading, it is not until the penultimate chapter that the protagonist reveals one of the reasons for his actions: his mother died of cancer. His reticence on this topic suggests that while he wants to confront himself, his disheveled emotions only allow him to do so incrementally. He is a complex character, in part demonstrated by the fact that critics have compared him to a variety of diverse figures in American literature.

Even though *Bright Lights, Big City* has, according to Kevin L. Ferguson, drawn comparisons to works such as J. D. Salinger's *The Catcher in the Rye*, Kingsley Amis's *Lucky Jim*, Saul Bellow's *The Adventures of Augie March*, and Truman Capote's *Breakfast at Tiffany's*,[19] it is far more indebted to Hemingway's *The Sun Also Rises*, particularly in terms of its structure and characterization. Like Hemingway's protagonist Jake Barnes, the narrator in *Bright Lights, Big City* begins and ends his story in the same physical and emotional state. Both men are sexually dysfunctional, albeit for different reasons.[20] *Bright Lights, Big City* is symmetrical, beginning early on a Sunday morning in a club and then ending almost exactly one week later, which is perhaps an extension of the fact that the novel is in essence the "middle" of "It's Six A.M." Near the physical center of book, the narrator first hears about Vicky, his friend Tad Allagash's cousin. His brief time with her proves to be the catalyst for the changes he begins to undergo at the end. Like Jake, the protagonist of *Bright Lights, Big City* offers only a faint hint that through his experiences he has attained a more advanced state of self-awareness. Jake's dismissal of Brett's hypothetical state of true love parallels the narrator's realization that he "will have to learn everything all over again" (182). Both men experience an epistemic shift, however slight, that adds depth to their respective tales.

As with *The Sun Also Rises*, the critical reception for *Bright Lights, Big City* was an odd mix of praise, criticism, and misunderstanding. John Duka represents the book as a "funny" take on nightclubs and fashion.[21] An anonymous reviewer in the *Atlantic* mentions two episodes, one involving a Cartier watch and another about a ferret, praising the latter as "satirical slapstick," but does not mention any of the more serious sequences that occur in the second half of the book.[22] Terence Moran writes in *New Republic* that it is an "accomplished and funny novel" that achieves profundity in the "quiet redemption of its main character."[23] On the contrary, reviewers who wrote negative appraisals of *Bright Lights, Big City* often dismiss it as a work that lacks substance. Kakutani praises McInerney's comedic sensibilities but concludes that "the book's heavily autobiographical flavor and its refusal to plumb the shiny surfaces of its characters' lives add up to a tale that's peculiarly slight."[24] Kakutani's statement suggests that she appreciates the entertainment value of the novel but does not ultimately find any discussion of profound themes. Her criticism results from McInerney's stylistic decisions; finding depth in *Bright Lights* requires multiple readings and extreme attention to detail. The humor is seldom lighthearted, often suggestive of the protagonist-narrator's struggles with depression and loneliness. In a review of McInerney's second novel, *Ransom*, David Remnick of the *Washington Post* retroactively savages *Bright Lights, Big City* as "a book admired most deeply, I suspect, by people who thought it was the novel they would write if they could get a year off from the horrific responsibilities of urban affluence. It tackled such universal themes as the fact-checking department of the *New Yorker* and the downtown rock club scene."[25] Remnick's criticisms suggest that he, like Kakutani, did not fully explore the ramifications of seemingly minor details and omissions. Assessing the efficacy of McInerney's characterization is often a function of determining the importance of what is not said.

In the mid-1920s, Hemingway was criticized for similar reasons. In a 1927 review of *Men without Women*, Joseph Wood Krutch argues that Hemingway's characters are "sometimes . . . the illiterate heroes of the prize-fight or the bull-ring, and sometimes they are the bankrupt intellectuals who wander disconsolately from bar to bar in the forlorn hope that a drink will be more refreshing somewhere else, but the two classes have this in common: they are all but inarticulate. The one has never learned to express itself, the other has grown tired of choosing words, and so both talk the lazy, monotonous, undifferentiated idiom which is the common denominator of the relaxed intellectual and the roughneck."[26] McInerney's characters would fall into the second of Krutch's categories, well-educated individuals who cannot overcome the inner pain that renders them "inarticulate." The pattern of behavior is the same: in McInerney's fiction, the club often replaces the bar. In his review of *The Sun Also Rises*, Allen Tate opines that Hemingway's focus on "physical object," or his reportorial manner of narration, is engineered at the expense of characterization: "Hemingway doesn't fill out his characters and let them stand for themselves; he isolates one or two chief traits which reduce them to caricature."[27] Tate and Kakutani are similar in their criticisms because neither seems to take into account the implicative nature of each text. The narrator's early reticence about the feelings that motivate his self-destructive behavior does generate a number of questions. The first two-thirds of the novel are often nothing more than a report on a series of sensations, many of which seem to have little meaning. While some of McInerney's characters, such as Clara Tillinghast and perhaps Tad Allagash, are decidedly two dimensional, his protagonist has a depth and humanity that can only be appreciated through a close reading.

Because Minimalist fiction often seems light on plot and characterization, scholars sometimes dismiss it as lacking a "message." This tendency has led critics to question whether McInerney's work is morally prescriptive or descriptive. He addressed the issue directly, saying in an interview that "students, I've been told, want to go to New York City and to live the life described in my novel. I've heard myself described as a Yuppie hero, as some kind of celebrant of a way of life and a set of values which I believe are actually held up for critical examination in my book. I don't feel I'm a Yuppie at all. Rather, I *thought* I was writing a book about someone coming to terms with failure, but it seems that the novel's been taken up by the people whose religion is success. They see *Bright Lights, Big City* as a guidebook to the world of fashion, to New York City's nightlife, to the pursuit of glamour. I was very shocked when magazines talked about the book as a wacky, funfilled [*sic*] romp through the fast lane."[28] In light of the rather moving and serious events of the last two chapters of the novel, it is interesting that some reviewers seize only on the humor. Despite what McInerney intended for *Bright Lights, Big City*, some saw the book as evidence of a greater social crisis, that it was an argument in favor of drug use and excess. John W. Aldridge, a scholar whose comments suggest he gave McInerney's work only cursory consideration, condemns McInerney and Bret Easton Ellis as promulgators of cultural superficiality: "The novels of Jay McInerney and Bret Easton Ellis . . . are by any serious critical measure artistically empty works that are best-sellers largely because they depict a spiritually empty world that is attractive to readers who are themselves spiritually empty and so in reading them experience a faint twinge of self-recognition."[29] The fundamental problem with Aldridge's position is that he assumes these works are reserved for the tasteless and vacuous, and that matters of content should negate any serious interest in their stylistic attributes. Additionally, Ellis's work is quite different from McInerney's, more catatonic and reportorial, so it is not helpful to talk about them together. A close examination of *Bright Lights, Big City* reveals a story about a young man who is trying to emotionally come to terms with loneliness, the elusiveness of love, and his mother's death.

For the narrator in *Bright Lights, Big City*, his eventual epiphanic shift is in part a response to his need to come to terms with who he is. The novel is necessarily ironic because the narrator is in a state of willful blindness until the end. The depth of his state of denial is evident in the first sentence of the book: "You are not the kind of guy who would be at a place like this at this time of the morning" (1). The instability of his character in part results from the tripartite division of his personality: he describes who he thinks he is, who his actions say he is, and who he wants to be. While talking to a "girl with the shaved head" and a "scar tattooed on her scalp," he concludes that his problem is that "for some reason you think you are going to meet the kind of girl who is not the kind of girl who would be at a place like this at this time of the morning" (3). The most suggestive passage in the first chapter, however, exhibits the depth of his disconnection with reality: "Your presence here is only a matter of conducting an experiment in limits, reminding yourself of what you aren't. You see yourself as the kind of guy who wakes up early on Sunday morning and steps out to cop the *Times* and croissants. Who might take a cue from the Arts and Leisure section and decide to check out an exhibition—costumes of the Hapsburg Court at the Met, say, or Japanese lacquerware of the Muromachi period at the Asia Society" (4). Despite his pretensions to cultural sophistication, his discussions of his "true" self lead him to pursue what he is genuinely lacking: companionship. In other words, his inflated image is a response to his loneliness. He wants to view himself as someone worthy of attention.

The scholarship dealing with *Bright Lights, Big City* as a story about "the self" tends to treat the protagonist as if he is "divided" into two parts rather than three. Gregor Wiebels-Balthaus proposes a postmodern version of the narrator, partitioning him into "the publicly presented self" and the "real self" and then concluding that McInerney is questioning whether "such a real, authentic self exists at all."[30] While this statement represents an interesting line of inquiry, it shifts focus away from the fact that *Bright Lights, Big City* is ultimately about coming to terms with personal failure rather than the cultivation of an "image." McInerney said in an interview that the book "is essentially an interior monologue," meaning that it is not a contemplation of selfhood but rather an ongoing, reactive report of what the main character is thinking.[31] In other words, there is no truly "public" self against which to judge a "private" persona. When the narrator says "you," he is speaking only to himself and not using the term as a substitute for external listeners or an "everyman."

Even though *Bright Lights, Big City* is in many ways focused on the protagonist's internal state, allusions to external places and situations are vital to the development of theme. The richness of McInerney's characterization is largely dependent upon his allusions to specific places. New York City brings with it a series of popular associations, the most important of which is that it is a place replete with opportunity. In the fifth chapter, titled "*Les Jeux Sont Faits*," a reference to a screenplay by Jean-Paul Sartre of the same name, the narrator thinks back on when he first met his ex-wife, Amanda. She was living in a trailer park in Kansas City, unaware that she had the look of a model. She is drawn to the protagonist because she saw him only as a means to enter into a world she envisioned as a glamorous escape. While engaged in an internal monologue about their time together, he remembers that "she seemed to think you came from Manhattan. Everyone in Kansas thought you came from New York City, whether you said Massachusetts, New England, or just East Coast. She asked about Fifth Avenue, The Carlyle, Studio 54. Obviously, from her magazine reading she knew more about these places than you did" (70). Throughout the novel, the narrator contemplates the nature of facades. New York City is presented as a real place but often in a purely sensorial manner.

McInerney's decision to present Kansas City as a rural dead end, the opposite of New York City, is an odd choice given that it is by no means a backwater town. In some of McInerney's other novels, such as *Story of My Life*, *Brightness Falls*, and *The Good Life*, he portrays New York as the figurative capital of the Western world. His inclusion of Kansas City makes sense, however, as an allusion to Hemingway. When the narrator talks about how he met his ex-wife, he mentions that he was a journalist in Kansas City at the time, the same job Hemingway held when he was a teenager.[32] In the moments preceding one of the more embarrassing episodes in the novel, the protagonist learns that his friend and coworker Megan Avery has a young son who lives with his dad in northern Michigan. The father works as a logger, a career that evokes images from "The Doctor and the Doctor's Wife" (138).

These examples seem to be token references to an author that McInerney respected, but Minimalistic fiction often includes allusions in order to emphasize the thematic focus of a work. McInerney's visual description of one club speaks to the leitmotifs of loneliness and isolation: "The glittering, curvilinear surfaces inside Odeon are reassuring. The place makes you feel reasonable at any hour, often against bad odds, with its good light and clean luncheonette-via-Cartier deco decor" (44). His references to bands such as Talking Heads place the story within a specific historical and spatial context, but it is this allusion to Hemingway's "A Clean, Well-Lighted Place" that clarifies what it is that the narrator is after. He is out at six in the morning because he wants to experience a meaningful connection with others, particularly a woman. While the serenity of a Spanish café at 2 a.m. is the atmospheric opposite of a dance club, the women and men who patronize these types of places pursue the same thing. McInerney's protagonist is different from Hemingway's Old Man, however. The former seeks not only to meet others but also to find himself. The most obvious reference appears at the beginning of the book. The epigraph in the novel is a quotation from Hemingway's *The Sun Also Rises*:

> "How did you go bankrupt?" Bill asked.
> "Two ways," Mike said. "Gradually and then suddenly."

The concept of "bankruptcy" plays an important role in *Bright Lights, Big City*. The narrator's financial insolvency, which it is implied will grow worse after he loses his job, is closely related to his moral bankruptcy. It is a term that, in the context of *Bright Lights, Big City*, speaks to the hazards of excess.

Cocaine is the most prominent vehicle for self-destructive behavior in *Bright Lights, Big City*, and it is an important object because it reflects the zeitgeist. McInerney omits much about the drug. The only earnest discussion of its effects does not occur until the end of the book. He treats it with both levity and seriousness, but the latter rarely seems to gain the notice of scholars. Characters in the novel are at times amusingly lighthearted about the drug, acting as if it is harmless. Tad Allagash narcissistically licks a mirror on Monday evening before going out in the hopes that its surface contains enough residue to give him a high, his logic being that "in this apartment the dust has better coke content than some of the shit we buy by the gram" (43). While clearing out his personal effects after being fired, the narrator casually offers Megan some of the remnants floating around in his desk drawer. Without hesitation, she snorts two lines (131). Even though "Bolivian marching powder" is ubiquitous, virtually none of the criticism written about *Bright Lights, Big City* seriously examines the actual effects of the narcotic, a glaring oversight given the importance it plays in character development.

In the 1980s, cocaine use was prevalent in the United States, especially among the wealthy elite. According to Belén Boville, a report in *The Economist* stated that Americans spent $60–70 billion on the drug each year during that decade. Like owning an expensive watch or driving an exotic car, possessing it "was surrounded by a halo of prestige and exclusivity."[33] Even though the protagonist in *Bright Lights, Big City* has not personally achieved astounding monetary success, he seeks to nurture a certain facade of wealth and sophistication. Cocaine is an affectation, and he uses it as a means to bolster his outer appearance in the same way he used his wife and his job: "Without getting too specific you imply that your job is extremely demanding and important. In the past you could often convince yourself as well as others of this, but your heart is no longer in it. You hate this posturing, even as you persist, as if it were important for these two strangers to admire you for all the wrong reasons. It's not much, this menial job in a venerable institution, but it's all you've got left" (46). The narrator displays a greater sense of self-awareness by saying that "his heart is no longer in it" when he lies as a means to inflate his image, but he continues to do it anyway, just as he continues to snort cocaine. His sense of resignation perhaps grows from a biographical parallel: McInerney was a part of the club-drug scene for many of the same reasons. He said in an interview that he, like his fictional counterpart, experienced a change in values: "I was young and that seemed to be a glamorous milieu—going to a club at midnight, being able to afford it, having enough cocaine to be able to stay up till 4 in the morning. I no longer think it's the height of human aspiration, but at the same time it seemed to be taken for granted among my friends as a great way to live."[34] McInerney, like his protagonist, seems to have been emotionally divided, caught between a desire to act and look a certain way yet not fall into a state of superficiality and self-destructiveness.

More important than conveying an image of success is the narrator's desire to be "likable." He says to himself that before his wife left him "you assumed you were very likable. That you had an attractive wife and a fairly interesting job seemed only your due. You were a good guy. You deserved some of the world's booty" (46–47). Given his desire to be and act a certain way, his choice of drug is ideal. Cocaine has been described as "expensive, energizing" and "esteem-boosting."[35] In *The Candy Machine: How Cocaine Took Over the World*, Tom Feiling includes accounts from people who use, or have used, the drug. Their stories often mirror that of the protagonist in *Bright Lights, Big City*; they took cocaine for the same reasons he does and experienced many of the same effects. "Gabrielle" (Feiling uses pseudonyms for all of his subjects) says that the narcotic enhanced the depth of her interactions with acquaintances, maintaining that "some of the best conversations I've ever had have been between close friends when we've had some charlie [cocaine]. You're on it, but there isn't that pressure to compete with other people for attention. You can have an earnest and honest chat about personal things." "Alan" emphasizes the camaraderie users felt when under the influence, saying that cocaine induced "a tribal feeling, doing it with your friends, and all going off into a little story together. Coke amplifies your personality and makes your conversation that little bit more amusing and sparkly, if only for a short period of time." McInerney's recollection of his own experience with cocaine aligns with Alan's and Gabrielle's accounts; in an interview, he likened it to "a kind of pursuit of an ideal state of sociability and mindless pleasure where somehow I thought, and lots of people I knew thought, that tonight was going to be the night when you were gonna meet the lover of your dreams and dazzle everyone with your conversation and get high enough and attain some perfect state of intoxication that was . . . like a prolonged orgasm. It's hedonism."[36] Alan's use of the phrase "a tribal feeling" is interesting. The narrator in *Bright Lights, Big City* employs similar language when describing the atmosphere at the first club he visits as having "a vaguely tribal flavor . . . pendulous jewelry, face paint, ceremonial headgear and hair styles" (2). He detects a uniformity to the way the club-goers act and look, a desire to conform as a means to feel part of a collective. The suggestion is that Alan, Gabrielle, and the narrator of *Bright Lights, Big City* share a common need to engage in meaningful exchanges with others to combat feelings of loneliness and inadequacy. In other words, they chose a drug that addressed what they perceived to be their primary weakness.

McInerney does not, however, imply that cocaine can be used without consequence. He suggests that it only momentarily counters feelings of isolation and insularity. Even though the drug can lead to garrulousness, not all users experience any real sense of camaraderie. "Ricardo" disagrees with Alan and Gabrielle over whether cocaine actually leads to meaningful interaction, arguing that "one of the main effects of coke is that everyone wants to talk and talk and talk. But after a point you realize that the words aren't working. You find yourself trying to describe your need to talk, but realizing that the words to do so barely exist. Words become useless, despite your fluency with them."[37] A conversation early in *Bright Lights, Big City* shows how cocaine offers verbal "fluency" but "words become useless." The narrator meets a girl in the club and they begin to dance. When the second song begins, she says she is tired, so he offers her some "blow." The immediate effect is a loss of inhibition: "A couple of spoons and she seems to like you just fine, and you are feeling very likable yourself" (7). As they head out of the ladies' room, they begin to converse:

> "I love drugs," she says, as you march toward the bar.
>
> "It's something we have in common," you say.
>
> "Have you ever noticed how all the good words start with D? D and L."
>
> You try to think about this. You're not quite sure what she's driving at. The Bolivians are singing their marching song, but you can't make out the words.
>
> "You know. Drugs. Delight. Decadence."
>
> "Debauchery," you say, catching the tune now.
>
> "Dexedrine."
>
> "Delectable. Deranged. Debilitated."
>
> "Delinquent."
>
> "Delirium."
>
> "And L," she says. "Lush and luscious."
>
> "Languorous."
>
> "Librium."
>
> "Libidinous."
>
> "What's that?" she says.
>
> "Horny."

> "Oh," she says, casting a long, arching look over your shoulder. Her eyes glaze in a way that reminds you precisely of the closing of a sandblasted glass shower door. You can see that the game is over, although you're not sure which rule you broke. Possibly she finds H words offensive. A purist. (7–8)

This passage is a good example of McInerney's wry sense of humor and preference for sparse yet implicative dialogue. It also illustrates his narrator's mental state when high on cocaine. His participation in the woman's word game indicates his desire to be charming and witty. On a more profound level, it demonstrates his need for companionship. He fancies himself to be a writer but he is unable to persuade through his use of words even though he has ingested something that he thought would help. He realizes that the word "game is over," and that despite all the talk, nothing meaningful has occurred.

The casual playfulness of cocaine use is only somewhat offset by allusions to the high human cost of its production and distribution. The turmoil it caused in the United States and abroad, however, forms part of the iceberg. During the late 1970s and early 1980s, the effects of cocaine extended well beyond the New York City club scene. Miami, for example, was in many ways a combat zone at the peak of the "drug wars": in 1979, the city averaged a murder per day.[38] The narrator's dark sense of humor about the origins of the narcotic is perhaps best on display when he randomly encounters Rich Vanier, a friend from his college days. Vanier says that he has just returned from South America after having "restructured" the finances of some unnamed "generals" so that they could "have a few more months of high living" (50). Because coca leaf production is greatest in remote areas of countries such as Colombia, Peru, and Bolivia, the leaders of populist militias are often among its primary beneficiaries.[39] Vanier's use of the phrase "high living" is a crass joke; he knows that the men he worked for are making it possible for their buyers to get "high." The narrator's response is a subtle indication that he is aware of the source of his cocaine: "I do a little South American business myself." When Vanier says that he had heard that the protagonist had married an actress, the protagonist shocks his friend with a false, macabre tale: "*activist.* I married a beautiful activist. She was the illegitimate daughter of Che Guevara. A few months ago she went home to visit her mother and got herself arrested and tortured by a series of rich South American generals. She died in prison" (50). This response shows an awareness of the atrocities that resulted from the drug trade, perhaps a sign of the narrator's feelings of self-loathing, but his knowledge does not lead him to stop. Not until the end does he begin to realize what has driven him to hedonistically self-medicate.

The final two chapters of *Bright Lights, Big City* are both serious and revelatory. The narrator acknowledges that the one-year anniversary of his mother's death has arrived and he must complete the grieving process (178–79). Shortly before he comes to this realization, he thinks back to the frank conversation he had with his mother shortly before she died. She talks about her own use of cocaine, saying that she took it along with morphine "to ease the depression" (165). The implication is that her son has been taking it for the same reason, but her revelation is somewhat ironic because if taken in high enough doses it can lead to "insomnia, apathy, anorexia, or depression."[40] In the final sequence of the novel, the narrator leaves a party early Sunday morning, shortly after weakly confronting his ex-wife, and reports that his nose begins to bleed. This occurrence is a physical indication of "chronic" use, signifying that if the narrator does not change he is going to kill himself.[41] The bloody nose was not included in "It's Six A.M.," suggesting that it shows the extent of the narrator's problem and reinforces the religious imagery that permeates the final paragraphs of *Bright Lights, Big City.*

The final sequences of *Bright Lights, Big City* are rife with symbolism. As he wanders through New York City early Sunday morning, just as he does at the end of the first chapter, the protagonist notices blood on his fingers and shirt. Walking down Canal Street, a "bum" looks up at him and says, "God bless you and forgive your sins" (180). The narrator then smells bread, reminding him of times when he was content with the important women in his life, his mother and Amanda. Finding the source of the aroma, he sees a man on a loading dock, perhaps preparing a bakery truck for deliveries. The narrator trades his well-worn Ray-Ban sunglasses, an item that functions both as a sensory barricade and a mask, for a bag of "hard rolls." He falls to his knees and gags as he eats, realizing that he will "have to go slowly" and that he "will have to learn everything all over again" (182). Blood, bread, an impromptu priest, kneeling: McInerney is not particularly subtle in his allusion, although virtually all of the critics that have analyzed the ending talk only about the bread, ignoring other important details.

McInerney distinctly alludes to the Eucharist, a rite that calls attention to his desire to belong. Kevin L. Ferguson somewhat derisively calls it a "final, choking communion of self-discovery."[42] Remnick is more acutely critical in his analysis, calling the narrator's actions "a redemptive, pathetically banal, epiphany."[43] Leypoldt offers a more nuanced, albeit conventional, reading: "the symbolism, of course, carries biblical pathos, as the symbol of yuppie values is traded in for the prime symbol of spiritual nourishment, the 'bread of life.'" He goes on to conclude that the "bread signifies both spiritual purification and the completion of the grieving process."[44] The final scene is not exclusively about remembrance and absolution but the narrator's need to belong.

The narrator implies early in *Bright Lights, Big City* that he comes from a Roman Catholic background, so his view has been shaped by the church's tradition. While trying to determine whether to leave the club, he tells himself that he is "a republic of voices tonight. Unfortunately, that republic is Italy. All these voices waving their arms and screaming at one another. There's an *ex cathedra* riff coming down from the Vatican: *Repent. Your body is the temple of the Lord and you have defiled it.* It is, after all, Sunday morning, and as long as you have any brain cells left there will be a resonant patriarchal basso echoing down the marble vaults of your churchgoing childhood to remind you that this is the Lord's Day" (6). His memory is stoked because he is in the midst of a minor ethical crisis. He is in no position to consider theological details in this moment, but the revelation of his background plays an important role in interpreting the ending. In the Roman Catholic Church, the Eucharist, along with Baptism and Confirmation, "completes Christian initiation."[45] It is one of seven sacraments performed as a means to "give expression to . . . faith and allegiance to God."[46] In other words, it is a means of outwardly expressing religious loyalty and affiliation.

Responding to a need he expresses earlier in the novel, the protagonist experiences an epiphany when he realizes his desire for community. During a midweek train ride, he notices a Hasidic Jew reading the Talmud and considers that "this man has a God and a History, a Community," things that he himself lacks. On Fourteenth Street he sees three Rastafarians and begins to feel that he is "the only man in the city without group affiliation" (57). He later has a similar experience when he wanders into an "anonymous Irish" bar and realizes that he knows nothing about the basketball game being shown on the television. He thinks that his "ignorance" keeps him "locked out of the largest fraternity in the country" (85). His cocaine use and his friendship with Tad Allagash equally reflect his hope of being included in a "tribe."

The speaker's feelings of isolation and his lack of "affiliation" motivate his desire to reform. The most common misconception about the ending is that it is catalyzed by the young man's need to mourn over the death of his mother.

This explanation is only partially true. McInerney's comments suggest that he achieved what he intended. He was asked in an interview to address whether the book was about self-destruction: "Given the number of readers who had turned *Bright Lights, Big City* into an etiquette book for the 1980s, are you glad you didn't write about suicide?" Contradicting the interviewer's presupposition, he said, "that's funny, in a way, because I thought I had. Or at least that I had gotten awfully close to the suicidal."[47] The novel tracks the narrator's process of coming to terms with his own mortality. The Eucharist is a ritual of remembrance, the symbolic consumption of someone believed to have died and then come back to life. Focusing heavily on the narrator's psychosexual relationship with his mother, as Ferguson does, detracts from the fact that the protagonist is on a personal search to find meaning and purpose in his own life. His feelings about his mother reflect his feelings about himself. He wants to find a woman not as a means to fulfill a Freudian maternal need but because he wants to feel loved. His insecurities force him to decide to choose a path that will not end in an early death.

The protagonist's contemplation of suicide is the most important implied yet omitted material. His thoughts about self-destruction are offhanded and indirect: "You think of Socrates, the kind of guy who accepted his cup and drank it down" (56); and when he is being terminated from his job, he imagines, "You are out the window with the pigeons" (103). McInerney's assertion that he had brought his narrator "awfully close to the suicidal" refocuses the novel on his narrator's internal conflicts and moves him away from the dominance of his mother's memory. In the final chapter, the protagonist comes to the realization that if he is to continue living, he must "start over" and reeducate himself to live life independently of the influence of others. He cannot worry about the past, the women who have hurt him, so he must reinvent his values and motivations. Rather than properly mourn the death of his mother, he must mourn the death of the "self" that has failed to achieve monetary and social success. His capacity to begin again, however, is suspect. The allusion to the Eucharist suggests a need for faith, a hope in what he cannot see or prove. His "redemption" invites cynicism, as it would not be any great surprise if he were in the same position again a week later. Imagining a rejuvenated, repaired narrator in a new job and a meaningful relationship with a woman may be, in the parlance of Jake Barnes, only a "pretty" thought.

The ending of *Bright Lights, Big City* is inconclusive, but the implication is that the narrator will begin the slow process of physical and emotional rehabilitation. The conclusion does not offer a concrete message or lesson, evidence that the book is not a how-to guide to living "the good life." It is not surprising that *Bright Lights, Big City* has been misconstrued as a prescriptive tome for those whose "religion is success" because it reflects many of the tendencies of American Minimalism. The novel is a powerful yet subtle description of how a life of excess cannot erase feelings of failure and inadequacy. McInerney's reportorial urban sequences, sparse dialogue, and allusiveness suggest that Carver and Hemingway were in many ways influential. McInerney's allusions to the latter suggest a stylistic affinity, a desire to build upon themes of isolation and loneliness in a subtle, understated manner. While the surfaces of the settings and characters do indeed seem superficial, a close reading reveals extraordinary depth. McInerney's protagonist is not a spiritually empty hedonist but a young man coping with the emotional realities of failure. His drug use is a means of compensation, a misguided attempt to transform himself into someone with a sense of belonging. He is in the end determined to change by going through the humbling process of reimagining himself.

4

Images, Fragments, and Little Moments

Susan Minot's *Monkeys*

Like the stories it precedes, the cover art on the first edition of Susan Minot's *Monkeys* is richly implicative. Five children in costumes stand on a grassy hill above the ocean, smiling as they have their portrait made. In contrast to their colorful surroundings, each is depicted in black and white. The two smallest are dressed as jungle cats, and a boy wearing a long coat over his outfit flanks them on their left. Casting a somber tone over what is largely a portrait of youth and innocence, two of the children depict skeletons. Through their presence, Minot, who created the artwork, subtly suggests that even within the idealized world of the young, death is a part of life. In juxtaposing vivaciousness and mortality, Minot visually adumbrates many of the themes and tensions she engages in her stories. Her fiction is reportorial, sensorial, and, as is her artwork, comprised of poignant individual images. Stylistically similar to the work of Hemingway and Carver, *Monkeys* stands as an important part of the American Minimalist tradition.

Early in her career, Minot favored Minimalistic style. Her first two works, *Monkeys* and *Lust*, are similar in technique. She wrote in this manner while in the creative writing program at Columbia University, and at times it made her the focus of harsh criticism. In interviews with Kelli Pryor and Anne O'Malley, Minot discussed how one of her instructors "was rather impatient with the elliptical way I was writing and used me as an example of what not to do."[1] In 2002, she said that her aesthetic is best suited to the mode, and she recalled that she "was learning how to write short stories when I wrote *Monkeys*, learning how to polish and be as brief as possible, which is an aesthetic that I prefer. If you can say it in a shorter amount of time, that's better. At the time, Raymond Carver was writing, and people were writing short stories that were full of those Hemingway simple sentences, but also the subjects were about little moments."[2] Minot resisted being tagged as a Minimalist, but her acknowledgment of Carver and Hemingway as influences places her firmly within the tradition. Her comment about "little moments" is particularly telling because her stories often take on the fragmentary quality common in austere and Impressionistic works. The tales in *Monkeys* are often comprised of implicative, allusive images held together by basic plots.

Even though it was marketed as a novel, *Monkeys* is best described as a short-story cycle.[3] It is composed of nine interrelated yet independent tales that follow a thirteen-year span in the life of the Vincent family.[4] Augustus "Gus" Paine Vincent, the father, is an emotionless, disengaged man who in many ways keeps his family on the perimeter of his world. The narrators in each tale reveal little about him, suggesting that he is inaccessible. Much is implied about him, however. For example, the casual disdain he displays for his spouse is in part based upon religious and social differences. He comes from a wealthy Protestant family, she from a Roman Catholic background. Rosie Vincent, his wife, provides her children with their day-to-day care. She is the emotional center of the family, vivacious and loving. After her death, the siblings carry a profound emotional burden they are never able to abandon completely. While much of the book focuses on the parents, each tale also involves the Vincent children. The three eldest, Caitlin, Delilah, and Sophie, are in a particularly precarious time of life, forced to make the difficult transition from adolescence to young adulthood while coping with their father's alcoholism and Mum's demise.

Structurally, the cycle is linear in that it is constructed according to the maturation of the children. The kids are relatively young during the first four pieces; Caitlin is eleven in "Hiding" and fifteen in "Wildflowers." The fifth story, "Party Blues," is particularly important because it is in many ways transitional. Sophie, the figure in the book on whom the narrator tends to focus most, comes to the realization that her childhood is effectively over and that she must begin to confront adult matters such as love, betrayal, and loneliness. The final four stories overtly explore sensitive issues such as alcoholism and death, topics indirectly examined in the first half of the work. The childhood innocence that dominates the opening half of the cycle gives way to the issues and themes that accompany adulthood.

Minot drew from her life experiences when writing the tales that comprise *Monkeys*. While it would be irresponsible to read the collection as pure biography, the occurrences that inspired key moments in the stories illuminate the iceberg. Much of the recent interest in *Monkeys* has grown from a continuing fascination with the artistically prolific Minot family. Susan has for many years remained silent on whether her cycle is based on familial events, but she said in an interview that she has not "figured out how to write about things" that she does not "have some sort of contact with."[5] With the publication of Eliza Minot's debut novel, *The Tiny One*, there has been a renewed interest in biographical parallels. The youngest Minot sister's book bears many similarities to *Monkeys*, although the father figure is not as emotionally distant as Augustus Paine Vincent. Susan's brother George Minot said in a 2004 interview that Eliza and Susan's works "were basically verbatim," a telling statement abundantly corroborated by Sam Minot's memoir *The Strange Poverty of the Rich*.[6] In the preface, Sam expressed consternation over the fact that his brother and sisters "hijacked" his "life and put" him "into their works of fiction." In directly addressing Susan's debut work, Sam maintains that *Monkeys* uses "different accounts from our childhood. Mum sometimes called us little ones 'monkeys.' She [Susan] kept the same first letter of our names for our fictitious characters."[7] Despite Sam and George's insistence that *Monkeys* is a near-factual account of their childhood, their respective views of past events are not always the same. The lack of overlap in each sibling's account of what happened poses myriad problems for the biographer but adds depth and possibility to a consideration of what Susan Minot omits.

While some of the early reviewers make brief mention of the autobiographical undercurrents of *Monkeys*, many comment on Minot's use of Minimalist techniques. An anonymous critic detects in Minot's work "the voices of the masters—the descriptive economy of Hemingway, the imaged delicacy of Virginia Woolf," authors whose work was in part shaped by literary Impressionism.[8] Three reviewers address Minot's use of Hemingway's iceberg theory. Jonathan Yardley maintains that she "writes in the minimalist style now fashionable in the writing classes" and criticizes her for attempting to "substitute" careful descriptions of objects for in-depth characterization, a common objection from those who do not fully comprehend the methods of the mode.[9] Anne Tyler demonstrates a more nuanced understanding of Minot's technique, praising her deft use of implication by omission.[10] Walter Bede places *Monkeys* among a "family of current writing in which nothing really happens" but acknowledges that "much in these nine stories about the Vincent family is left vague or hidden below the surface, as major events occur offstage and characters change in the white spaces between chapters."[11] Reviewers express near unanimity about the directness of Minot's prose:

A. R. Gurney Jr. praises Minot for her "fine economy"; Michiko Kakutani observes that "Ms. Minot has a gift for delineating her characters' inner lives with economy and precision"; and Roxana Robinson and Thomas Hinde note how Minot renders day-to-day experiences with an eye for minute detail.[12] Remarkably, *Monkeys* has elicited little response from the academic community and has not been assessed in the context of American Minimalism. James Nagel's "Susan Minot's *Monkeys* and the Cycle Paradigm" is the only serious scholarly examination of the cycle. He offers a brief discussion of Minot's technique, but the primary purpose of his essay is to examine matters of genre. Nagel explores many key allusions and explains how Minot's leitmotifs help unify the work.

"Hiding," the first story in *Monkeys*, introduces many of the book's central themes and is in many ways a model Minimalist short story. As Nagel observes, the first sentence suggests that there are religious and familial divisions.[13] Sophie begins her narrative by informing her audience that "our father doesn't go to church with us," an immediate indication of parental disagreement.[14] The first two words are an ironic allusion to the Lord's prayer; Mr. Vincent is in no way a dependable "fatherly" force who responds to the needs of his children. Within the family dynamic, he has none of his wife's grace and charisma. As Rose Vincent (who is usually referred to as "Mum") and her six children are "all downstairs in the hall at the same time, bumbling, getting ready to go" (1), Dad is absent. He often stays away from his children when they are not physically static, suggesting that he is annoyed by noise and motion. While driving the car home after ice-skating, he turns the radio "off because there's enough racket already" (10). The children, bundled up in their winter coats, are led from the house by Mum, who wears a funereal "black lace veil" (1). Gus stands motionless in the cold while Mum leads the processional, the children obediently "filing . . . out the door" (2). Minot artfully balances the vibrancy of life with the inevitability of death throughout *Monkeys*, and the opening scene of "Hiding" serves as a prime example of how she accomplishes equilibrium through precision and subtlety.

The narrator, Sophie, describes a series of images that resonate throughout all of the tales. Her narration is unusual in that she at times speaks for herself but just as often represents all of the children, similar to the technique William Faulkner uses in "A Rose for Emily." For example, she explains the children's lack of vigor by reporting that "everyone's in a bad mood because we just woke up" (2). In accord with the narrators who follow her, Sophie is most closely attuned to the emotions and attitudes of the children. Her consistent physical proximity to her mother allows for a fuller picture of Rose, but this intimacy is not shared by all of the narrators in *Monkeys*. As a result of her youth and innocence, Sophie does not always seem to grasp the meaning of what she is seeing and hearing. This limitation is, in part, why Dad remains a mystery. Sophie talks about what he does but she reveals little about his motives. It is telling that even though she at times speaks for the collective, her omniscience is confined to her peers. The information she shares about her parents demonstrates that she has a limited understanding of the adult world she observes and reports about.

Sophie communicates the division between her parents through contrasting images of heat and coldness. "Hiding" is set during winter. Mum is, literally and figuratively, an agent of warmth, "the one who's warm-blooded" (2), working against the various forms of frigidity that distress her home life. As she dresses her children to face the elements, her husband, the chief representative of cold and detachment, stands "outside already on the other side of the French doors, waiting for us to go. You can tell it's cold out there by his white breath blowing by his cheek in spurts" (2). While in church, a domain that exclusively belongs to Mum, the kids do not remove their coats (3). The priest, the only other adult male figure in "Hiding," tellingly "leaves" Mum feeling "cold" (4). Even in summer, Dad is associated with winteriness as he spreads "white fertilizer on the lawn," making it look as if it is covered with "frost" (6). In a rare instance of leadership, Dad takes the family skating at a nearby outdoor pond. When he finishes his clean, powerful laps around the ice, "tears leak from the sides of his eyes and there's a white smudge around his mouth like frostbite" (9). The opposite of Dad's isolated power, Mum's graceful figure skating seems fiery and inviting: "Whirring around, she lowers into a crouch, ventures out one balanced leg, a twirling whirlpool, hot pink, rises again, spinning, into a blurred pillar or a tornado, her arms going above her head and her hands like the eye of a needle" (9–10). Dad, consistent in his indifference, takes no notice of Mum's performance (10).

Sophie's description of her father's past demonstrates the allusiveness common in Minimalist fiction. Sophie mentions that Dad "played hockey in college and was so good his name is on a plaque that's right as you walk into the Harvard rink" (9). This information carries an important biographical parallel with considerable bearing on how Gus is characterized. Susan Minot's father, George R. Minot II, was an accomplished hockey player at Harvard University through the spring term of 1950. The plaque that Sophie mentions is likely the same as a real one that honored winners of the John Tudor

Memorial Cup, an annual award given to "the most valuable member of the Harvard hockey team." George Minot received the cup for his performance during his final season. It was not simply to commemorate his talent but also to reward him for exhibiting "sportsmanship, leadership, and team cooperation." More importantly, it was given to him because he possessed "the vague quality which John Tudor called 'the old come through in the pinch.'"[15] While Sophie's mention of the plaque seems like a relatively minor detail, it is highly implicative. Her father was honored with an award for attributes that he consistently fails to demonstrate within his home. He is in no way a "valuable" member. He does not lead or cooperate, and throughout *Monkeys* he shows that when life becomes tangled and difficult, he is unreliable. Sophie's observation is thus bitterly ironic; his qualities as a "good" hockey player have not led to success in domestic roles.

Mr. Vincent's unreliability fuels the emotional climax in "Hiding." After several failed attempts to earn her husband's attention, Mum and the children hide in an upstairs linen closet while Dad is away at the store with the hope that he will come looking for them once he realizes they are missing. They wait in anticipation, and it is telling that they are unsure of what Dad will do. Minot creates a sense of immediacy through direct sensory description: "The motor dies and the car shuts off. We hear the door crack, then clip shut. Footsteps bang up the echoing porch, loud, toe-hard and scuffing. The glass panes rattle when the door opens, resounding in the empty hall, and then the door slams in the dead quiet, reverberating through the whole side of the house. Someone in the closet squeaks like a hamster. Downstairs there isn't a sound" (19). By focusing on a brief moment in time, Minot accentuates the depth of the family's feelings. They want to know that they are appreciated and safe, that their father-husband cares about them. True to his character, however, he does nothing. Through subtle imagery, Minot implies that Mr. Vincent's coldness causes feelings of emotional confinement. Sophie observes how "the light from downstairs shines up through the railing and casts shadows on the wall—bars of light and dark like a fence." The play of shadow and light also changes the appearance of their clothing: "Standing in it we have stripes all over us" (21). Home has become a figurative prison for the kids, and the overall sense is that nothing is going to change. Speaking again for the collective, Sophie reports that she and her siblings listen for their parents "with the football drone in the background, even though this isn't anything new—we always see this, holding out your arms and seeing the stripes" (21). Echoing the religious connotations of the "our father" in the first sentence, extended arms and "stripes" allude to divine pain and persecution. Even though these images border on the sentimental, Minot's stark prose maintains a remarkable level of tonal control. The overwhelming message of "Hiding" is that the Vincent children suffer for reasons they do not fully comprehend.

The theme of emotional coldness and stagnation continues in "Thanksgiving Day," a tale that reveals some of the reasons for the divisions within the Vincent family. Because of a lack of familial warmth, the Thanksgiving tradition has lost its vibrancy, although it is unclear whether it ever had any. Life for the Vincents seems to have become a series of customary gestures. The children realize that they are to greet their grandfather, Pa, upon arrival because "every year it was the same" (23). The entire clan has gathered—aunts, uncles, and cousins—to dine together. The scene is strikingly funereal, however, because everything within the elder Vincent's home seems to be in a state of decay. Sophie, for example, ponders the dead rabbit used to make her cousin Bit's muff. The children venture into the attic to see a dead lion shot by Ma's father, the fur on its head almost gone from "being touched, or from being old" (31). The narrator juxtaposes the image of Ma as a young woman before marriage, "holding a plume of roses at her waist, her chin to the side, her dark eyes and dark hair swept up," with a conversation about a neighbor who, in a manner allusive to Hemingway's "The Snows of Kilimanjaro," "died after she cut her finger on a splinter from a Christmas-tree ornament" (28). The speaker seems to suggest that the photos and memories are fading, that the glory of the family name is no longer what it was.

The objects in the home are essentially miniature monuments to a fading era of accomplishment and prosperity that once came easily to the Vincent family. As Nagel explains, many of the details Minot includes reveal that the family is, or was, wealthy and well educated. Pa was a "dollar-a-year man," academically trained at a New England prep school and then Harvard University, and his brother was a "famous doctor who discovered the cure for a disease" (32).[16] The latter was likely based on Susan Minot's great-uncle, George R. Minot, the man her father was named for, "who won a Nobel Prize in Medicine in 1934, for finding the cure for pernicious anemia."[17] Despite all the material objects that serve as reminders of American nobility, conversation among those present at dinner tends to shift toward dissolution. Pa's health is fading, and his mind is not what it once was. He does not remember his children skating on his frozen-over "sunken garden" (32–33), and his wife must cover for him when it is alluded that he was responsible for a fire that destroyed the "piazza" on their old home in Cassett Harbor (35). When

Ma attempts to calm him, he asks, "why don't you go shoot yourself?" (37). Pa's disillusionment perhaps stems from the onset of senility, a condition that does not allow him to maintain the mythical level of competence he exhibited in his youth.

The deterioration implied in "Thanksgiving Day" carries over into "Allowance," a tale that suggests that Dad is having monetary problems. He is not a "dollar-a-year man" like Pa; he must be paid for his work in order to provide for his wife and kids. To some degree, a similar financial downturn occurred in the Minot family. Despite their Brahmin ancestry and the appearance of familial wealth, the Minots experienced something of a "reversal of fortune." Seemingly without irony or self-awareness, George Minot said in an interview that "the money ran out on us . . . we didn't go to Gstaad. We went to Bermuda. It was tight."[18] George's comment speaks to the central tension in "Allowance": the Vincents are worried about their financial state but do not act accordingly. This story is about excess, the inevitable conflicts that arise when perception and reality are grossly misaligned. When things are "tight," the price of a trip to both Gstaad and Bermuda are prohibitive. The depth of Dad's financial problems leads to his increased drinking and desire for solitude.

Consistent with Minimalistic technique, Minot does not offer explicit detail about the family's money shortage. Much is communicated through brief, implicative images. "Allowance" begins in the middle. While "trapped" in their cottage at a resort in Bermuda because of persistent rain, the kids understandably grow restless. They are loud and full of energy, so it is no surprise that Dad is hidden away in his room. Mum's eventual emergence is greeted by silence, further proof of her importance to the children. Her appearance immediately suggests that something is wrong; the narrator reports that she "came out in a bathrobe—something she'd never be wearing at home" (44). She is "distracted," also unusual, and is unable to exhibit the easy confidence she displays in "Hiding": "'It's Dad,' Mum said. 'He—' Her eyes were shiny with visions. . . . 'He thinks—' But she couldn't go on and was overtaken by little sobs and jumpy breaths. . . . 'It's okay. It's just things at the bank, and he thinks . . .'" (45). Even though the children do not understand the full extent of the problem, they again show that they are closely attuned to their mother's emotional state. Caitlin asks if they should go home. Mum's halts and starts, her inability to articulate what is at issue, and her incomplete state of dress poignantly illustrate the depth of her anguish and helplessness. As is often the case in *Monkeys*, the sense is that Dad should be the one to deal with these kinds of issues, but he is conspicuously hidden away.

One of the most memorable scenes in the cycle illustrates the depth of Dad's detachment and emotional immaturity. Because he has been drinking from his requisite "gallon of bourbon" for much of the afternoon (46), he is drunk at the start of the family dinner. The kids are "careful not to look straight at him," perhaps out of respect for Mum. As the children skeptically ponder their green pea soup, Mum anachronistically alludes to the 1971 "Mikey likes it!" advertisement for Life cereal when she declares, "Look . . . Dad likes it," letting them know that "it was okay to look at Dad now" (49).[19] Because he is acting immaturely, his face "one inch from the bowl," Mum calls "yoo-hoo" in order to rouse him from his stupor. She is trying to negotiate a difficult situation. The suggestion is that she wants to somehow maintain her husband's dignity in the eyes of their children and that his poor behavior is not serious enough to elicit fear or a lack of confidence. This need is nowhere more apparent than when in the moments after Dad has poured his ice water over his head, Mum "dipped her fingers into [her own glass] as if it were holy water, but instead of crossing herself, absentmindedly, the way she did when arriving late for church, she purposefully dabbed the water around her neck like perfume" (51). Dad at times calls Rose "Mum," and it is indicative of the fact that he needs her to care for him not as a wife but often as a maternal figure.

The absurdity of Dad's behavior at dinner carries over into a third image, set at the ocean. While his kids play, Gus yelling at him to gain his attention much the way Mum does at dinner, Dad sits "behind the girls in a rickety chair he'd found on the beach, wearing sneakers and socks" (53). Similar to the suggestive power of the empty rocker at the end of "Thanksgiving Day," which implies that Pa will soon pass away, the "rickety" state of Dad's chair reflects the state of his relationship with his family. His shoes indicate that he is again to be treated with distance, that he does not intend to play. He provides money for ice cream when called upon and during a trip to a fort commands the kids to obey their mother, but he seems more mascot than active participant. In the final action of the story, Gus steals his father's wallet and then tries to hide his misdeed. While Nagel argues that Gus's thievery "suggests that the inherent pathology in the relationship between the parents is having its effect on the children,"[20] it also seems a calculated attempt by Gus to gain his father's attention. On the beach Gus yells "watch me!" to no effect, so he makes a weak attempt at portraying himself as a hero by "finding" the lost item in the bushes, a ploy that if successful would garner fatherly appreciation. Because it is apparent that Dad gives the kids money whenever they want something, it is unlikely that Gus is motivated by greed. Mr. Vincent says nothing when his billfold is recovered, taking time only to confirm whether anything is missing, and Gus begins to look panicked because everyone "knew what he'd done" (57). His extreme measures do not even elicit him the negative attention of a punishment. Dad's emotional frigidity has become insurmountable.

In "Wildflowers," it is Mum who goes to extreme measures in an attempt to gain her husband's attention. In the sixteen months since the trip to Bermuda described in "Allowance," it is implied that Mum has begun an affair with a weapons manufacturing magnate named Wilbur Kittredge. The third-person narrator is closely aligned with Mum's consciousness. The events of the story take place in North Eden, Maine, an island community that swells in population during the summer months. The girls have all reached their teenage years and are increasingly aware of the problems between their parents. They also notice a newfound sexual and emotional vibrancy in Mum, and Caitlin and Sophie understand the reason for it. Early in the story, the narrator observes that "Mum had brought wildflowers—loosestrife and buttercups and queen anne's lace. There was no space for a garden at the Vincents', with the dock in front and Main Street just up the steps—the vegetable garden was in another place entirely—so Mum gathered flowers up island. She found fields everywhere shimmering down to the sea, flowers scattered and random, not boxed inside walls. On her bedside table she kept a small vase, always fresh." Sophie remarks that Mum is "feeling her oats," reflective of the elder woman's newfound sense of purpose. Both girls know, however, that it is because Mum has been invigorated by Kittredge's attentions. Sophie says that "guess-who must be racing today" (60), a reference to Kittredge and the boat races, and her statement is an indication that the young women are no longer oblivious to the intricacies of love and betrayal. Because of the depth of their allegiance, they do not express anger toward Mum, suggesting that any emotional ties they may have once felt with their father have been severed.

Understandably, the Minots have not commented publicly on whether their father and mother had marital problems of the sort alluded to in "Wildflowers," but they have spoken extensively about their summers. Their vacation house, first mentioned in "Thanksgiving Day," was in a town called North Haven, Maine. Sam Minot describes the place in detail:

> Our house on the island was right on the water, literally. A wharf house remodeled since its earliest days of catering to the big

> schooners, the cargo ships of the era. The house was a long rectangular, cedar shingled, two storied triplex that balanced on wooden pilings and granite blocks. At high tide the ocean comes entirely under the house, making it feel like you're on a boat. My grandparents, my dad's parents, purchased this place back in the late 1930's for they had learned about the island through friends. We called them Ma and Pa and they lived at one end of the house with their live-in Irish cook, Sheila. . . . The opposite end of the house, a four bedroom unit, was where we stayed in as children. The in between area, a three bedroom unit, was known as the middle house. All these units were under the same roof, a unique antique house that easily accommodated the likes of a large family like ours.[21]

Sam's account suggests that the house was extremely important to the family, but it was also highly partitioned. It is in many ways reflective of the emotional state of the Vincent family: everyone could be in the same building yet maintain their distance from one another. Sam had fond recollections of the time he spent there as an adolescent and talked about the nearby structure that served as the island yacht club.

Mum is in her element when she is at the club, greeting her friends, catching up, doing the kinds of things that Dad avoids. Her spirit is not one of division but of a desire to create and maintain a sense of community. The summer people gather at the afternoon races "clustered together; they'd known each other a long time" (60–61). While on its surface "Wildflowers" seems to be about Mum's affair and eventual disillusionment, it is in actuality about the nature of motherhood. Minot depicts the bond between mother and child as far more substantial than that between lovers: it is a relationship with meaning and sustainability. Mum is not conflicted about her roles, however. She is relatively young at thirty-nine years old, and she still desires passion.

Minot omits many of the details of Mum's relationship with Kittredge. The narrator of "Wildflowers" reveals that they "went on rides" in his carriages when Dad was back home in Marshport. Her commitment to him seems primarily physical: her politics are decidedly left-wing and antiwar while he is wealthy because he "made bombs" (69). The relationship is similar to her marriage in that it mirrors the religious division between her and Dad. Kittredge is for Mum a mythical idealization, someone who allows her to forget the realities that weigh on her. The narrator reveals much about Mum's state of mind during the "silver fox" sequence. The speaker contrasts the mundane duties of motherhood with the allure of a man with a "grayish-white spot on the back of his dark head," a figure later identified as Kittredge. As Mum stands near him, her "eyes were lit with brightness" (62). The narrator juxtaposes this image with that of a silver fox Mum claims to have seen while on Boxed Island, an event that her husband dismisses as false because he does not believe the animal exists.[22] Foxes in some contexts possess mythical qualities; in *The Golden Bough*, James George Frazer talks about how they were sometimes burned during European summer festivals. Some believed foxes were particularly dangerous because witches were known to shift into their shape.[23] The narrator describes Mum as if she is returning home after a night taking part in a pagan rite of spring, saying that she "came flying out of the cricket darkness, her nightgown luminous, a fiery look in her eye. She was panting" (62). Mum's reaction to Kittredge carries base connotations as well. The term *fox* is slang for someone who is attractive, and Mum's giddiness around him is proof that she finds the silver-haired Kittredge alluring. She is "thrilled" with him just as she was when "the silver fox streaked across" her path on Boxed Island (63). Unfortunately for her, her experiences with both man and beast prove ephemeral.

Like foxes, carriages take on particular imagistic importance within "Wildflowers": they represent both pleasure and intense pain. Mum's carriage rides with Kittredge are for sexual liaisons, and it is later implied that he used them for this purpose with other women as well. The narrator mentions that during a late-night ride home Caitlin and Sophie spot Kittredge's carriage outfitted with "red lamps," objects commonly associated with prostitution, and he is sitting next to "a woman with a hat on" (69). It is unclear who this woman is, though the girls seem to think it is their mother. Mum later spots her lover in a carriage with an unidentified blonde woman, and she knows that her relationship with him is effectively over.

Minot broadens the imagistic relevance of carriages by suggesting that for Mum they are a source of maternal suffering. The implicit idea is that for Mum sex is not simply for pleasure, as it is for Kittredge, but also for procreation. It is not an inconsequential act. The narrator reveals that Mum gave birth to a daughter named Frances in 1961, nine years before the events described in "Wildflowers," and that the newborn died in a "baby carriage" (66). While there is little if anything redemptive about the Kittredge episode, Mum gives birth to another child in the end, a daughter named Miranda, and her paternity is ambiguous. The "thrill" Rose feels while being near Kittredge early in the tale gives way to the maternal satisfaction of feeding her newborn:

"There is nothing so thrilling as this. Nothing" (73). She affirms that the failings of her romantic dealings are far outweighed by the joy she derives from motherhood.

While Rose revels in her contentment as a mother, her teenaged daughters are learning to cope with a complex adult world. In "Party Blues," Sophie ponders her own sexual awakening and learns about betrayal firsthand. The third-person narration focuses on Sophie, and the plot closely mirrors that of "Wildflowers." Sophie's boyfriend Duer flirts with a fifteen-year-old girl who parallels the young blonde with whom Kittredge betrays Mum. The difference, however, is that Sophie has likely been tolerating her boyfriend's behavior for a long time. Mum returns to Dad and the children in the wake of her affair with Kittredge, but Sophie stays with Duer because she does not have a similar alternative. She has given her heart to someone unequally committed, whose drives are purely physical, but her infatuation dictates that she stay with him even though he is destructive emotionally.

The depth of Sophie's understandable discontentment with love and life manifests itself in the contemplation of suicide. The narrator demonstrates a profound sensitivity to Sophie, saying that "she'd taken it hard—the discovery of her faults. Death was never far from her mind. One evening, Mum asked her to promise she wouldn't commit suicide until she was eighteen. 'I think you'll outgrow it by then,' she explained, casually doing her needlepoint in front of the TV" (81). Mum's nonchalance suggests that she feels self-destructive thoughts are a normal part of growing up, something that she herself pondered during difficult stretches of her life. As Nagel observes, a "suicide motif . . . surfaces in virtually every story."[24] The overall suggestion, however, is that Sophie will eventually learn to cope with the vicissitudes of daily experience once she achieves a true sense of independence.

Minot's reference to Ludwig Bemelmans's *Madeline* stories in the final paragraph of "Party Blues" is particularly important because it indirectly suggests that Sophie has realized that her childhood is over. Minot conflates the original *Madeline* with *Madeline and the Gypsies*.[25] Both plots follow the experiences of a young orphan named Madeline. Her adventures are often set among the monuments of Paris, and Bemelmans's tales are in many ways a celebration of the city itself. Like Minot, he was both an author and painter. In *Madeline*, the title character needs an emergency appendectomy, and it is Miss Clavel's seemingly telepathic knowledge of her girls that leads her to awake in the night and cry out that "something is not right!" For Sophie, this exclamation reflects her own ineffability. Like so many characters in Minimalist works, she is unable to articulate what she feels and thus begin the process of coming to terms with her problems.

The idea of disappearance grows from Sophie's recollection of *Madeline and the Gypsies*. When a day at the Gypsy Carnival is disrupted by a violent storm, Madeline and Pepito, the son of the Spanish ambassador, are forgotten as they ride the Ferris wheel during a storm. They are rescued, drugged, and kidnapped by a "Gypsy Mama," who despite her dubious actions is presented as a benign and protective figure. They travel throughout France and learn various circus skills until they are returned to the orphanage. This story likely resonates with the eighteen-year-old Sophie because she too played circus when she was young: "They used to put on circuses next door with the Birches. She'd liked that." Reflective of her precarious state as a teenager coping with a fickle lover, she used to pretend to be a "trapeze artist" (77). The narrator's harrowing final statement, that "one of the little girls is gone" (89), is an indication that Sophie now realizes that her youthful innocence has faded and that she can no longer rely upon her mother to resolve her problems for her. In a figurative sense, Sophie, like Madeline, has been orphaned.

Sophie's sense of abandonment is exacerbated by her father's unreliability, an attribute glaringly on display in "The Navigator." Because of its serious tone and direct treatment of Dad's escalating problem with alcohol, "The Navigator" was later included in an anthology of short stories titled *The Invisible Enemy: Alcoholism and the Modern Short Story*.[26] Set in North Eden, Maine, in August 1977, all of the children have at least entered their teenage years, the lone exception being six-year-old Miranda. They are preparing dinner and talking about their parents. Mum has somehow convinced Dad to spend an evening playing games at the Irvings', and the kids laugh when they determine that the alternative was a Sunday clambake at the Kittredges'. Delilah reflexively calls her father a "poor guy," a label replete with meaning. While they do not seem to begrudge their mother's affair with Kittredge, they share a sense of pity about Dad. Because they are no longer children, they now see him as a pathetic figure. Sophie offers only a hollow show of support, replying that "he can handle it" (92–93). As the narrative progresses, it becomes starkly evident that Dad can "handle" little.

Alcohol is a ubiquitous object in "The Navigator," and it is invested with deep and divisive emotions. Ma, who is now without Pa, enters the plot already drunk and "wobbling" after an afternoon spent drinking sherry in her living room. The evening begins well for Dad but ends poorly. Caitlin and Sophie encourage their father when he finally appears wearing a yellow blazer, complimenting him on his "snappy" appearance (96–97). The next time they see him, he is so drunk he needs help from his "Mum" in order to get back in the house. The third-person narrator mentions that Dad calls his wife "Rosie" as an allusion to "the schoolteacher in *The African Queen* who dumps out all of Humphrey Bogart's gin in order to get them down the river" (97–98). Mum abstains from drinking, and the implication is that she "never drank" because of the abiding sense of responsibility she feels toward her "monkeys."[37] Minot communicates much through the use of imagistic correlative. As Ma vacantly smiles at her surroundings, Gus stands at the window and says "foggy." As everyone busily moves around the kitchen, he concludes that "everything's disappearing" (97). His ominous observation suggests that the family is caught in a "fog" of denial, a general lack of awareness that mirrors the physical cloudiness of a person under the influence. A lack of vision, or a refusal to acknowledge the situation for what it is, ultimately leads to the disappearance of interfamilial faith.

The "fog" that pervades this early sequence is snapped by an equally poignant image at the end of the tale. After Dad returns from the Irvings' drunk, the family confronts him about his problem and encourages him to seek help. He seems receptive. The family decides to take the boat out to a favorite picnic spot for lunch, and Dad competently guides them through rocky waters without the aid of a spotter. Once there, however, the peaceful outing is disrupted by a shotgun-like "*crack*" (107). Minot describes the scene masterfully:

> Some heads jerked toward Dad; some looked down. Above them, Dad was facing the root screen, his back to the family. Mum didn't move, lying on the life jacket, eyes hidden behind her sunglasses. Sophie hugged her shins and bit her knee. Gus's neck was twisted into a tortured position; he glared at Dad's back.
>
> Dad turned around. He gazed with an innocent expression out over the snaking water. If aware of the eyes upon him, Dad did not betray it, observing the scenery with contentment; nothing more normal than for him to be standing in the shade at a family picnic holding a can of beer. He twisted the ring from its opening and, squinting at a far-off view, stooped to lap up the nipple of foam at the top of the can. (108)

The power and meaning of the moment are communicated through imagery alone. Consistent with Minimalist technique, the narrator does not comment on the significance of the scene: the passage is purely reportorial. The closest she comes to indicating an emotion is in the description of young Gus's neck, which is "twisted in a tortured position." Dad's nonchalant "contentment," his overwhelming sense of normality, sharply contrasts with the family's unspoken feelings of betrayal. The final sentence of "The Navigator," possibly an allusion to the last sentence of Carver's "Vitamins," suggests that Dad's problem is, in the eyes of his family, insurmountable.[28] The narrator talks about how the kids would throw rocks into the "thorofare" and "the darkness would swallow up a stone and they'd wait, but no sound would come. It seemed then as if the stone had gone into some further darkness, entered some other dimension where things went on falling and falling" (108). This well-crafted ending successfully synthesizes the concept of disappearance, introduced by Gus's comments about the fog, with the family's seemingly inexorable decay.

The Vincents' metaphorical fall continues in "Accident," a tale about the aftermath of Mum's death. The title refers to a car accident involving Sherman, but it also alludes to an event that, even though omitted, represents the emotional apogee of the cycle: Mum's death. Minimalistic plots often focus on characters in the midst of unspoken crises, the causes of which are subtly implied, and Nagel maintains that "it is indicative of Minot's minimalist methodology that the most important event in the book is never directly portrayed and is revealed only through partial memories obliquely described."[29] The children are understandably forlorn, and Sherman's mishap occurs because both his drinking and anger toward his father have intensified. Sherman confronts Dad moments after wrecking his car and asks him why he does not "act like a faddah" (125). Consistent with his character, Dad weakly retreats. Because "Accident" is part of a collection of interrelated stories, much can be discerned about the possible reasons Mum drove her car into a train.

In the decades since the original publication of "Accident" in the *New Yorker*, the emergence of new biographical information has complicated the interpretation of Mum's actions.[30] Based solely on the text of *Monkeys*, it is most likely, although not absolutely certain, that Mum has taken her own life. Even though she seems relatively content with Dad in the wake of her failed affair with Kittredge, it is possible that she suffers from a lingering depression. Dad's drinking, and the considerable embarrassment it continues to cause, has not abated with time. Nagel maintains that Mum has killed herself, and his argument is compelling given the references made to suicide in earlier stories such as "Hiding," "Thanksgiving Day," and "Party Blues."[31] The actual death of Helen Minot, however, was likely an accident. Although Sam Minot, like his fictional counterpart Sherman, also has "certain theories about the accident," Susan does not agree with him, and her rejection of his version of events makes it unlikely that she would construct a fictional scenario that suggests she accepted it. Although Sam was away from home when his mother died, he contends that "our mother was killed in a bizarre car accident, colliding in her car head on into a train that ran nearby our house in Manchester. She was forty-eight years old when it happened on that sunny, January Monday morning. It was deemed that the lights weren't working at the railroad tracks crossing due to an icy storm over the weekend. In any case, the engineer stated in the newspaper that he saw her coming down the hill and that he had sounded the train's horn. It was a direct head to head collision and her little Ford Fiesta was demolished, causing her instant death. The priest who blessed her body said that she had a content smile on her face; unlike he had ever seen on a corpse."[32] Sam essentially dismisses the facts of the case: the roads were treacherous and the signage dysfunctional. Many details that he includes in his memoir suggest that he felt a latent anger toward his father, and his "theories" seem to be a mechanism for casting blame.[33] "Accident" is about Sherman's frustration with Dad, and their confrontation near the end seems both pointless and cathartic. Sam is alone in his interpretation because "his siblings, for the most part, become exasperated when he raises this chain of events. Their mother, they say, drove her car into an oncoming train entirely by accident; a winter storm had broken the warning signals at the crossing. The bells never rang; the red lights failed to flash. 'Sam is—whatever,' Susan Minot told me recently, in her terse way. 'He's got his own thing. And people in the family kind of do this. They sort of act like they have a little inside information, somehow.'"[34] Mum's accident also occurs in January, so it is plausible that the roads would have been dangerous at the time of her collision (130). Despite his seeming confidence in his position, Sam eventually retreats: "Many things were under the surface and all her children, except for Eliza, were out of the house. Her job as homemaker and mother of seven was pretty much over and the future prospects of living alone with an alcoholic must have depressed her. I don't know what happened. It could have been, and probably was, a freak coincidence for her Catholic upbringing surely shunned any thoughts of suicide since our lives aren't our own in belonging, but that of God's."[35] Sam demonstrates a deep level of empathy and insight when talking about his mother. Because Rose is, like Helen, a devout Catholic, it is unlikely that she would commit a mortal sin. Regardless, the iceberg is remarkably complex. While biographical evidence supports the argument that Mum's death is in fact an accident, Susan Minot's choice of a suicide leitmotif provides considerable evidence to the contrary. The only certainty at the end of "Accident" is that the Vincent siblings must now negotiate the difficulties of adulthood in the absence of the one parent they could depend upon for guidance and love.

In "Wedlock," the intense sadness the Vincents feel manifests itself in mundane objects and events. The original version of the story is titled "The Silver Box," a more appropriate name because it refers to an important physical item that appears in the tale rather than a diffuse concept.[36] "Wedlock" is set during Christmas, the first the family has celebrated since Rose's death. The plot is quite weak; little happens other than conversation. Dad drifts in and out of the story, at one point appearing "puffy-eyed" and "awful" (131). Because the family has not completed the mourning process, they feel an intense absence: "The house was filled with missing things" (130). Material items carry intense memories and emotions they are unprepared to confront. When looking for the decorations, they find some of Mum's clothes and "a shoebox of postcards from Mr. Kittredge" (131). Dad leaves the house to buy himself some shaving cream, something he used to get in his stocking. Dad may have also visited Pat Meyer, the woman he later marries, a prospect Sherman finds upsetting.

The implication of the ending sequence is that the Vincents will only survive Mum's death if they maintain their familial bond. The daughters, with the exception of Minnie, talk about their own romantic travails. Caitlin and Delilah have visited with their boyfriends, admitting that they will eventually marry. In talking about their relationships, they begin to empathize with their father, to appreciate the loneliness he must feel. Even though he has failed them repeatedly because of his drinking, they do not hold him to any standard of conduct. As the girls chat, a drunken Dad appears at the door not wearing "pajamas" (137). They tell him to return to bed, and Sophie whispers "he had a lot tonight" (138). While Dad's coping mechanism is self-destructive, it seems that the siblings will to some degree be able to rely upon one another for support. The girls share a closeness, however, not matched by Gus, Sherman, and Chicky. "Wedlock" is essentially a story about the power of love.

The closeness expressed in "Wedlock" is concretized in the final tale in *Monkeys*, "Thorofare." While it would be inaccurate to say that *Monkeys* ends happily, the story includes subtle themes of redemption and restoration. Dad's marriage to Pat has set into motion a new outlook within the Vincent home. About one-third of the way into the plot, Sophie moves into the living room and notices that Pat has been cleaning and rearranging. The curtains have been sent out and a rug has been removed, "revealing a polished wooden floor Sophie had never seen before." The narrator reveals that while Sophie was given the unfair burden of filling Mum's role "things had deteriorated," but Pat has "brought painters in for the upstairs bedrooms, and Mr. Parsons had been over to look at the rot on the front porch" (147). Throughout the cycle, homes reflect the family's collective emotional state. The implication is that Pat has played a role in literally and figuratively halting the Vincents' descent. One result is that Dad's attitude toward the children improves, and it is significant that he does not drink in "Thorofare." When Delilah requests that they spread some of Mum's ashes in Marshport, Dad rebukes her. He relents, however, and determines that the best place for the ceremony is his garden, a space that he has protected and considered his own throughout the book (150).

The final sequence of events illustrates both the family's sadness over Mum's death and the potential for rejuvenation. The Vincents gather in Maine in order to fulfill Mum's desire to have her ashes spread in the "thorofare" near their summer home. After much bustle and preparation, a scene reminiscent of the opening of "Hiding," Dad and the children embark. In a moving ceremony, each family member throws a handful of Mum's remains into the sea.[37] On the way home, Caitlin asks her father, "do you think it will get nice?" In an uncommon show of optimism, he replies, "I know it will" (158). By throwing Mum's "bones" into the ocean, the Vincents feel that restoration may be possible. Minot subtly alludes to imagery used in Ezekiel 37:1–14, the passage in which God tells the prophet to speak over dry bones in order to bring them back to life. In doing so, Ezekiel restores hope to Israel. While the ending does not affirm that the Vincent family's troubles are fully resolved, the suggestion is that they have earned a new sense of freedom. Less clear is whether they will know what to do with it.

The Minot children have revisited the events of the past in both fictional and nonfictional accounts, suggesting that they are still attempting to come to terms with their adolescence. Much has been revealed about the family in the past decade, and these facts provide essential insight into what Minot has implied but omitted from *Monkeys*. While biographical parallels do not necessarily provide absolute interpretive certainty, they often generate a deeper appreciation for the profundity of what may seem on the surface to be nothing more than a collection of well-crafted but mundane vignettes. Additionally, these new revelations form the basis of a fresh appreciation of Minot's formidable ability as a stylist. Even though her tales primarily explore domestic content, her precise sentences and eye for detail are in many ways equal to Hemingway's finest work. The simplicity of Minot's prose enhances the sensorial impact of her stories. Given the emotional magnitude of the events that inform *Monkeys*, it is remarkable how Minot avoids the pitfalls of sentimentality.

5

Transnational Minimalism

Sandra Cisneros's *Caramelo*

Sandra Cisneros's *Caramelo* is a stylistically innovative work of fiction. An unconventional novel, it is best described as a lengthy collection of vignettes and stories that achieves unity through thematic continuity and interconnected imagery. The chapters are compact, well crafted, and nonchronological. Although it is not directed at adolescents, it is similar to Cisneros's most famous work, *The House on Mango Street*, in that it requires a heightened level of interpretive insight. Even though it at times seems incomplete, a work that lacks a distinct design, the book achieves profound richness. It is a fragmentary, impressionistic collection of memories and historically based reminiscences shaped by American and South American Minimalist traditions.

Cisneros incorporates poetic devices and techniques into her prose, reflective of the fact that she is an accomplished poet. She uses dense imagery and precise language in the many vignettes that comprise the novel, and her style is at times reminiscent of the work of Hamlin Garland, Ambrose Bierce, and other literary Impressionists. Her devotion to craft in part explains why it took her nine years to finish the book.[1] In an interview with Renee H. Shea, Cisneros said, "I write in such a way that every syllable matters; maybe that's why the book took me so long. But I don't know how else to write; my unit has always been the syllable. Sometimes Dennis [Mathis, her fiction editor] tells me to take bigger strokes—but in essence I'm still a miniaturist."[2] In calling herself a "miniaturist," she may have been attempting to avoid the "Minimalist tag." During an interview with Gayle Elliot, Cisneros was asked, "Do you classify yourself in a particular way: minimalist, magical realist, postmodernist? It would seem to me that you classify yourself maybe more as a storyteller." Cisneros responded, "I don't classify myself as any of those things because I don't know what that means, and I don't have to know. It's not my job to be classifying my stories."[3] Regardless, she values precision and directness, saying, "I think I write about very complex things in ways that are simple and poetic."[4] While there is nothing epic about the book in a classical sense, it achieves a remarkable level of emotional forcefulness while maintaining prose-poetic efficiency. Aspersive names such as *deadpan domestic* and *catatonic realism* do not apply.

Cisneros said that *Caramelo* began as a story she told to her friends about a family trip to Acapulco, a tale she thought would be fairly simple to include in her collection *Woman Hollering Creek*. During the writing process, however, the piece expanded and she came to the realization that it was likely going to be a novel.[5] Considering that *Caramelo* is over 440 pages long, it may seem absurd for her to refer to herself as a "miniaturist." The chapters in *Caramelo* are finely wrought stories that combine to form a unified, well-crafted work of prose.

Structurally, *Caramelo* is in many ways unusual. All eighty-seven chapters, many of which are brief, stand alone as individual stories, although some, such as "Echando Palabras," would seem incomplete if left on their own because important information is omitted only to be revealed later. This type of deferral, a technique Jay McInerney also uses in *Bright Lights, Big City*, is akin to the "big reveal" commonly found in detective fiction and melodrama. Cisneros published some chapters as short stories, although when placing them within *Caramelo* she had to add material in order to establish continuity.[6] All of the pieces that comprise the work feature recurring characters, and the fact that Celaya "Lala" Reyes narrates all of the tales unifies a seemingly disjointed, fragmented plot.

Caramelo is divided into three sections woven together by common themes, characters, and images. Part 1, "Recuerdo de Acapulco," describes a Reyes family road trip from Chicago to Mexico City that transpires when Lala is four or five years old. Her exact age is omitted; she at one point says to her grandfather, Narciso, that she does not "go to school yet."[7] Cisneros uses many of the episodes in this portion to establish the central characteristics of individual family members. For example, Soledad, also known as Awful Grandmother, fulfills the expectations of her nickname and makes life prickly for everyone except her beloved son, Inocencio. Lala introduces her many uncles, aunts, and cousins, but they are flat characters who ultimately have little impact on the plot. The second segment, titled "When I Was

Dirt," explains the genesis of the Reyes family. Much of the action is set in the besieged Mexico City, a dangerous place reduced to rubble by the ongoing Mexican Revolution. The final third resumes where the "cliffhanger" ending of part 1 leaves off. Lala becomes a young teenager who must confront a complex society that both accepts and rejects her because of her race and ethnicity. Her father's love, as well as his ongoing struggle to realize the American Dream, sustains and enervates his family.

Generally avoiding the subject of fatherhood, the initial reviews of *Caramelo* tend to address matters of tone, specifically the exuberance of Cisneros's storytelling. Several reviewers comment on structure and style but do not make an explicit connection with the Minimalist tradition. Betsy Kline compares the book to *The House on Mango Street*, writing that Cisneros's "choppy, episodic style, which served her so well in the astoundingly brief and breezy 'The House on Mango Street,' turns her new novel into a string of firecrackers, sudden bursts of color and character development."[8] Keir Graff refers to it as a series of "coming-of-age vignettes," and Adriana Lopez likens it to "a mosaic of hundreds of sepia snapshots of stories."[9] In a particularly insightful review for the *Toronto Star*, Elizabeth Johnston writes that "structurally, the novel is composed of short, bite-sized chapters that can, most of the time, stand on their own as prose poems—an approach used to delightful ends in her much shorter novel, *The House on Mango Street*." Johnston continues on to suggest that Cisneros frequently employs the technique of implication by omission, stating, "each chapter is a snapshot that is complete in itself, but also leaves something out, creating suspense and questions that make you turn the page."[10] Ana Lopez speaks to the efficiency of Cisneros's prose, echoing Susan Minot's statement about the centrality of "little moments": "The real triumph of *Caramelo* is its author's ability to paint the big picture while capturing the trifles of everyday life, giving them profound and tender meaning."[11] Much of *Caramelo* seems large in scale, but it is, like many Minimalist works, a testament to the beauty that can be found in the mundane. Lala's world is full of small, seemingly irrelevant moments.

While *Caramelo* is at times rather simple, beneath the surface it is, among other things, a complex examination of racial, ethnic, and political boundaries. The opening third is representative of the many types of "border crossings" that occur throughout the plot. Much of the scholarly criticism about *Caramelo* tends to focus on theoretical and social concerns, saying little about Cisneros's style or contribution to the development of American literary aesthetics. The book is a conventional bildungsroman, but it is about the coming of age of a young girl who must negotiate societal divisions and prejudices that she does not fully understand. Juanita Heredia posits that *Caramelo* is an attempt to in a broad sense preserve the histories of immigrants, writing that "Cisneros is concerned with telling the transmigratory experiences of families who wish to maintain their culture alive [*sic*] for the younger generation—products of a hybrid identity."[12] In "Sandra Cisneros and Her Trade of the Free World," Gabriella Gutiérrez y Muhs discusses how many of the objects incorporated into *Caramelo* reflect historical and cultural hybridity.[13] Heather Alumbaugh, James Phelan, and María José García Vizcaíno all explore narrative technique, but none of them talk about how Cisneros traverses the line between prose and poetry.[14] Her authorial choices about narration carry much interpretive weight, particularly because Lala expresses deep emotional ties to both the familial and political significance of the stories she is telling.

Part of Cisneros's Minimalist experimentation involves a measure of authorial intrusion. She occasionally talks about herself in her notes, at times referring to herself as "the author."[15] While this in one sense makes her an exception to the Minimalist practice of self-effacement, it is important to recognize that the narrator in *Caramelo* does not tend to explain or moralize. Lala does not describe a scene and then offer an explanatory divergence, which is why the book is not overtly political. Jessica Magnani opines that "if this novel is dedicated to Cisneros's father, as well as to emigrants like him, then it seems logical to assume that the didactic inclusion of historical references is an attempt at recovering a familial and cultural past."[16] Cisneros did not talk about writing as an act of "recovery," however, but rather as a means to preserve, to prevent her father from being forgotten. Allusions to name brands, places, and historical events also serve as a means of conveying details about time and setting.

Caramelo is typical of Minimalist works in that it is autobiographical and replete with historical and cultural allusions. It is atypical, however, because Cisneros includes a number of explanatory footnotes, many of which seem to offer her unique perspective on past events. She has been vocal about the idea that history is highly subjective and that those who have traditionally been marginalized must tell their own stories or, to use one of the central metaphors in *Caramelo*, "weave" their own tales. She talked about her research process in several interviews and suggested that she at times made use of unorthodox sources.[17] Cisneros's lengthy descriptions of historical events are not necessarily objective; "truth" in *Caramelo* speaks more to the realities of the human condition. The epigraph to the book, "cuéntame algo, aunque sea una mentira" or "tell me a story, even if it's a lie," implies that factual accuracy is a secondary concern. She is playful with the past, and her focus does not always seem set on conveying sound historical data. On the other hand, in multiple interviews Cisneros said that she was concerned with honoring and preserving the memory of her father: "I really wanted to write about my father because I felt as if his life didn't count. . . . He served in World War II, but people don't think about men like my father when they think about American history. That hurt me very deeply, to have someone I cared about so much erased and forgotten once he died, as if he meant nothing."[18] While Cisneros assumes a degree of irreverence when it comes to the murky line between truth and fiction, natural and supernatural, *Caramelo* cannot be dismissed as "healthy lies" alone. Even though it is a tribute to a man she loved, it is neither autobiography nor hagiography. She admittedly confronted some of her own family's most sensitive secrets in writing the book. For example, Alfredo Cisneros, Inocencio Reyes's counterpart, also fathered an illegitimate daughter, and the fictional rendering of this fact provides one of the most intriguing plot turns.[19] Even though the events Lala describes have a direct impact on her life, she often reports what she sees as if she is providing play-by-play commentary for a film.

In the opening lines of the novel, Lala appropriately describes a brief moment in time, or *vistazo*, manifested in the form of a photograph that hangs above her father's bed. She Impressionistically reports what was happening when it was taken: "Here are the Acapulco waters lapping just behind us, and here we are sitting on the lip of land and water. The little kids, Lolo and Memo, making devil horns behind each other's heads; the Awful Grandmother holding them even though she never held them in real life." She implies the light and position of the sun, declaring, "here is Father squinting that same squint I always make when I'm photographed. He isn't *acabado* yet. He isn't *finished*, worn from working, from worrying, from smoking too many packs of cigarettes" (3). Lala uses the "historical present" to both render the scene and intimate what is to come. In other words, she defines the past in terms of the present. Surprisingly, she admits that she is absent from the photograph, and she laments that she is "off by" herself "building sand houses" (4). It is a fitting situation given that *Caramelo* is a novel in which much is omitted yet implied. Lala describes events in generous detail but often leaves out her own emotional responses. In the end, the photograph serves multiple purposes. It is the preservation of an incomplete "memory" as well as a contemplation of all that has happened in the years since it was created.

The techniques Cisneros employs in this opening sequence, and throughout the novel, reflect a transnational stylistic hybridization. Her style in part grows from the intersection of South American and US Minimalism, a literary nexus that scholars in the United States have neglected. In combining these traditions, Cisneros makes an important contribution to the vitality of the American mode. When asked during interviews about influences, she mentioned three South American authors: Argentine Jorge Luis Borges, Brazilian Clarice Lispector, and Uruguayan Eduardo Galeano. While Cisneros's prose is not a complete technical departure from Ernest Hemingway's or Raymond Carver's, she instead mentioned Borges, Lispector, and Galeano as writers whose aesthetic affected her during the years she was writing *Caramelo*. During a 2002 interview with Robert Birnbaum, she made a specific reference to Galeano's *The Book of Embraces*; in 1987, she said that she was "greatly impressed" with Borges's *Dreamtigers*.[20] Each is comprised of brief, prose-poetic pieces that generally include descriptive imagery and contemplation.

While Cisneros does not explicitly refer to *Book of Embraces* and *Dreamtigers* in *Caramelo*, some of her primary presuppositions seem to have been molded by Borges's and Galeano's views of history and memory. One of Cisneros's central philosophies about subjectivity and the act of remembrance is embodied by the epigraph to *Book of Embraces*: "*Recordar*: To remember; from the Latin *re-cordis*, to pass back through the heart."[21] The title of the opening section of *Caramelo* is titled "Recuerdo de Acapulco," or "Memory of Acapulco," and Lala's description of events demonstrates how emotional context shapes historical perspective. Galeano expands on this idea in many of his pieces. One of the most poignant vignettes in *Book of Embraces*, "Christmas Eve," illustrates a human need that Cisneros frequently talked about in interviews. The "doomed child" expresses the same desire, a hope that someone will know that he was alive and that his life mattered. The power of Galeano's piece is in part derived from its basis in reality; the doctor who runs the hospital has a name and a family, and lives in a real place, Managua, Nicaragua. The dying boy's request takes place within the context of an important holiday, a day that typically reinforces deep familial bonds. Cisneros, like Galeano, is careful to construct specific contexts for the brief episodes that comprise *Caramelo*. Her father died of cancer while she was writing it, a fact she said motivated her.[22] *Caramelo* is essentially a manifestation of her desire to "tell" about the life and contributions of her father.

Given the intensely personal nature of Cisneros's motivation for writing *Caramelo*, her choice of influences is fitting. Galeano's "Christmas Eve" is an example of a type of prose poem Latin American authors often use called a *crônica* (in Portuguese) or *crónica* in Spanish.[23] In his preface to a collection of *crônicas* by Brazilian author Clarice Lispector, Giovanni Pontiero describes them as "aphorisms, diary entries, reminiscences, travel notes, interviews, serialized stories, essays, loosely defined as 'chronicles': a genre peculiar to Brazil which allows poets and writers to address a wider readership on a vast range of topics and themes."[24] They are often personal in nature, and the author tends to use them as a means to publicly contemplate the enigmas of daily experience. While some of them are brief, a few lines or a single paragraph, they can go on for pages. *Crônicas* are often Impressionistic, and they generally deal with intense sensorial experience; Lispector's "Rebellion" illustrates this.[25] The acuteness of her imagery is matched by the potency of her reaction. While "Rebellion" is in some ways similar to the work of literary Impressionists such as Stephen Crane and Anton Chekhov, it is different because they do not generally include a clearly stated philosophical conclusion. Lispector suggests that she has transferred her intense physical pain into the mental processes of memory and a contemplation of her future, making her body subservient to the power of her imagination. Impressionists seek to capture sensation in a moment of time whereas the writers of *crônicas* want to preserve both sensory experience and the resulting contemplation of its meaning. Cisneros draws from the latter tradition in her desire to chronicle, and thus subjectively shape, history.

One function of the *crônica* is to combat the tragic loss of individual memories that accompanies death. In other words, it is a mechanism used to safeguard experiences that do not qualify as worthy of publication in a widely read textbook. Cisneros explained in an interview that she viewed her family and friends as figurative museums: "I found myself drawing from families' memorias, their memoirs, as well as doing some research by doing interviews with the real people, the walking Smithsonians as I like to put it, sitting down and talking to people, and then doing the research to add to that."[26] Borges suggests a similar view of the richness of individual experiences in his prose poem "The Witness":

> Events far-reaching enough to people all space, whose end is nonetheless tolled when one man dies, may cause us wonder. But something, or an infinite number of things, dies in every death, unless the universe is possessed of a memory, as the theosophists have supposed.
>
> In the course of time there was a day that closed the last eyes to see Christ. The battle of Junín and the love of Helen each died with the death of some one man. What will die with me when I die, what pitiful or perishable form will the world lose? The voice of Macedonio Fernández? The image of a roan horse on the vacant lot at Serrano and Charcas? A bar of sulphur in the drawer of a mahogany desk?[27]

Borges's contemplation of loss at first seems hopeless, but in the end he speaks to the value of mundane, yet valuable, moments. The final paragraph of "The Witness" begins with an evaluation that favors events that have shaped art and destiny. It concludes, however, with a recognition that there is something beautiful, and worth preserving, in everyday occurrences. Cisneros approaches her subject matter in a similar spirit. Her father was an upholsterer by trade, and she observed that the novels she has read do not include any famous upholsterers.[28] The point implicit in *Caramelo* is that prophets and generals, the victors who earn the spoils, are not the only people who deserve monuments. Cisneros, like Borges, not only draws attention to the richness of common life, but also redefines notions of what, and who, is worth preserving.

Cisneros's incorporation of the mundane into her fiction does not, however, result in an absence of drama, a fact in part attributable to the influence of the *fotonovela* and telenovela. The thesis of so-called reality television seems to be that everyday life is as entertaining as programs filmed using scripts and various high-dollar production techniques. Lala at times works along similar lines in that she captures the visual drama of passionate arguments and tender moments, although it would be a disservice to Cisneros to state that her fiction is at all comparable to what passes for reality television. Inocencio Reyes is a dedicated fan of *fotonovelas*, perhaps best defined as love stories "told in photographs with balloon captions presenting the dialogue . . . omnipresent among the masses in Latin America, Northern Africa, France, and Italy."[29] Awful Grandmother pampers her favorite son by giving him *fotonovelas* and comic books she has kept locked away in her treasured "walnut-wood armoire." One of Cisneros's footnotes reveals that Soledad's favorites include "Wives There Are Plenty, But Mothers—Only One" and "He Doesn't Give a Damn What You Feel" (63). As these titles suggest, often lurking below the surface of these entertainments is a tidy moral lesson.

The telenovela, a medium in some ways similar to the *fotonovela*, is comparable to a typical American soap opera.[30] *Caramelo* is melodramatic, but more importantly it resembles these forms because it is often narrated in a highly visual manner. Lala creates an overt connection among genres. Chapter 83, for example, is titled "A Scene in a Hospital That Resembles a Telenovela When in Actuality It's the Telenovelas That Resemble This Scene" (402). In a broad sense, the novel follows the basic formula of the telenovela: "Contemporary melodrama typically narrates tales in which, after a number of problematic events, misunderstandings and sufferings, the main character—a hero or a heroine (who is normally a good and tender-hearted young woman)—comes to a happy ending. The audience are well aware of the outcome. But they want to know *how* that ending will be produced and delayed—what forms of suspense will delay the resolution of the problem until the very end. That has been the structure of melodrama throughout Latin American cultural history."[31] While Cisneros's men and women tend to be both heroic and deeply flawed, Lala's narratives are often organized around dramatic events that find resolution in empathic moments. Cisneros uses these instances, however, to conceal "truths" that reside beneath the surface of the plot.

Cisneros uses melodrama as a device, a means to submerge important information. O. Hugo Benavides articulates how this technique works when he asserts that "melodrama in itself is invested in exploring the emotions and sentiments, not the hidden rationality behind human relationships and interactions."[32] As is so often the case with the protagonists in Minimalistic fiction, Lala sometimes responds to her inability to verbalize her feelings about the occurrences she is describing by omitting essential facts. For example, the fifteen-year-old's decision to elope to Mexico with her boyfriend, Ernesto Calderón, is in part motivated by an intense, unstated need for paternal affection. While she knows that she is her father's favorite child, work monopolizes his time while the family lives in San Antonio. One of the leitmotifs in her narration is that she is constantly being passed over or ignored, such as when her father introduces his six sons and single daughter as his *siete hijos*, or seven sons. Lala's running away demonstrates a need for attention, similar to the episode in Susan Minot's "Allowance" when Gus steals his father's wallet and then dramatically "finds" it in the bushes during the family's search with the hope that his father will give him some type of positive consideration. Rarely does Lala struggle with ineffability, but when her father comes to Mexico City to "rescue" her after Ernesto has abandoned her, she is unable to tell him how much she loves him. She embraces him and explains, "my mouth opens and closes and the only thing that comes out is a thin, slippery howl, like raw silk unspooling from my belly" (395). Even though the scene is sentimental, Lala's visceral reactions are honest and sincere.

"St. Anthony," the seventy-third chapter of *Caramelo*, illustrates how Cisneros synthesizes the philosophical and stylistic conventions of the telenovela and the South American *crônica* with techniques common to the American Minimalist tradition. Lala describes a simple domestic occurrence. In the first paragraph-stanza, she juxtaposes the image of Inocencio's worn hands with an explanation of why his sacrifice is significant: "Father's hands are numb from working on a set of lounge chairs for the Saint Anthony Hotel. Leather is rough on the hands. His hands calloused from tugging the twine hard and taut. After six days, he comes home and can't untie his own shoes, his hands swell as fat as a mattress of needles. It's a good job, one he can't afford to pass up. We need the money, and landing the hotel account is something Father is proud of" (358). Lala sees what her father has given for his family, although she does not have any illusions about what he is working for: security. The beginning of the next paragraph subtly suggests the passage of time: "But now his hands are as big as Popeye's. He's so tired he eats his dinner on a TV tray in the living room.—Please, a bucket of hot water for my feet and another one for my hands. . . . Then Father just lies there splayed in his La-Z-Boy" (358). Zoila respects Inocencio, and in this moment she acknowledges him for his dedication to the family. This scene takes place in part 3 of the novel, after she has learned that her husband fathered Candelaria with Awful Grandmother's washerwoman, Amparo. Zoila's caring approach suggests that she is willing to "mother" her ailing husband in light of his labor. Lala's careful descriptions are reflective of Cisneros's respect for her father's industriousness. She said in an interview that "I've done what I set out to do, which is to honor my father. I wanted to honor him and all the hard work that he did. At the end of his life, he said the meaning of his life was to labor honorably. Well, I had to labor very hard to write this book. I think my father showed me a lot about taking pride in your craft—he taught me a lot."[33] "St. Anthony" is in multiple ways a tribute to craftsmanship. Despite its brevity and seeming simplicity, it is a complex narrative.

Through the use of allusion, Cisneros adds interpretive density to "St. Anthony." The title refers to the Portuguese Saint Anthony of Padua, considered by Roman Catholics a patron of travel, lost items, and against starvation, all of which are pertinent to Cisneros's primary themes.[34] In the prose poem, Lala subtly addresses concepts of loss: Inocencio is in obvious pain, and the fact that his wife must feed him like "a baby" suggests that the situation is somewhat humiliating. St. Anthony was venerated in part because he continued his ministry despite ongoing sickness, a fortitude Inocencio emulates.[35] Lala's narrative choices indicate how as a young teenager she is on the figurative borderlands of maturity and immaturity. Her reference to Popeye, a cartoon character who gains superhuman strength by eating spinach, reflects her own youthfulness at the time she is telling the story. Her description of her father "splayed in his La-Z-Boy" chair is imagistically contradictory; he is tired because of industriousness and deserves a few quiet moments of "laziness."

Cisneros frequently alludes to popular culture, particularly name brands like La-Z-Boy, as a means to differentiate among cultural settings. In chapter 4, "Mexico, Next Right," she uses a compact, paratactic style along with a sensorial reportage common in Minimalist fiction. This passage subtly suggests the differences Lala sees when crossing the border from the United States into Mexico: "No more billboards announcing the next Stuckey's candy store, no more truck-stop donuts or roadside picnics with bologna-and-cheese sandwiches and cold bottles of 7-Up. Now we'll drink fruit-flavored sodas, tamarind, apple, pineapple; Pato Pascual with Donald Duck on the bottle, or Lulú, Betty Boop soda, or the one we hear on the radio, the happy song for Jarritos soda" (17). In this passage, Lala's narration is direct and synesthetic. Her thoughts and feelings reflect the physical process of realizing that she has moved into a different world. As the chapter progresses, Cisneros's prose becomes more fragmentary, her sentences poetic, sensorial bursts: "Sweets sweeter, colors brighter, the bitter more bitter. A cage of parrots all the rainbow colors of Lulú sodas. Pushing a window out to open it instead of pulling it up. A cold slash of door latch in your hand instead of the dull round doorknob. Tin sugar spoon and how surprised the hand feels because it's so light. Children walking to school in the morning their hair still wet from the morning bath" (17). Similar to Garland's "Chicago Studies" and sections of McInerney's *Bright Lights, Big City*, Lala describes brief moments in time. The last line is the most traditionally Impressionistic because of its reference to the time of day, a detail that implies the position of the light. Lala's reportage indicates that she does not synthesize any of the things she sees, hears, feels, or imagines herself tasting. In other words, she is neither contemplating the social or cultural significance of the moment of crossing the border nor attempting to explain what her sensations mean. In an interview with Fritz Lanham for the *Houston Chronicle*, Cisneros offered an explanation of why she includes these types of "lists": "I remember things viscerally in my body. So I always start there. It might be just a smell. I don't know where it's going to take me or why it's important, but I trust that if it stayed in my body, it's important."[36] Lala's first-person, present-tense narration conveys a strong sense of immediacy.

One of the subtle, well-crafted adjustments Cisneros makes as the novel progresses is in the voice of Lala. The youthful exuberance of the first part is matched by a distinctly teenaged malaise in the third. Cisneros continues her use of parataxis, but Lala's impressions are more negative, reflecting her general sense of purposelessness at this time in her life. While the family is in San Antonio, Lala begins at a Catholic school called Immaculate Conception. Because of the Reyes' ongoing financial problems, she is ultimately allowed to leave the school she despises and move to "Davy Crockett, the public school across the freeway." She is not initially content with her new surroundings, calling it "Davy Crock-of-shit Vocational. Home of the Future Farmers of America. Livestock shows. Rodeos. Majorettes twirling batons. Home Ec. Machine Shop. The Davy Crockett marching band with cheerleaders in raccoon hats and fringed booties. Creeps in nerdy glasses and crew cuts. Girls still wearing their hair poufed into a Patty Duke bubble. Super-straight. Like they escaped from the fifties, I'm not kidding" (352). The energy of the young Lala's sense of discovery is rerouted into absurd images that betray her feelings of discontent. The scenes she describes imply that she is superior to her new classmates, that they are not "cool" enough, but her reactions are evidence of her own misgivings about being in a new place. Her peers have goals, and it is interesting that she disapproves of their ambitions even though they are, like her father's, vocational. More accurately, she rejects her classmates' choice of work because they remind her of her father. Lala subtly directs her anger at Inocencio, motivated by his decision to move the family to San Antonio only to continue to struggle financially, at the kids around her. The "St. Anthony" chapter, which follows Lala's rant about Davy Crockett, represents Lala's maturation in that she is able to put aside her selfish pride and see her father's assiduousness.

Lala's emotional reconciliation with her father reflects the central theme of the novel, which is that seemingly disparate strands of human experience are inextricably "interwoven." Minimalist authors frequently imbue everyday possessions with profound emotional significance, often because these objects represent feelings the protagonist is unable to verbalize or explain. The material item invested most with physical and emotional feeling is the *caramelo rebozo*, or traditional striped shawl, woven together and passed down from its maker, great-grandmother Guillermina, to Awful Grandmother, and then to Lala. One of the most poignant images in the book occurs when Lala sucks on the fringes of the unfinished shawl as a means to calm herself, using physical sensation as a means to transport herself to another time and place (388). Cisneros's quality as a storyteller is in part attributable to her ability to craft a cohesive piece of art from incongruous, generationally divided characters in the same way a weaver creates a masterpiece from different threads.

Lala does not speak of her treasured rebozo as simply a symbol of happiness or as a quaint cultural artifact. Great-grandmother Guillermina died before she could finish it, so it was created under tragic circumstances and stands incomplete. The elaborate design represents a full range of human experience, the ugly and the ebullient. Cisneros promulgates a distinctly anti-Manichaean view of good and evil and illustrates how humans are a paradoxical mixture of destructive and constructive impulses. Awful Grandmother's near-universal rudeness is countered by her stern toughness in the midst of trying circumstances; Narciso's brazen sexuality and disloyalty are offset by his gentleness; and Inocencio's careless immaturities are often forgotten when he shows love for his favorite child, Lala. The Reyes family's history draws its vibrancy from lives that metaphorically reflect the intricacy of a striped rebozo.

Cisneros's ability to infuse complexity into seemingly simple images and objects places her among the best of the American Minimalists. While she adheres to the central techniques of the tradition, she brings to it a new vitality by incorporating the aesthetic philosophies of South American authors. As chapters such as "St. Anthony" illustrate, *Caramelo* is not purely a collection of imagistic renderings but a work of art that leans more toward the subjective than the objective. In other words, it is a novel with a distinct testimonial purpose. The compactness of her chapters mirrors that of the *crônica*, and the novel is thus structured as a series of "little moments" valuable not only for their cultural importance but also for their individual and collective beauty. The fragmentary pieces that comprise the novel synergistically combine to form a cogent examination of cultural and political themes. Due in part to the fecundity of the traditions that influenced it, *Caramelo* is a stylistic tour de force. In the context of one of Cisneros's central metaphors, her writing crosses borders and transcends simple classifications. Her fiction is not a complete stylistic departure from that of Hemingway, Carver, Galeano, and Borges, but possesses a unique character and emotion.

6

The State of the Art

Cormac McCarthy's *The Road*

In an interview with Oprah Winfrey, Cormac McCarthy recounted that a single image inspired him to begin *The Road*. Staring out the window of an El Paso hotel room, his young son John Francis McCarthy asleep on a bed behind him, he wondered how what he saw might be different five or ten decades into the future. He imagined "fires up on the hill and everything being laid waste" and "thought a lot about" his "little boy." McCarthy wrote a couple of pages, thinking the fragments might be incorporated into a longer piece, but during a trip to Ireland four years later he realized they were the beginnings of a new work.[1] In comparison with two of his earlier books, *Suttree* and *Blood Meridian*, *The Road* is unusually efficient, perhaps best classified as a long prose poem.[2] The compactness of the language is more reminiscent of Ernest Hemingway's Minimalist fiction than that of maximalists such as William Faulkner and Thomas Pynchon. *The Road* is anomalous to its era, a piece that returns to a literary mode dismissed as passé nearly two decades earlier. True to the aesthetic legacy of the Imagists, McCarthy includes no ancillary words or insignificant images, achieving depth through allusion and implication.

The Road is a typical McCarthy novel, as it does not feature a particularly intricate plot. The protagonists are referred to as "the man" and "the boy," although the latter often refers to his father as "Papa." The man's sacrificial love for his son generates emotional depth and power, and it is remarkable how the tenderness of their relationship transcends the violence and poverty of the world they inhabit. About eight years have passed since a cataclysmic event led to the destruction of the ecology of Earth. Given that the boy was born in the days immediately following the occurrence, he is probably seven or eight. The narrator suggests that the man may be in his mid-forties: when he is in his childhood home, he feels the mantle and sees "the pinholes from tacks that had held stockings forty years ago."[3] All animal and plant life has died off, and fires have reduced much of the landscape to ash. Food is scarce, and most of what remains is preserved in jars and cans. Father and son begin somewhere in the American South, probably in what once was Kentucky, and head to the southeastern coast in the hopes of finding a warmer climate.[4] Early on, the man coughs into the snow and leaves "a fine mist of blood," indicating that he is suffering from a lung condition that will soon cause his death (30). The path father and son travel is perilous, and they are in a constant state of fear mixed with vigilance. After encounters with marauders, thieves, and castoffs, the two finally arrive in a swampy area near the ocean, likely somewhere in southern Georgia or northern Florida. Weakened by his lung condition, the man passes away. After three days, a well-armed survivor and his family find the boy; the suggestion is that they have been tracking the father and son and decided to approach. The child has been "rescued," but it seems to matter little given the fragility of the planet. On the other hand, he and his father have been "carrying the fire" (83), an inner power that represents a vibrant love, and there is hope in knowing that his "quest" will continue.

The father and son's journey is narrated in a terse, poetic style characteristic of works of American Minimalism. McCarthy's descriptions of landscapes tend to be reportorial, emphasizing sensorial experience over narrative exposition. In sharp, staccato sentences the narrator says that "they moved on east through the standing dead trees. They passed an old frame house and crossed a dirt road. A cleared plot of ground perhaps once a truckgarden. Stopping from time to time to listen. The unseen sun cast no shadow. They came upon a road unexpectedly and he stopped the boy with one hand and they crouched in the roadside ditch like lepers and listened. No wind. Dead silence" (68–69). McCarthy deftly sustains a sense of foreboding by implying the emotional state of his characters. Images of "standing dead trees" and "a cleared plot of ground" are objective correlatives that speak to the lifelessness of the land and the physical decay that has been brought about by the passing of time. McCarthy employs a technique common in literary Impressionism when he indirectly describes the darkness of the scene by referring to "the unseen sun." Passages such as these exemplify the Imagist axiom that calls for "direct treatment," which is in part a call for efficiency and concision. In a review of *The Road* for the *Grand Rapids Press*, Laura Philpot Benedict maintains that "there are no extraneous words here, no oblique references or irritating inside jokes."[5] Cliff Froehlich posits that the content and style are well matched, writing that "form sharply mirrors content, a basic story of survival related in terse sentences, telegraphic dialogue and surprisingly simple language."[6] McCarthy uses many of the same devices common in polyphonic prose, incorporating poetic techniques such as simile and alliteration: "they crouched in the roadside ditch like lepers and listened." Kenneth Lincoln identifies "anapests, reverse spondaic feet, and alliterative rhythms" in his scansion of the opening sentence of the book: "When he *woke* in the *woods* in the *dark* and the *cold* of the *night* / he'd *reach out* to *touch* the *child sleep*ing be*side* him."[7] Arranged differently on the page, many of McCarthy's lines could pass for verse.

Stylistically consistent with the descriptive passages, conversations between father and son are generally brief and direct. Given the emotional and physical energy the boy and his Papa expend each day, the laconic nature of their discussions reflects their mental state. Mark Schechner of the *Buffalo News* opines that the dialogue "is a little like Ernest Hemingway on Valium, and in a world in which articulate conversation is really beside the point, why even bother? The catastrophe appears to have robbed people of the power of speech, or created a habitation that is not very interesting to talk about."[8] Schechner's dismissive comments suggest that he did not fully consider the effects of the environment on the father and son. It is not that the man and the boy have nothing to say, or that they have lost a desire to speak with each other, but that their reality is not conducive to intellectual and philosophical banter. They are usually tired, hungry, and afraid. The man sleeps little at night. The boy often says that he is scared, but he is unable or unwilling to articulate the cause of his fears. Early in the novel, the man visits his childhood home, a decision that causes the boy to feel a deep unease. The last words they share before leaving the house provide a typical example of their dialogue:

> We should go, Papa. Can we go?
> Yes. We can go.
> I'm scared.
> I know. I'm sorry.
> I'm really scared.
> It's all right. We shouldnt have come. (27)

The boy is most nervous when his father explores the unknown interiors of abandoned enclosures. His apprehension is not so much based on the possibility of his own death but rather that something will happen to his father, leaving him alone. He knows that his dad is dying, however, and his reticence is in part driven by his desire to assure his mentor that he is committed to learning how to survive. As is often the case in Minimalistic works, much meaning can be derived from what is left unsaid.

The laconic dialogue is also attributable to the disappearance of the objects signified by words. Because the boy was born into a burned-out environment, he does not know what a "neighborhood" is or the meaning of the phrase "as the crow flies," as he has no point of reference for either thing (95, 156). One evening while sitting by a fire, the man "tried to think of something to say but could not." The narrator relays his thoughts: "The world shrinking down about a raw core of parsible entities. The names of things slowly following those things into oblivion. Colors. The names of birds. Things to eat. Finally the names of things one believed to be true. More fragile than he would have thought. How much was gone already? The sacred idiom shorn of its referents and so of its reality" (88–89). The man is a far more developed character than the boy, in part because the narrator is closely attuned to him, but the implication is that there is a persistent linguistic divide separating father and son. Papa is older and better educated, but the gap between them is in some respects most acute because they see the world differently. One night the man wakes and looks at his child, and the narrator says that "maybe he understood for the first time that to the boy he was himself an alien. A being from a planet that no longer existed" (153). In order to communicate, they must slowly build a language derived from common experiences.

Because the narration is composed of brief, independent sensorial moments rather than a fluid, tightly constructed sequence of events, *The Road* is structurally fragmentary. McCarthy said in an interview that he does not "plot things out" beforehand when he writes, suggesting that chronology and setting are matters he deals with later in the compositional process.[9] *The Road* is unified by characters, themes, and the geographical movement of the central figures. The timeline is generally linear but the perspective sometimes shifts into the man's mind, leading to either remembrances of dreams, his thoughts in the moment, or expository flashbacks. This discontinuity is likely a product of the fact that McCarthy wrote each part separately and then integrated them as he progressed. For example, the dream about the sightless, translucent creature described in the opening pages of the book was, in an early manuscript, part of a section called "Cave." The scene in which the man and boy enter a large, relatively well-preserved home and find a group of captured people about to be cannibalized is titled "The Manse."[10]

The fragmentary quality of the plot mirrors the state of the man's mind, particularly his memory. The narrator is a conduit for the man, a third-person observer with "limited omniscience," who tends to remain outside of the consciousness of the boy. Hemingway often employs the same technique in his Nick Adams stories, and the mixture of reminiscence and current action found in *The Road* is similar to Hemingway's episodic short story "Fathers and Sons." McCarthy is at times able to meld thought and sensory experience seamlessly without the opacity endemic to stream of consciousness. Near the middle of the novel father and son are starving and desperate, and the narrator says that "they scrabbled through the charred ruins of houses they would not have entered before. A corpse floating in the black water of a basement among the trash and rusting ductwork. He stood in a livingroom partly burned and open to the sky. The waterbuckled boards sloping away into the yard. Soggy volumes in a bookcase. He took one down and opened it and then put it back. Everything damp. Rotting. In a drawer he found a candle. No way to light it. He put it in his pocket." McCarthy transitions from pure reportage into the man's thoughts, a paratactic description of his bleak mental perceptions: "He walked out in the gray light and stood and he saw for a brief moment the absolute truth of the world. The cold relentless circling of the intestate earth. Darkness implacable. The blind dogs of the sun in their running. The crushing black vacuum of the universe. And somewhere two hunted animals trembling like groundfoxes in their cover. Borrowed time and borrowed world and borrowed eyes with which to sorrow it" (130). The man does not express a consistent personal philosophy, but in his most desperate moments he embraces the "absolute truth" of an indifferent, uncaring universe.[11] He is broken by both the disappearance of a world he is slowly forgetting and the constant possibility of death. The structure of the novel aptly reflects the fluctuations of his mindset, the tensions within him generated by a desire to live in the present rather than sentimentally mourn a world that has been lost.

The precision with which McCarthy explores the psyche of a man constantly under duress is in part a product of his judicious editing. The "Cave" dream sequence underwent numerous changes early in the compositional process. On the first of thirteen pages of the "first draft," McCarthy writes four heavily marked paragraphs. The first speaks of a woman, perhaps a figure that represents the man's deceased wife: "A mere and ~~substanceless~~ ((spectral)) elflet squatting upon the red windowbench watching her sleep with those incendiary eyes pooled like hot slag in the hairless skull."[12] He keeps little of this in the handwritten version, expanding on the image of the "elflet": "Something white and translucent caught in the momentary light ~~of~~ ((where)) a visitor ((has)) fallen through by chance into a nameless grotto, a thing blinking with ~~blind~~ eyes, its white ((alabaster)) bones ~~secluded in shade~~ ((repeated)) upon the rock behind it, its brain beating in a glass bell, looking up from a rimstone pool with that she water dripping from its bloodless mouth and then loping off * into the (soundless) millennial dark."[13] In subsequent drafts, McCarthy uses a number of adjectival phrases and similes to describe the creature's eyes, including "eyes opaque and whited," "eyes dead white and sightless," "blank and lidless attic eyes," "eyes as bald as eggs," and "eyes the color of a spider's eggs."[14] McCarthy's drafts demonstrate that he is a scrupulous editor who tries a number of word combinations before settling on the best rhythmical fit. The final product achieves poetic mellifluence and sonority: "And on the far shore a creature that raised its dripping mouth from the rimstone pool and stared into the light with eyes dead white and sightless as the eggs of spiders. It swung its head low over the water as if to take the scent of what it could not see. Crouching there pale and naked and translucent, its alabaster bones cast up in shadow on the rocks behind it. Its bowels, its beating heart. The brain that pulsed in a dull glass bell. It swung its head from side to side and then gave out a low moan and turned and lurched away and loped soundlessly into the dark" (3–4). The beast itself suggests a wearied, mutated horse, an animal that McCarthy writes about frequently in his novels, perhaps most memorably in the Border Trilogy. While the image is a product of the man's subconscious, it may be associated with something he saw in a vignette cut from the final version of the book. In his second draft, he writes a scene in which father and son watch "the last horse" cornered "by a horde of ragged starvelings" and its throat cut. The mob tears open and eats the carcass, evidence of their barbarity and desperation.[15] Even though the creature in the dream is not aggressive, there is something discomforting about it because it seems to have survived a crippling, near-death experience. The man's imagining of the beast's internal organs also suggests his former occupation.

McCarthy follows Hemingway's iceberg theory in *The Road*, using a series of implicative images and details to suggest that the man was once a doctor. His former occupation is significant in terms of character development, particularly because it influences the many ethical decisions he makes during his journey. The earliest indication that the man once practiced medicine occurs during the "Cave" dream sequence. He has studied the internal map of the human body and would be able to easily envision a creature's innards, "its bowels, its beating heart," and a brain in a "dull glass bell," images that perhaps hark back to his days studying cadavers and medical-school specimens. During a flashback to the boy's birth, a scene reminiscent of Hemingway's "Indian Camp," the man uses "gloves meant for dishwashing" to deliver the baby, and the narrator says that his wife's "cries meant nothing to him" (59).[16] His seeming indifference to her pain is a product of his training; he is focused on the task at hand and feels comfortable with what he is doing. His even emotions suggest that he is a professional, not that he does not care about his wife. He exercises a similarly stoic demeanor near the end of the novel when he sutures a deep, three-inch laceration in his own leg after being grazed by an arrow: "He took a clamp from the kit and caught the needle in the jaws and locked them and set about suturing the wound. He worked quickly and he took no great pains about it" (266). The implication is that this is something he has done numerous times and is now a natural part of his skill set.

Passages that appear in the manuscripts but that are omitted from the final version of the novel also suggest the man once practiced medicine. Ruminating on the new state of civilization, the narrator says he "knew that there were doctors and other men of skill who would not come forward in that world. Doctors who would pass the dying in a ditch and move on. So that there was no one to fix the simplest thing. You worked on your own problems in the dark and you couldnt let anyone know you could do special things. If you were a doctor or an engineer or had some other skill and it were found out you would be enslaved by one of the communes for their own purposes. So no one could do anything. No one had any skills."[17] In an earlier draft, possibly a version of the same paragraph, McCarthy's narrator says that "there were men of skill who would never come forward in that world. He'd been one himself. Doctors who would pass the dying in a ditch."[18] Offering further evidence that the man was once "a doctor or an engineer," McCarthy wrote that the man "would have gone to one of the communes long ago ((and offered his services)) but he knew what would happen to the boy."[19] The implication is that his skills are a commodity that can lead to enslavement, but McCarthy also suggests that the man would find emotional relief by acquiescing to his humanitarian impulses. Physicians are no doubt in high demand as no one in *The Road* is physically healthy; environmental hazards and a lack of fresh food have left all survivors bodily and mentally degraded.

In one of the most important scenes in the novel, the man is given the opportunity to declare that he is a doctor but declines. Father and son are hiding from a truck driven by a group of marauders and accidently come upon one of them in the woods. During an intense standoff, the man aims his revolver at the cannibal, to which the latter responds,

> You aint got but two shells. Maybe just one. And they'll hear the shot.
>
> Yes they will, but you wont.
>
> How do you figure that?
>
> Because the bullet travels faster than sound. It will be in your brain before you can hear it. To hear it you will need a frontal lobe and things with names like colliculus and temporal gyrus and you wont have them anymore. They'll just be soup.
>
> Are you a doctor?
>
> I'm not anything. (64)

The man renounces his former career because his context no longer allows him to act in response to his desire to help others. His use of medical jargon, terms such as "colliculus" and "temporal gyrus," is an attempt to intellectually intimidate the other man. When the soldier grabs the boy and threatens to kill him with his knife, the man shoots him in the forehead. As he later explains to his son, his purpose in life has changed according to his circumstances: "My job is to take care of you. I was appointed to do that by God. I will kill anyone who touches you. Do you understand?" (77). He does not have the time, resources, or security to help those in need, so he must distance himself from his past and from others. The boy often wants to help starving fellow travelers, but the father knows that doing so could jeopardize his survival and that of his son. After a violent storm, the pair comes upon a ragged man walking in the road. The child asks,

> Papa? . . . What is wrong with the man?
>
> He's been struck by lightning.
>
> Cant we help him? Papa?
>
> No. We cant help him.
>
> The boy kept pulling at his coat. Papa? he said.
>
> Stop it.
>
> Cant we help him Papa?
>
> No. We cant help him. There's nothing to be done for him. (50)

Although the narrator does not reveal the man's reasons for refusing his son's request, the suggestion is that ignoring the injured man runs against his instincts. His situation, however, does not allow him to act according to his precatastrophe conscience. The extremity of his shift into being "not anything" is also reflected by his modification of the tenets of the Hippocratic oath, specifically the promise that a doctor "will not give a drug that is deadly to anyone if asked [for it], nor will" he "suggest the way to such a counsel."[20] Even though this part of the creed warns physicians against murder, the man is not in violation for killing an aggressor or refusing to help those in obvious need. His willingness to take his son's life lest he be captured, raped, and killed, however, is a much more complicated matter.

Suicide and euthanasia are prominent in *The Road*, ethical topics that the man begrudgingly contemplates as his surroundings darken. During a flashback to a conversation between the man and his wife, he ruminates on the night she determined to kill herself. She tells her husband that he is unable to protect her and their son and that "sooner or later they will catch us and they will kill us. They will rape me. They'll rape him. They are going to rape us and kill us and eat us and you wont face it" (56). Her "only hope is for eternal nothingness" (57), and it drives her to disappear into the wilderness and slit her wrists with a shard of obsidian. The mother is placed in opposition to her light-bearing husband and son, those who have determined that there is something worth seeking in a burned-out world. The man is not entirely unsympathetic to her position, however, in that he often gives the gun to his son when he leaves him. The understanding they have is that if something happens to the man and the "bad guys" discover the boy, he is to put the barrel in his mouth and shoot himself (113). At other times, the former doctor ponders whether he could take his son's life if circumstances call for it: "Can you do it? When the time comes? When the time comes there will be no time. Now is the time. Curse God and die. What if it doesnt fire? It has to fire. What if it doesnt fire? Could you crush that beloved skull with a rock? Is there such a being within you of which you know nothing? Can there be? Hold him in your arms. Just so. The soul is quick. Pull him toward you. Kiss him. Quickly" (114). The man's ethical struggle is shaped by the tension between his faith in his "mission" and his assessment of reality. He has determined that even though he is emotionally disgusted with the thought of destroying the boy, the unraveling of a civil society and the threat of violence make such an action necessary. Proclamations about the sanctity of life no longer seem applicable; endless visions of sadistic acts suggest that sacrality has become an empty concept.

McCarthy modeled the lawless, depraved social atmosphere depicted in

The Road upon biblical source material. He openly acknowledged that his works are influenced by others, saying in a 1992 interview that "the ugly fact is books are made out of books. . . . The novel depends for its life on the novels that have been written."[21] The manuscripts suggest that McCarthy was interested in the Old Testament story of Abraham, recounted in chapters 11 through 22 of the book of Genesis. In his first draft, he wrote "Kierkegaard: Abraham and Isaac" on leaf fifty-one, perhaps as a note to himself.[22] Søren Kierkegaard published an essay titled "Fear and Trembling" under the pseudonym Johannes de Silentio, and it is an exploration of whether Abraham acted ethically in agreeing to sacrifice Isaac in response to God's request. Even though Isaac was pardoned, Abraham was willing to carry out the command, a fact that suggests that he harbored murderous impulses. Kierkegaard concludes that Abraham was a "Knight of Faith," a man who transcended natural laws against murder and "as the single individual . . . became higher than the universal."[23] The protagonist in *The Road* is similar to Kierkegaard's Knight of Faith in his belief that he is "appointed by God" to care for his son. The divine sanctification of his acts informs all of his moral thought processes, trumping whatever humanitarian impulses he may feel. Like Abraham, he too is spared from having to kill his son.

The parallels between *The Road* and the story of Abraham extend far beyond the episode involving Isaac. Even though the plots are set nearly two thousand years apart, the social contexts are similar. Abraham was born nine generations after the flood that destroyed the earth, and Isaac was brought into the world not long after the fiery destruction of Sodom and Gomorrah. In other words, they lived in barbarous, violent times. In one episode, Abraham is called to rescue his nephew Lot when he is kidnapped in the aftermath of a battle fought in the Valley of Siddim. The lawlessness and sexual predation described in Genesis 19 is mirrored in McCarthy's postcataclysmic world. In the years after the war, the "cities of the plain" were razed because of the iniquities of the citizenry. When Lot harbors two angels in his home in Sodom, they are besieged by "all the men from every part of the city of Sodom—both young and old." The townsmen surround the house and demand that Lot release the angels so that they can rape them. Desiring to show his loyalty to his divine visitors, Lot offers them his daughters instead, but the mob refuses.[24] In that moment, the guests assure Lot that Sodom will be destroyed. McCarthy iterates a theme common in the Old Testament: humankind is inherently destructive and often brings evil upon itself.

While the destruction described in Genesis can be attributed to human sin and a resulting expression of divine wrath, the cause of the conflagration that has destroyed much, or perhaps all, of the surface of the earth in *The Road* is not explicitly revealed. It is implied, however. The details McCarthy offers suggest that the man and his family are surprised at what has happened and that they were in no way expecting a cataclysmic event. In a brief flashback, the narrator says that "the clocks stopped at 1:17. A long shear of light and then a series of low concussions. He got up and went to the window. What is it? she said. He didn't answer" (52). The configuration of the collisions would be consistent with a nuclear missile equipped with multiple warheads. The man's refusal to answer his wife's question suggests that the attack was unexpected and unlike anything he had experienced before. The man immediately fills his tub, knowing that drinking water may become scarce (52–53). In his essay "Life of War, Death of the Rest: The Shining Path of Cormac McCarthy's Thermonuclear America," Tim Blackmore writes that "McCarthy's book opens after some kind of undetermined human-created global spasm of destruction," a reading that implicitly dismisses the possibility of an asteroid or comet strike.[25] While the ecological effects of such an event would be similar to that of nuclear fallout, a militaristic, man-made cause is more likely given that human depravity is one of the central concepts explored in *The Road*.[26] Manuscript evidence also supports the theory that McCarthy considers war as the catalyst.

McCarthy composes two lines in an early draft that suggest that the natural world has been destroyed by a global conflict. In what he titled "Old Road Notes," he writes "~~So pale and thin. These dead have seen an end to war~~."[27] Devoid of context, these sentences probably refer to some of the many corpses the father and son see during their journey. On the next leaf, the narrator describes survivors as "children of the late last wars shuffling through the ashes."[28] McCarthy eventually cuts all references to war with the lone exception of a description of a barbaric group marching with pregnant women and leather-collared catamites in tow (91–92). *The Road* is thematically consistent with the rest of McCarthy's oeuvre. From Marion Sylder, the whiskey-running murderer in *The Orchard Keeper*,[29] to the bloodthirsty Judge Holden in *Blood Meridian* and the cannibalistic "bloodcults" that constantly threaten the man and the boy, McCarthy shows no restraint in his portrayals of human depravity. People fight and enslave because, he suggests, such actions are inherent to human nature.

The Road is thus about two people coping with the emotional and physical wounds of a war the narrator says virtually nothing about. Father and son survive because they adhere to a strict code of behavior, committing to heart rules about when to hide, when to travel, and what to look for when scouring various enclosures such as homes and cars. The man maintains his sanity by focusing his mind on the minor tasks and rituals that fill his day; when he synthesizes the meaning of what he is seeing and doing, his thoughts often tend toward violence and hopelessness. His psychological state, as well as his coping mechanisms, is remarkably similar to that of Hemingway's Nick Adams, the protagonist in "Big Two-Hearted River." Stylistically similar to *The Road*, the tale is about Nick's fishing trip into the Michigan woods, a journey devised as a means for him to maintain a frail hold on his psyche. He has returned from World War I emotionally splintered, and the implication is that the methodical actions of setting up camp, eating, cooking, and fishing are therapeutic.[30] In the first paragraph of "River," Hemingway describes the burned-out town of Seney, Michigan.[31] The image perhaps reminds Nick of the battlefield, of villages he has seen during his service, but as Thomas H. Schaub posited, he "takes reassurance in knowing that 'the river was still there.'" The man and his son have nothing similar to offer them solace.[32] All three figures, however, have the promise of simple but necessary rituals.

McCarthy's and Hemingway's characters carry out tasks with ease and industry. Following the code and doing things the "right way" means survival. After arriving at a proper site, Nick sees that "between two jack pines, the ground was quite level. He took the ax out of the pack and chopped out two projecting roots. That leveled a piece of ground large enough to sleep on. He smoothed out the sandy soil with his hand and pulled all the sweet fern bushes by their roots. His hands smelled good from the sweet fern. He smoothed the uprooted earth. He did not want anything making lumps under the blankets. When he had the ground smooth, he spread his three blankets. One he folded double, next to the ground. The other two he spread on top."[33] Nick takes pleasure in these tasks, and the suggestion is that they allow him to take his mind away from the war, allowing him to feel "happy." His actions also imply that if he chooses a proper place to sleep he will rest well and enjoy his time fishing, meaning that his mind will ultimately benefit from his attention to detail. McCarthy includes many similar passages. The narrator of *The Road* describes how during a search of a wrecked ship the man "unlatched and raised the hatch to the engine compartment. Half flooded and pitch dark. No smell of gas or oil. He closed it again. There were lockers built into the benches in the cockpit that held cushions, sailcanvas, fishing gear. In a locker behind the wheel pedestal he found coils of nylon rope and steel bottles of gas and a toolbox made of fiberglass. He sat in the floor of the cockpit and sorted through the tools" (226–27). The father's diligence in looking for useful items means the difference between death and survival. He is deliberate in his search, constantly weighing the potential usefulness of what he sees. The unfortunate difference between the man and Nick is that the former rarely feels anything resembling happiness. He is, however, "stirred" when he comes across a brass sextant, an object pleasing in itself but one that also reminds him of the beauty of stars he can no longer see (227–28). He does not contemplate for long, knowing that he must soon return to his emotionally fragile son.

The man's deliberate actions, his commitment to structure, are also intended to help his son maintain some semblance of his innocence, to be able to have some sort of childhood despite the ugliness of their environment. Of the many texts alluded to in *The Road*, a list that might include Milton's *Paradise Lost*, Dante's *Inferno*, and T. S. Eliot's *The Waste Land*, Hemingway's "Indian Camp" is perhaps the most influential in terms of thematic development. McCarthy makes two overt references to the tale, both of which subtly aid in the construction of theme. The first occurs during the flashback in which the man delivers his son. The second is when the man thinks back to when he was a boy and he and his grandfather went out on the lake together in search of firewood. The man remembers "sitting in the back of the rowboat trailing his hand in the cold wake while his uncle bent to the oars" (12). The image echoes the final scene of "Indian Camp" in which Nick sits in the stern while his father rows: "The sun was coming up over the hills. A bass jumped, making a circle in the water. Nick trailed his hand in the water. It felt warm in the sharp chill of the morning." The idyllic atmosphere is somewhat illusory, however, given that the young Nick, probably seven or eight years old, has seen an impromptu caesarean section and a bloody suicide.[34]

The serene surface of McCarthy's image is also in part shadowed by violence. The narrator says that this memory was for the man "the perfect day of his childhood. This to shape the days upon" (13). It is interesting, however, that he built his ideal upon an outing engendered by a catastrophic event. The firewood that the boy and his grandfather are out collecting is the stumps from "the windfall trees of a hurricane years past" (13). In his notes, McCarthy set this scene at the man's "grandfather's summer house on the lake in Maine," and the abundance of timber is more specifically attributed to "windfall trees from the hurricane of 1938."[35] The allusion is to the Great

Hurricane of 1938 that devastated New England, killing 564, injuring 1,700, and causing 306 million dollars in damage.[36] The image of a man and young boy wending their way through the aftermath of a catastrophe is a common one in *The Road*, but in this scene it is presented in a starkly different context. McCarthy suggests that even in the most peaceful environments, destruction is an inextricable part of human experience.

The parallels between *The Road* and "Indian Camp" are much more profound than these two allusions suggest. Both works are about a father-doctor and son, and each portrays a child who is inadvertently exposed to grotesque violence and death too early in life. Near the beginning of the novel, the man warns his son, "you forget what you want to remember and you remember what you want to forget" (12). This idea resonates in the Nick Adams stories as well; "Big Two-Hearted River" is in many ways about a man trying to replace horrific remembrances with new experiences. While it is arguable whether Dr. Adams is right to allow Nick to assist him with the operation, he distinctly attempts to keep his son from seeing the dead father, telling his brother, George, to "take Nick out of the shanty" once he discovers what happened.[37] *The Road* is replete with similar occurrences. Upon discovering a barn, the boy insists that they search it, but the father abruptly says, "let's go" when he sees that there are "three bodies hanging from the rafters" (17). Passing burned "figures half mired in the blacktop, clutching themselves, mouths howling," the man tells his son to take his hand, adding, "I don't think you should see this" (190). In what is the most tragic scene in *The Road*, the boy sees "a charred human infant headless and gutted and blackening on" a "spit" before his father is able to intervene. The man responds with love and sadness: "He bent and picked the boy up and started for the road with him, holding him close. I'm sorry, he whispered. I'm sorry" (198). The man's apology is not an acknowledgment of his failure as a parent but a lamentation about the state of their world.

The ending of *The Road* does not imply that there is a possible means of redemption for the planet, at least not materially. The boy's innocence and empathic nature are apparent, but he is a messianic figure only in a limited sense. Children have become food for many people, so the perpetuation of the human race is unlikely. On the other hand, father and son carry "the fire," a spirit of hope and love. In *The Road*, "carrying the fire" is not exclusively a state of goodness, however, and brings with it implications of violence. Fire has destroyed the earth, but it is also a source of light and refinement. The Christic implications of "shining in the darkness" speak to the way the boy is characterized, but the father in the end represents the destructive impulses of fire. While his inevitable death is tragic, he must die because his "original sin" is his complicity, direct or indirect, in the destruction of the world. He does not conform to the ways of his son, choosing instead to apply the same logic that led to the demise of his civilization. Near the end of the novel, an amputee steals most of the man and boy's belongings. After catching up to him, Papa orders the perpetrator to strip naked and surrender his clothes. Boy and criminal plead for mercy, a subtle reference to the pardon Christ offers to the repentant thief crucified next to him, but the man exercises retaliatory justice, responding, "you didnt mind doing it to us" (257).[38] The implication is that the man is irreversibly part of a cycle of behavior that only the boy may be able to defy.

The final sequence of events suggests a further cyclicality and reflects the Minimalistic tendency of investing profound meaning in common objects. Three days after the man's death, the boy is "rescued" by another family. The boy is approached by a man wearing a "yellow ski parka" and carrying a shotgun along with a "bandolier filled with shells," an image of plenty given the dearth of ammunition. He is a "veteran of old skirmishes," scarred, bearded, and with "one eye wandering" (281–83). While there is an element of relief in knowing that the child is being adopted by a man who is experienced and well armed, there is nothing to suggest that he is someone who will help the boy bring about a spiritual or moral renaissance.

If there is anything redemptive about the man, it is the fact that he has a wife and family who accept the boy (284). McCarthy suggests that any future for humanity rests upon children who see the world in a way radically different from the corrupted vision of their war-ravaged parents. In "talking" to his father, the boy sanctifies his memory and effectively forgives the elder man for his acts of cruelty. The presence of a new mother figure is also suggestive of restoration, and the spiritual guidance she provides for her new son will no doubt aid him as he seeks to rebuild a destroyed world. However, she is also a reminder of what has been forever lost: nothing can bring back the boy's mother.

The introduction of a new maternal figure, a replacement for what has long been missing in the boy's life, provides a fitting thematic transition into the final paragraph of *The Road*. If there is a biblical parallel or allusion at work in this scenario, it is likely rooted in the book of Job. After all of his suffering, the terrifying result of a bargain made between God and Satan, Job's wealth and possessions are partially restored. Like the boy, Job was given a new family, but at the end of Job's story there is also a subtle yet pervasive sense of permanent deprivation. The near-mythical "brook trout in the streams in the mountains" described in the last lines of the book are objects of life and nature that form part of what the narrator describes as a "thing which could not be put back. Not be made right again" (286–87). The mystery of *The Road*, the treacherous and wondrous journey at the heart of human experience, resonates in images of beauty and irrecoverable loss. The final passage, what Allen Josephs refers to as the "epilogue,"[39] raises unanswerable questions about the reasons for suffering and pain that McCarthy addresses neither implicitly nor explicitly.

The fragmentary, episodic structure of *The Road* reflects the fading vision of a failed civilization, and the subject matter matches well with McCarthy's Minimalistic style. The reduction of language is a symptom of a dying world, one that the boy and his young cohorts will have to reimagine and rebuild, and yet the lessons of the father imply that there is something useful in the ruins. *The Road* itself is the product of a tested but enduring literary tradition. McCarthy omits important information but implies what is missing, submerging facts that are essential to understanding the ethical ramifications of the man's actions. The novel is a testament to the author's axiom that "books are made out of books," and despite its efficiency it generates considerable depth. Through allusions to the book of Genesis and the short stories of Hemingway, McCarthy develops a thematic kinship with works that are an indelible part of the Western canon. In spare but vibrant prose, McCarthy illustrates a principle that Hemingway's work often examines: even in the face of certain defeat, there is reason to continue. Abraham's trials suggest that the reason is seldom, if ever, well defined, but there is virtue in continuity. Although McCarthy does not offer assurances or certainty, the ending of *The Road* implies that even in the wake of catastrophe, love and hope endure.

Conclusion

Despite being scattered among eleven decades, American Minimalists share a common aesthetic. Their work does not suggest that they were blindly enamored with the idea that "less is more," but that it is possible to write compact prose that achieves depth of setting, characterization, and plot without including long passages of exposition. Like the haiku poets who stand among their influences, they draw attention to their art rather than themselves. In other words, precision and craftsmanship transcend the allure of egoism. Writers working within the tradition did not invent new techniques but rather used a unique combination of storytelling methods to an extreme degree. When stylistically successful, their stories, poems, and novels evoke intellectual and emotive richness.

The effectiveness of a Minimalist story depends upon the successful use of three central techniques: allusion, implication, and efficiency. In order to create fiction that achieves thematic and linguistic gravity, authors working within the mode are economical in their use of language. Every word matters. The images they render are consequential; details about setting often serve as objective or imagistic correlatives. Because of these characteristics, the fiction often has the compression of poetry but the structure of prose.

Even though they have much in common stylistically, Minimalist writers do not share a unified philosophy, perhaps because they do not form a school in the sense that they all knew one another, gathered, and produced a manifesto. They generally do not place their characters in the midst of ethical crises or use their fiction to level social criticism. The Imagist credo that was written by Ezra Pound and then expanded upon by Richard Aldington and Amy Lowell is the nearest thing to a formal set of rules for the movement, and it deals strictly with technique. In a broad manner, those who participated in the movement reacted against what they perceived to be excesses in literature, such as the flowery abstractions of British Romanticism and the assertive, moralizing narrators common in Victorian novels. The progenitors of the tradition—Pound, Ernest Hemingway, and Raymond Carver—are united by a common adherence to imagistic precision. All were dedicated to craft, to creating art that matched the intensity of their aesthetic vision.

The tenets that govern the Minimalist aesthetic developed over the course of the twentieth century; they were certainly not "new" in the 1980s. Neglecting to acknowledge the line of influence that extends from the Imagists to Cormac McCarthy and beyond, critics such as Madison Smartt Bell, John W. Aldridge, and Richard Ford dismiss the mode as a fad or superficial "tag." The style is not, however, so historically narrow. As the twentieth century progressed, writers such as Hemingway began to explore and adapt what proved to be a versatile category.

The depth found in the best Minimalist works is in part attributable to the fact that authors in the tradition embrace the idea that, in McCarthy's words, "books are made out of books."[1] In a broader sense, writers within the mode exploit multiple facets of culture without regard for what is considered "low-brow" and "high-brow." If T. S. Eliot, Pound, and the other "high modernists" wanted to ensure that literature needed to be studied in the classroom in order to be understood, then the writers of austere fiction are in many ways their opposites. The writing of McCarthy and Cisneros suggests that references to popular drinks, advertisements, and department stores, as well as other literary works, elicit emotional responses and are an indelible part of everyday life. Ann-Marie Karlsson misses this fundamental point, arguing that "in the new fiction . . . the overwhelming profusion of details, objects and brand-names does not deepen our knowledge or understanding of characters or plot. Despite their prominent presence these details do not communicate but conversely display uncommunicativeness."[2] On the contrary, a well-placed reference enhances the efficiency of a piece, effectively achieving a contextually relevant, poetic depth. In a paratactic passage in *The Road*, McCarthy's narrator spots a barn with the words "See Rock City" written "across the roofslope," a detail that could easily be dismissed.[3] However, it is an important geographical indicator that implies that the father and son are traveling through the American southeast, at that moment somewhere in the vicinity of Chattanooga, Tennessee. Perhaps it would have been simpler if McCarthy had directly identified where the man and his child were headed, or at least where they begin, but it would allow for a lesser degree of engagement from his audience. Similarly, Cisneros's allusions to specific drinks and candies in *Caramelo* accentuate the physical and sensorial differences that occur when crossing various types of borders.

Even though he is primarily responsible for reviving the style during the 1970s and 1980s, Carver is something of an anomaly among the Minimalists because he seldom refers to actual places or cultural artifacts. His tendency was to rely more heavily on suggestive language and omission than allusion when developing setting and characterization. The subtle narrative style used in "Cathedral," for example, suggests that the protagonist-narrator has experienced a profound change in attitude since Robert's visit. Hemingway wrote a number of first-person retrospective narrations, the Mons interchapters in *In Our Time*, *The Sun Also Rises*, and *A Farewell to Arms* among them, and an interpretation of each demands consideration of the speaker's temporal point of view. Carver uses the same approach in "Cathedral." During the course of the telling, the main character does not admit that he has changed, but he demonstrates the shift in his perspective toward Robert when he says, "I wasn't enthusiastic about his visit. He was no one I knew. And his being blind bothered me."[4] The subtle implication is that each of his objections has been quelled by the epiphanic, highly sensorial moment he shares with Robert at the end. Using the same kinetic, Impressionistic language found in Chekhov's and Hemingway's fiction, the protagonist describes that he "put in windows with arches. I drew flying buttresses. I hung great doors. I couldn't stop."[5] The pacing of his language increases, suggesting that he is reliving an intense experience. He is unable in the end, however, to articulate a lesson learned. The moment was far too complex emotionally, and he understands what happened in only an abstract sense.

All of the stories in *Cathedral* examine a form of figurative blindness, and Carver's characters commonly struggle with ineffability. Despite the fact that he often used dramatic irony, portraying figures who could not see their lack of comprehension even though an outside observer might be able to, Carver insisted that he did not feel he was holding his characters up for examination.[6] Carver's position is sincere, but he seems to either miss or ignore the fact that many of his protagonists experience growth because of an expansion in vision. Authors within the tradition commonly depict characters in similar situations, but Carver is right in the sense that it is not so that they can be analyzed and judged as part of a broader critique of societal ills.

Minimalist authors frequently employ irony in their fiction, perhaps attributable to the legacy of Stephen Crane and other Impressionists, but it seldom communicates a condemnatory tone. In Crane's *Maggie: A Girl of the Streets*, for example, after Maggie has been murdered, her mother, Mary, hypocritically declares that she will "fergive" the young girl for becoming a prostitute[7]—the hypocrisy lying in the fact that Maggie only chose that occupation because her family cruelly rejected her after Pete seduced her. Crane's depiction of Maggie's brutal, uncaring household calls attention to destructiveness of religious legalism and, more broadly, the spiritually corrosive effects of poverty. Because their work does not tend to resemble social commentary, rarely will characters such as Mary appear in a work by Hemingway, McCarthy, or Susan Minot. On the contrary, writers in the mode often seem to have a profound respect for their figures.

Hemingway's Nick Adams, for example, is not portrayed as a fool or hypocrite. Nick is frequently confronted with situations that prove formative even though he is not intellectually or psychologically prepared to handle them: "Indian Camp" is a strong example. In the concluding scene, when Nick trails his hand in the water as he and his father move across the lake and feels "quite sure that he would never die," it is a stark adumbration of the violence he is yet to experience.[8] The irony is that he has no idea how much he will suffer in the future, how close he will come to death as he sits against a church with a wound to his spine.[9] He does not yet comprehend mortality, and it is understandable given what he saw at the camp. The inclusion of the "Three Shots" material, in which Uncle George calls his nephew a "coward" and a "liar," would have brought a condemnatory atmosphere to the tale.[10] Because Hemingway excised George's pejorative assumptions about Nick, the writer and his audience do not have a conspiratorial relationship that necessitates judgment.

The lack of cutting irony in Minimalist fiction is perhaps attributable to two different things. First, many of the best works in the tradition are heavily autobiographical. For Hemingway to write something that made Nick Adams look foolish or hypocritical would have, on some level, meant casting aspersions upon himself. Hemingway is not Adams, but, as the many biographies about the author attest, the latter is loosely based on the former. Carver wrote about the people he knew, and he said they were familiar to him because he was one of them. "Cathedral" is an autobiographical tale, but it has a moment of insight that in the end reflects well on the nameless central figure. He learns from the experience and, to an extent, sheds his blindness. Jay McInerney comes close to open disparagement of his autobiographically based main character in *Bright Lights, Big City*. Like the protagonist in

"Cathedral," McInerney's central figure is in many ways repulsive. However, he is ultimately redeemed by an epiphanic moment.

While the ending of *Bright Lights, Big City* suggests the possibility of redemption, it is not in any way didactic. The second reason for the lack of critical irony is that it is a device often used as a means to teach a lesson, to instruct readers not to act in a certain way. Minimalist authors are far more subtle in their attempts to educate, although they seldom seem to try. Gus Vincent, the alcoholic father in *Monkeys*, could easily have become a caricature, a "cautionary tale," or an object of ridicule. While the narrators in *Monkeys* do not excuse the father's actions, they tend to give him a voice and a perspective. In the end, it is telling that he is given the opportunity to provide a hopeful sentiment during the boat ride home from the ash-scattering ceremony, affirming that he knows that "it will get nice" in the future.[11] Gus is a destructive force in most of the narratives, but Minot's narrators show rather than tell how his problems generate and perpetuate the various interpersonal fissures that divide the family. One of the central implications in *Monkeys* is that no experience can be explained in simple terms. As is also the case in many Impressionist works, human existence proves too complex to be reduced to unsophisticated ethical axioms.

Minot's and McInerney's uses of Impressionistic techniques also involve stringing together sensorial montages, brief moments in time that emphasize experience over intellectual contemplation. Hemingway does this in his combat narratives, but it works equally well in depictions of domestic scenarios energized by suppressed emotional tension. McInerney's *Bright Lights* is, among other things, a novel about impulse and narcissism. The narrator's self-destructive drives, his inability to cope with the death of his innermost personal ambitions, compel him to self-medicate with drugs and club life. He also surrounds himself with people who enable his behavior. In sparse, direct terms, the narrator describes how the self-absorbed Tad Allagash "goes over to the mahogany-and-gilt framed mirror that you inherited from your grandmother, the one Amanda was so afraid your cousin was going to nab. He runs his tongue over the glass."[12] The implications of the scene, however, are more complex. As Carver so often does, McInerney inserts a mundane object into a situation and imbues it with emotional significance. The mirror awakens the speaker's memory of his grandmother, a member of his family and thus a part of the past he attempts to bury within himself. He then remembers that his estranged wife prized the item and is therefore reminded of one of the women who had caused him pain. The final image, Tad licking a reflection of himself, is a gross act of self-indulgence that implies that the person he cares about most is himself. In addition, it is a repudiation of the narrator's refusal to forget the past and live in the moment, a brazen act of indirect disrespect. In Tad's code of conduct, overstimulation of the senses is an acceptable way to form a protective barrier against a discomforting contemplation of reality.

The emphasis upon the senses in Minimalist fiction suggests that immediate experience is more pressing than the need to contemplate the past. The implication is that memories, in order to be understood, must be intellectually synthesized before they have meaning. This is not to say that characters in the fiction of McInerney, Carver, and Hemingway are incapable of complex thought, but that they are more interested in "living in the moment." A figure's desire to focus on the present rather than the past often has profound psychological ramifications. In Hemingway's *In Our Time*, characters such as the protagonist in "On the Quai at Smyrna" and Nick Adams in "Big Two-Hearted River" have not yet come to terms emotionally with their personal histories. The narrator is a conduit rather than an interpreter, making no attempt to mediate in the relationship between character and listener.

Despite the fact that there is an aesthetic reason for emphasizing sensory experience over synthesis, the reticence of narrators and protagonists, their lack of philosophizing, is often misattributed to a dearth of intelligence on the part of the author. Minimalists have often been undeservedly attacked as anti-intellectual. In 1934, polymath Wyndham Lewis wrote a disparaging piece on Hemingway titled "The Dumb Ox: A Study of Ernest Hemingway." Lewis could not dispute the craftsmanship of Hemingway's writing but complained that he was figuratively "*submerged*" when it came to the pressing social matters of the day: "But *political significance*! That is surely the last thing one would expect to find in such books as 'In Our Time,' 'The Sun also Rises,' 'Men Without Women,' or 'Farewell to Arms.' And indeed it is difficult to imagine a writer whose mind is more entirely closed to politics than is Hemingway's. I do not suppose he has ever heard of the Five-Year Plan, though I dare say he knows that artists pay no income tax in Mexico, and is quite likely to be following closely the agitation of the Mexican matadors to get themselves recognized as 'artists' so that they may pay no income tax. I expect he has heard of Hitler, but thinks of him mainly, if he is acquainted with the story, as the Boche who went down into a cellar with another Boche and captured thirty Frogs and came back with an Iron Cross."[13] Hemingway was seldom politically inclined, although he did participate in the production of Joris Ivens's film *The Spanish Earth* in 1937 and write *For Whom the Bell Tolls* in 1940, works relevant to the Spanish Civil War.[14] Regardless, Lewis's assertions lack merit. Hemingway addressed major themes such as death and love, ideas that inform and transcend the machinations of government and nationalism.

After the advent of the grandiose, self-reflexive literature of the 1960s and 1970s written by authors such as Thomas Pynchon and Vladimir Nabokov, the accusations of superficiality continued. In addressing a question of whether his fiction reflects a broad sense of disengagement, Frederick Barthelme said in an interview that "I don't like being called a minimalist, which I am called I think because my characters don't get up on boxes and shout out their views of the world. This is not because they do not have views of the world, but rather that they recognize that we make views of the world the same way we make cars—we produce a great many, but they're not very reliable. So the characters shut up. This pleases me."[15] Barthelme's position suggests a postmodern apathy that does not universally apply to all authors working within the tradition. His comments indicate that attempting to examine meaningful content is in effect pointless because the objective has been superseded by the subjective. If anything, the work of later Minimalist authors such as Cisneros and McCarthy indicates that stylistic austerity does not diminish the power of precise images and major themes. In other words, there is nothing small or uniform about their ideas.

Minimalism is stylistically homogenous, but the subjects that authors within the tradition write about cannot be generalized. This fact has not stopped some critics from trying. In the introduction to *The Best American Short Stories 1988*, Mark Helprin wrote a lengthy diatribe, asking,

> why are so many minimalist stories about despicable people in filthy unkempt garden apartments filled with ugly bric-a-brac, where everyone smokes, drinks, stays up all night, and is addicted to coffee? Why are the characters almost uniformly pudgy, stiff, and out of shape, even if they are in their twenties? Why do they watch so much television? Why do they have so many headaches? Why are they impotent, frigid, promiscuous, or all three combined? Why are their lives intertwined inextricably with brand names? Why are almost all of them divorced, never married, or, if married, remembering, having, or about to have an affair? Why is their hair dirty? Why

> don't they work at a profession or a trade? What are they doing in university towns in their middle age? Why do they seem to exist as if there were no landscape, or as if they were living in tunnels under ground?[16]

Read in the context of the works of Hemingway, Cisneros, and Minot, none of which involve headaches or tunnels, Helprin's list of queries proves inaccurate. No topic, theme, or character type is endemic to the mode. Settings and character types differ greatly, and the idea that works within the mode tend to feature blue-collar workers who do little more than shop at the local Kmart is pure myth. Minot and Carver wrote tales using remarkably similar styles yet dealt with families and individuals from diverse backgrounds. The fact that the term *dirty realism* originated in England suggests that America's reputation as a hard-working, no-frills society somehow trumped the actual content of the fiction when considered from abroad. Robert Rebein maintains that the title was motivated by marketing demands, that "for the British, in short, dirty realism was a kind of truncated documentary naturalism that told the 'truth' about America in the 1980s, even as imported television shows such as *Dallas* and *Dynasty* traded in 'lies.'"[17] Many Americans seem to have adopted a similarly limited view of austere fiction.

While the "real" America may not reside in the fictitious worlds of soap operas and dramas, it is indisputable that melodrama is an important, and appealing, genre in North and South American countries. In *Caramelo*, Cisneros embraces television and popular culture, perhaps more than any Minimalist who preceded her. Like Minot, Cisneros artfully portrays the beauty of "little moments," the minor daily rituals that are for so many of their characters a source of sustenance. Cisneros demonstrates that popular culture is not necessarily mindless. In fact, it is the vehicle she uses to communicate one of her central themes: every person is worth memorializing.

Cisneros's *Caramelo* is a somewhat unusual example of Minimalism, however, because it is not austere in terms of setting and characterization. Some passages border on sensory overload, such as when Lala recounts objects and events that appealed to her in Mexico: "Fireworks displays, *piñata* makers, palm weavers. Pens,—Five different styles, they cost us a lot! A restaurant called—His Majesty, the Taco. The napkins, little triangles of hard paper with the name printed on one side."[18] The rapidity of Lala's thoughts reflects her active mind, a technique that Hemingway also uses in "Big Two-Hearted River" when Nick Adams sits inside his tent with nothing left to accomplish: "He had not been unhappy all day. This was different though. Now things were done. There had been this to do. Now it was done."[19] *Caramelo* is exceptional because the central techniques of the mode typically operate more effectively within sparse, or mundane, settings.

Hemingway and McCarthy, for example, present "waste land" motifs in their narratives. For Hemingway, it is a logical choice because he was writing about the emotional and psychological landscapes of World War I. In capturing the zeitgeist, he created fiction that reflected the most rudimentary elements of daily life, and his work depicts the search for a lost sense of purpose. The emotional frigidity of Hemingway's speakers matches well with the declarative, reportorial style. McCarthy's desolate, burned-out setting in *The Road* is also a world destroyed by combat, but the expansive vocabulary of his narrator operates as the last vestige of a dying civilization. McCarthy implies that even though "the names of things" are "slowly following those things into oblivion," words themselves are one of the few aesthetic pleasures that can be preserved.[20]

McCarthy's technical mastery in many ways bolsters the thematic depth of *The Road*. In some cases, however, authors achieve poor results because they attempt to use the central techniques of the mode to explore topics that lack sufficient depth. The sharpest criticism of Minimalism is often centered on a disdain for the superficial content of a specific work rather than the style itself. Rebein, for example, takes Amy Hempel to task for her tale "Tonight Is a Favor to Holly" not because it is technically unsound but because he does not care for the plot. However, he does not adequately identify the actual problem. Focusing on the nebulous concept of "reader response," Rebein opines that "what we are to make of all this is hard to say. Considerable energy has gone into creating a mood of impending doom, but other than the rather obvious idea that these women are waiting around for men and hate themselves for it, nothing much seems to be behind this mood. We know as little about the narrator at the story's end as we did at the beginning. No explanation is offered for why these women live the way they do, why it's so important for Holly that the narrator go on the blind date, what in their previous relationships has gone so wrong, or what, if anything, they intend to do about it. To be sure, we are given plenty of Hemingway's tip of the iceberg, but by the time we finish the story we are far from believing that anything substantial remains below the surface."[21] Hempel is not, in other words, an ineffective practitioner of the mode. The problem is that she does not write about topics that interest Robert Rebein, who tellingly takes the liberty of speaking for a collective rather than himself alone. Detractors of the tradition often confuse matters of method with elements of taste.

Hempel's fiction, and perhaps even Carver's to some extent, sometimes raises questions about the difference between omission and complete absence. John W. Aldridge declares that Carver,

> along with writers like Joan Didion, Ann Beattie, and Donald and Frederick Barthelme, may be said to be the contemporary progenitors of the minimalist method, in which what is barely stated about a person or an experience is given a kind of subaqueous luminescence. . . . The ghostly presence of the eliminated is absolutely vital to the successful minimalist effect. But it is essential to know whether there is material that has been eliminated or material that is simply absent. The distinction is crucial and is perhaps best illustrated by the example of Hemingway, the minimalist Papa of them all. His famous short story, "A Clean, Well-Lighted Place," is conventionally cited as a piece of highly effective minimalist fiction, and it is so in large part because in planning the story Hemingway composed, but in the actual writing omitted, several elaborately detailed histories of the characters, even of the soldier and the girl who are briefly seen as they pass in the street outside the café.[22]

Aldridge's assertions raise a number of issues, and Hemingway addresses some of them in *Death in the Afternoon*.[23] His position was that the writer must know what has been left out, but he offered no provision that suggests the material had to have actually been written and then excised. Hemingway left the issue open in that only a writer can confirm or deny whether he actually knows what has been withheld. Manuscripts, notes, letters, and interviews are not always available, and it would be disingenuous to argue that a narrative is ineffective only because there are no available means to confirm what precisely is absent.

Another important consideration is that knowledge of the omitted material is not always aesthetically beneficial. "Indian Camp" is an interesting story, and is perhaps enhanced, without the context of "Three Shots." Nick Adams's delusional conclusion that he would never die is a more complex realization if it is attributed to what he has seen in the shanty rather than to a hymn. Minimalist authors are exacting editors, and the most successful among them have exceptional instincts. "Big Two-Hearted River" is a better work of fiction because the "meditations" that comprised the original ending were removed.

The concept of absence is also pertinent to the discussion of whether Minimalist fiction addresses ethical, social, and political topics. In a round-table discussion of his play *Death of a Salesman*, Arthur Miller explicates the role of omission from a slightly different perspective. Several of his copanelists debate Willy Loman's moral complexities and whether the play itself was intended as social criticism. Miller responds that "not only drama, but literature in general—and this goes back a long, long distance in history—posits the idea of value, of right and wrong, of good and bad, high and low, not so much by setting forth, but by showing so to speak, the wages of sin. In other words, when, for instance in 'Death of a Salesman,' we are shown a man who dies for the want of some positive, viable human value, the play implies—and it could not have been written without the author's consciousness that the audience did believe something different. In other words, by showing what happens where there are no values, I at least, assume that the audience will be compelled and propelled toward a more intense quest for the values that are missing."[24] Hemingway and the other writers within the movement use this technique, often achieving the result Miller articulated. In *Deep Surfaces: Mass Culture and History in Postmodern American Fiction*, Philip E. Simmons addresses the same question in the context of statements Ann Beattie made, saying that she "explains her avoidance of an editorializing narrator by saying, 'I don't think I have an overall view of things to express.' To those critics and readers who expect a writer to have 'an overall view of things,' Beattie's statement is an admission of failure: of moral vision, perhaps even of intelligence and skill."[25] Simmons's point is pertinent but accentuates a problem with the depth of particular content more than style.

Although it follows in the Minimalist tradition of nonintrusive narration, McCarthy's *The Road* is in many ways an acute social commentary. He does not evade difficult and complex issues but rather explores serious themes such as death, empathy, and ethical responsibility. He does so in the manner Miller described, showing "what happens where there are no values." The narrator in *The Road* reports the action with a poetic sensibility, using elaborate language to describe dark landscapes and brutal events, but does not engage in lengthy contemplation or synthesis. He presents an atmosphere marked by loss. Animals are gone and the trees are dead. Clean water is a rarity. In a depleted natural world, an earth devoid of governments and geopolitical development, day-to-day existence is reduced to core emotions and experiences. In McCarthy's postwar world, the importance of love and empathy is magnified through poignant illustrations of what human experience is like when such things are missing.

Throughout the last eleven decades, American Minimalist fiction has effectively provided a counterbalance to more verbose prose styles. Rather than engaging in long-standing political arguments or choosing sides in debates over morality, both of which have been done with aplomb by contemporary authors such as Michael Chabon and David Foster Wallace, writers within the tradition have tended to write pieces that invite a wide range of interpretations. Through authorial self-effacement and the use of nonintrusive narrators, they direct attention to the intricacies of their art. If there is one central philosophy in the mode, it is that enduring literature results from superior craftsmanship. Content is subservient to style. In *Hemingway's Craft*, Sheldon Norman Grebstein articulates a "truth" about Hemingway that applies to all of the authors in the category when he wrote that "if we approach Hemingway's fiction primarily by way of its craft, we will discover that the work offers its own reply to the major and persistent complaint that it is narrow in range and intellectually thin. In sum, the very structure or pattern of Hemingway's stories comprises a form of thought, perhaps for an artist the most cogent kind: form *as* thought."[26] The consistent abstention from social criticism is in effect an insistence that such things are essentially abstractions that draw attention away from the intricacies of a well-written narrative. Regardless of what they write about, authors within the movement are meticulous with words and careful in their use of devices, demonstrating a dedication to meticulous editing and refinement.

Notes

Introduction

1. Roland Sodowsky, "The Minimalist Short Story: Its Definition, Writers, and (Small) Heyday," *Studies in Short Fiction* 33, no. 4 (1996): 539.

2. Cynthia Whitney Hallett, "Minimalism and the Short Story," *Studies in Short Fiction* 33 (1996): 487.

3. Frederick Karl, *American Fictions, 1940–1980* (New York: Harper and Row, 1985), 384.

4. Karl, *American Fictions*, 384.

5. Kim A. Herzinger, "Introduction: On the New Fiction," *Mississippi Review* 40–41 (Winter 1985): 8.

6. See, for example, William L. Stull, "Matters of Life and Death," in *Conversations with Raymond Carver*, ed. Marshall Bruce Gentry and William L. Stull (Jackson: University Press of Mississippi, 1990), 184–85; and Richard Ford, "A Symposium on Contemporary American Fiction: Richard Ford," *Michigan Quarterly Review* 2, no. 4 (1987): 730–31.

7. Herzinger, "Introduction: On the New Fiction," 8.

8. James Nagel, *The Portable American Realism Reader*, ed. James Nagel and Tom Quirk (New York: Penguin, 1987), xxv.

9. Bill Buford, "Dirty Realism: New Writing from America," *Granta* 8 (1983): 4–5.

10. Buford, "Dirty Realism," 4.

11. Sven Birkerts, "David Foster Wallace," in *American Energies: Essays on Fiction* (New York: William Morrow, 1992), 388–89.

12. Cynthia Whitney Hallett, *Minimalism and the Short Story—Raymond Carver, Amy Hempel, and Mary Robison* (Lewiston, NY: Edwin Mellen Press, 1999), 25.

13. Kerry McSweeney avoids the term *Minimalist* throughout his study. See McSweeney, *The Realist Short Story of the Powerful Glimpse: Chekhov to Carver* (Columbia: University of South Carolina Press, 2007).

14. Hallett, *Minimalism and the Short Story*, 25.

15. Ibid.

16. Edward Hoagland, "A Symposium On Contemporary American Fiction: Edward Hoagland," *Michigan Quarterly Review* 26, no. 4 (1987): 745.

17. Russell Banks, "Raymond Carver: Our Stephen Crane," *The Atlantic* 268, no. 2 (1991): 101.

18. Donald Pizer, *Realism and Naturalism in Nineteenth-Century American Literature* (Carbondale: Southern Illinois University Press, 1984), 9.

19. Sinda Gregory and Larry McCaffery, "An Interview with Raymond Carver," in *Raymond Carver: A Study of the Short Fiction*, by Ewing Campbell (New York: Twayne, 1993), 110–11.

20. James Dishon McDermott, *Austere Style in Twentieth-Century Literature: Literary Minimalism* (Lewiston, NY: Edwin Mellen Press, 2006), 96–97.

21. See, for example, John W. Aldridge, *Talents and Technicians: Literary Chic and the New Assembly-Line Fiction* (New York: Scribner's, 1992), 8, 32–33, 39.

22. Kirk Curnutt, *Wise Economies: Brevity and Storytelling in American Short Stories* (Moscow: University of Idaho Press, 1997), 246.

23. See James Nagel, *Anthology of the American Short Story* (Boston: Houghton Mifflin, 2008), 1–3.

24. John Barth, "A Few Words about Minimalism," *New York Times Book Review*, December 28, 1986, 2.

25. Hallett, *Minimalism and the Short Story*, 12.

26. See Edgar Allan Poe, "The Philosophy of Composition," in *Poe: Poetry, Tales, and Selected Essays* (New York: Library of America, 1996), 1375.

27. Hamlin Garland, "Impressionism," in *Crumbling Idols: Twelve Essays on Art Dealing Chiefly with Literature Painting and the Drama*, ed. Jane Johnson (Cambridge, MA: Belknap Press of Harvard University Press, 1960), 97–98.

28. Garland, "Impressionism," 104.

29. Ibid., 105.

30. James B. Stronks, "A Realist Experiments with Impressionism: Hamlin Garland's 'Chicago Studies,'" *American Literature* 36, no. 1 (1964): 49–50.

31. James Nagel, "Literary Impressionism and *In Our Time*," *Hemingway Review* 6, no. 2 (1987): 19.

32. Nagel, "Literary Impressionism and *In Our Time*," 19.

33. Sodowsky, "The Minimalist Short Story," 535.

34. James J. Kirschke, *Henry James and Impressionism* (New York: Whitston, 1981), 9.

35. Maria Elizabeth Kronegger, *Literary Impressionism* (New Haven, CT: College and University Press, 1973), 61.

36. Jay McInerney, *Bright Lights, Big City* (New York: Vintage, 1984), 86–87.

37. See Nagel, "Literary Impressionism," 19–20.

38. Ezra Pound, "Imagisme," in *Ezra Pound: Early Writings, Poems and Prose* (New York: Penguin, 2005), 209–10.

39. Robert Pope and Lisa McElhinny, "Raymond Carver Speaking," in *Conversations with Raymond Carver*, ed. Marshall Bruce Gentry and William L. Stull (Jackson: University Press of Mississippi, 1990), 22.

40. Jim Spencer, "Raymond Carver: No Shortcuts to a Good Story," in *Conversations with Raymond Carver*, ed. Marshall Bruce Gentry and William L. Stull (Jackson: University Press of Mississippi, 1990), 24.

41. Ezra Pound, *The ABC of Reading* (New York: New Directions, 1987), 32.

42. See, for example, Michael Reynolds, *Hemingway: The Paris Years* (New York: W. W. Norton, 1999), 22–27; and chapter 4 of Carlos Baker, *Ernest Hemingway: A Life Story* (New York: Macmillan, 1988).

43. In Edmund S. de Chasca, *John Gould Fletcher and Imagism* (Columbia: University of Missouri Press, 1978), 142.

44. J. B. Harmer, *Victory in Limbo: Imagism, 1908–1917* (New York: St. Martin's Press, 1975), 17.

45. Harmer, *Victory in Limbo*, 22.

46. Ibid., 41.

47. T. E. Hulme, *Selected Writings*, ed. Patrick McGuinness (New York: Routledge, 2003), 38–39.

48. De Chasca, *John Gould Fletcher*, 152–53.

49. Peter Jones, introduction to *Imagist Poetry* (New York: Penguin, 2001), 22.

50. De Chasca, *John Gould Fletcher*, 39.

51. The title page of the book explains that *Cathay* is "for the most part from the Chinese of Rihaku, from the notes of the late Ernest Fenollosa, and the decipherings of the professors Mori and Ariga." Ezra Pound, *Cathay* (London: Elkins Matthew, 1915).

52. Ezra Pound, "Liu Ch'e," in *Des Imagistes* (New York: Albert and Charles Boni, 1914), 44; Pound, "Fan-Piece for Her Imperial Lord," in *Des Imagistes*, 45.

53. Noguchi lived from 1875 to 1947.

54. Yoshinobu Hakutani, *Haiku and Modernist Poetics* (New York: Palgrave Macmillan, 2009), 2–3. In his article "Ezra Pound, Yone Noguchi, and Imagism," Hakutani publishes a letter from Pound to Noguchi in which the former acknowledges having read *The Pilgrimage*.

55. Yoshinobu Hakutani, "Ezra Pound, Yone Noguchi, and Imagism," *Modern Philology* 90, no. 1 (1992): 47.

56. Yone Noguchi, *The Pilgrimage*, vol. 2 of 2 (Kamakura: Valley Press, 1909), 137n.

57. Hugh Kenner, *The Pound Era* (Berkeley: University of California Press, 1971), 510.

58. Yone Noguchi, *The Spirit of Japanese Poetry* (New York: E. P. Dutton, 1914), 21.

59. De Chasca, *John Gould Fletcher*, 145.

60. Hakutani, *Haiku and Modernist Poetics*, 9.

61. See Noguchi, *The Spirit of Japanese Poetry*, 92–93, for an explanation of ancient and contemporary usages of syllabic patterns in haiku.

62. Noguchi, *The Pilgrimage*, 2: 114.

63. Mark Helprin, "Introduction: The Canon under Siege," in *The Best American Short Stories 1988* (Boston: Houghton Mifflin, 1988), xx.

64. Hakutani, *Haiku and Modernist Poetics*, 9.

65. See, for example, Bladen's *The X* and Morris's *Untitled, 1967*. Photos of each can be found in Gregory Battcock, ed., *Minimal Art: A Critical Anthology* (New York: E. P. Dutton, 1968), 22, 229.

66. Hallett, *Minimalism and the Short Story*, 1.

67. For an insightful statistical analysis of Minimalism during the 1980s, see Sodowsky, "The Minimalist Short Story: Its Definition, Writers, and (Small) Heyday," 529–40. Sodowsky takes a common approach in choosing a narrow sample set. Based on his numbers, he concludes:

> Herzinger's lengthy definition functions fairly well in isolating the stories and authors considered here, with the exception of the terms "hyper-realistic/superrealistic," which, unless they are meant to apply to the flat, colloquial language—representational language—of most minimalist narrators and characters, I do not find descriptively useful. Minimalist writing is simply representational. If we take note of setting and of the importance of narrative voice in many of the "form" traits named by Herzinger, a somewhat more concise definition is possible: published primarily between 1975 and 1989, most minimalist short stories are set in present-time America; their effaced narrators report action and dialogue, some exposition, and occasionally introspection in the same nonliterary language used by their self-focused blue collar or yuppie characters. (539)

His point about most Minimalist stories being set in America is particularly troublesome, even if he would have been correct about the time frame. Some of Tobias Wolff's and Raymond Carver's stories, for example, make no mention of town, state, or country. Others, such as Carver's "The Compartment," are clearly set outside of the United States. Sodowsky's final point is most helpful because it suggests the connection between Minimalism and Impressionism.

68. Aldridge, *Talents and Technicians*, 8–9. Carol Ianonne writes what is perhaps one of the most lucid, albeit charged, responses to the backlash against Minimalism, arguing that it in many ways was the end product of postmodern critical theory:

> In even a casual observer of the recent cultural scene, such remarks are liable to inspire anything from bemusement to incredulity. After years of a Left-inspired literary criticism that attacked the possibility of narrative authority; the possibility of shared moral and cultural values in literature; the possibility of rendering a comprehensive world view in fiction; the possibility of conveying any definitive meaning whatsoever in literary texts; the possibility of even knowing reality itself through language—after all this, now we hear denunciations of "literary passivity," "moral confusion," and the "lack of a shared conceptual system." After years of assaults on literary standards as hierarchical and imperialistic; of assertions that a literary canon supposedly devised by white males could not reflect the experience

> of "marginal" groups; of vehement demands for a separate literary criticism to evaluate the work of women, of blacks, of homosexuals—after all this, now we are instructed that identification through "surface details" is spurious and that we need to go deeper to find "the shared human ground" where "our resemblance to one another becomes apparent."

The fundamental problem with Ianonne's statement is that Minimalistic fiction is not, as she maintains, superficial or devoid of a deeper moral foundation. In other words, it is not a manifestation of "Left-inspired literary criticism": the style was established long before the advent of Jacques Derrida, Michel Foucault, and various other poststructuralist theorists. It has been, and continues to be, misunderstood in this regard. From Ianonne, "The Fiction We Deserve," *Commentary* 83, no. 6 (1987): 61.

69. David Kaufmann, "Yuppie Postmodernism," *Arizona Quarterly* 47, no. 2 (1991): 96–97.

70. John Updike, "A Symposium on Contemporary American Fiction: John Updike," *Michigan Quarterly Review* 27, no. 1 (1988): 126.

71. Joe David Bellamy, "A Symposium on Contemporary American Fiction: Joe David Bellamy," *Michigan Quarterly Review* 26, no. 4 (1987): 695–96.

72. T. Coraghessan Boyle, "A Symposium on Contemporary American Fiction: T. Coraghessan Boyle," *Michigan Quarterly Review* 26, no. 4 (1987): 707.

73. Herzinger, "Introduction: On the New Fiction," 10.

74. Raymond Carver, "A Symposium on Contemporary American Fiction: Raymond Carver," *Michigan Quarterly Review* 26, no. 4 (1987): 711.

75. Stephen Koch, moderator, "Throwing Dirt on the Grave of Minimalism," *Columbia: A Magazine of Poetry and Prose* 14 (1989): 46.

Chapter 1

1. Ernest Hemingway, *Death in the Afternoon* (New York: Scribner, 1932), 191.

2. See Hemingway, *Death in the Afternoon*, 192.

3. Ernest Hemingway and George Plimpton, "The Art of Fiction XXI: Ernest Hemingway," *Paris Review* 18 (Spring 1958): 75.

4. James Nagel, "Literary Impressionism and *In Our Time*," *Hemingway Review* 6, no. 2 (1987): 19.

5. Linda Welshimer Wagner, *Hemingway and Faulkner: inventors/masters* (Metuchen, NJ: Scarecrow, 1975), 41, 55–65.

6. Frederic Svoboda, "Who Was That Black Man?: A Note on Eugene Bullard and *The Sun Also Rises*," *Hemingway Review* 17, no. 2 (1998): 105; and H. R. Stoneback, *Reading Hemingway's* The Sun Also Rises: *Glossary and Commentary* (Kent, OH: Kent State University Press, 2007), 70.

7. Ernest Hemingway, *The Sun Also Rises* (New York: Scribner, 1926), 69. Subsequent references are to the same edition.

8. Svoboda, "Who Was That Black Man," 105–7.

9. Ibid., 108.

10. Svoboda incorrectly argues that the song was "Aggravatin' Papa (Don't You Try to Two Time Me)." Stoneback writes that "Aggravatin' Papa" does not contain the lyrics "you can't two-time," but that they can be found in Ida Cox's "Cherry Picking Blues," a song with numerous thematic implications. Stoneback, *Reading Hemingway's* The Sun Also Rises, 108–10.

11. Ida Cox, "Cherry Picking Blues," *Complete Recorded Works, 1923–1938: Volume 2, 1924–1925*, compact disc, Document Records, 1995. Subsequent references are to the same recording.

12. Carlos Baker, *Ernest Hemingway: A Life Story* (New York: Scribner, 1969), 27.

13. Quoted in Charles A. Fenton, *The Apprenticeship of Ernest Hemingway: The Early Years* (New York: Viking, 1960), 30–31.

14. Quoted in Matthew J. Bruccoli, *Ernest Hemingway's Apprenticeship: Oak Park, 1916–1917* (Washington, DC: Microcard Editions, 1971), xvii.

15. Constance Cappel Montgomery, *Hemingway in Michigan* (New York: Fleet, 1966), 43.

16. David Marut, "Out of the Wastebasket: Hemingway's High School Stories," in *Ernest Hemingway: The Oak Park Legacy*, ed. James Nagel (Tuscaloosa: University of Alabama Press, 1996), 82.

17. Marut, "Out of the Wastebasket," 89–90.

18. George Francis Thomas, *Legends of the Land of Lakes; or, History, Traditions, and Mysteries, Gleaned from Years of Experience among the Pioneers, Voyageurs, and Indians* (Chicago: G. F. Thomas, 1884), 56–57.

19. Ernest Hemingway, "Judgment of Manitou," *Tabula* 22 (February 1916), 9–10. Reprinted in facsimile in Bruccoli, *Ernest Hemingway's Apprenticeship*, 96–97. David G. Mandelbaum describes the role of "Manito" in the Cree culture, explaining that "the concept of a single all powerful creator was dominant in Plains Cree religious ideology and ceremonialism. Every prayer for supernatural aid, every ritual addressed to divine powers, had to begin with an invocation to *kıce•manito•*, Great *Manito*. All the phenomena of the universe are considered to be under His control and everything was created by His will. He was not personalized, nor given any definite abode other than a general empyrean locale; He did not appear to men in visions. Moreover, He was conceived as being too great, too awesome, to be asked directly for His blessing." Mandelbaum, *The Plains Cree: An Ethnographic, Historical, and Comparative Study* (Regina, SK: Canadian Plains Research Center, 1979), 157. It is interesting, and consistent with his Cree heritage, that Pierre does not address Manitou or ask him for mercy once he realizes his fate. His decisiveness in part extends from the fact that he knows that there is no possibility of divine intervention or chance for mercy.

20. Ernest Hemingway and Fred Wilcoxen, "Athletic Verse: The Tackle," *Tabula* 23 (March 1917): 39. Reprinted in facsimile in Bruccoli, *Ernest Hemingway's Appren-*

ticeship, 107. Also printed in Ernest Hemingway, *Ernest Hemingway: 88 Poems*, ed. Nicholas Gerogiannis (New York: Harcourt Brace, 1979), 11.

21. Carlos Baker, *Ernest Hemingway: A Life Story*, 31–34.

22. James Nagel, "Hemingway and the Italian Legacy," in *Hemingway in Love and War: The Lost Diary of Agnes Von Kurowsky* (New York: Hyperion, 1995), 201–2.

23. Nagel, "Hemingway and the Italian Legacy," 216–26, 239. Of the many accounts written about Hemingway's service in the American Red Cross and subsequent wounding, Nagel's is among the most carefully written and researched.

24. Michael Reynolds, *The Young Hemingway* (New York: W. W. Norton, 1986), 93–94.

25. Reynolds, *The Young Hemingway*, 95.

26. Ernest Hemingway, "Crossroads—An Anthology: Pauline Snow," reprinted in Peter Griffin, *Along with Youth* (New York: Oxford University Press, 1985), 124; and Stephen Crane, *Maggie: A Girl of the Streets*, *The Portable Stephen Crane*, ed. Joseph Katz (New York: Viking, 1977), 20.

27. Reynolds claims that Hemingway had not yet read *Winesburg, Ohio* in the fall of 1919, but does not cite a source for his information. Reynolds, *The Young Hemingway*, 96.

28. Hemingway, "Crossroads—An Anthology: Pauline Snow," 124.

29. Ernest Hemingway, "A Free Shave," in *By-Line: Ernest Hemingway*, ed. William White (New York: Scribner, 1967), 5–8. The piece is dated March 6, 1920.

30. Quoted in Nancy R. Comley and Robert Scholes, *Hemingway's Genders: Rereading the Hemingway Text* (New Haven, CT: Yale University Press, 1994), 24–25.

31. Carlos Baker, *Hemingway: A Life Story*, 84–85.

32. Richard Hasbany, "The Shock of Vision: An Imagist Reading of *In Our Time*," in *Ernest Hemingway: Five Decades of Criticism*, ed. Linda W. Wagner (East Lansing: Michigan State University Press, 1974), 224.

33. In *A Moveable Feast*, Hemingway discusses his exposure to Cézanne and other Impressionists, recalling that "if I walked down by different streets to the Jardin du Luxembourg in the afternoon I could walk through the gardens and then go to the Musée du Luxembourg where the great paintings were that have now mostly been transferred to the Louvre and the Jeu de Paume. I went there nearly every day for the Cézannes and to see the Manets and the Monets and the other Impressionists that I had first come to know about in the Art Institute at Chicago. I was learning something from the painting of Cézanne that made writing simple true sentences far from enough to make the stories have the dimensions that I was trying to put in them. I was learning very much from him but I was not articulate enough to explain it to anyone. Besides it was a secret." Hemingway, *A Moveable Feast* (New York: Scribner, 2009), 23. Also see Nagel, "Literary Impressionism and *In Our Time*," 18–19.

34. See Hemingway, *A Moveable Feast*, 177.

35. Scott Donaldson, *By Force of Will: The Life and Art of Ernest Hemingway* (Lincoln, NE: iUniverse, 2001), 247.

36. Harry Levin, "Observations on the Style of Ernest Hemingway," in *Hemingway and His Critics*, ed. Carlos Baker (New York: Hill and Wang, 1961), 115.

37. Ernest Hemingway, "IN OUR TIME," *Little Review* 9 (Spring 1923): 3–5.

38. Carlos Baker, *Hemingway: The Writer as Artist* (Princeton, NJ: Princeton University Press, 1972), 411n8.

39. See Carlos Baker, *Hemingway: A Life Story*, 97; and Hemingway, *By-Line*, 49–60.

40. Hemingway and Plimpton, "The Art of Fiction XXI: Ernest Hemingway," 74.

41. Ernest Hemingway, "On the Quai at Smyrna," in *In Our Time* (New York: Scribner, 1930), 11. All subsequent references to the stories and interchapters in *In Our Time* are to the same edition.

42. Louis H. Leiter, "Neural Projections in Hemingway's 'On the Quai at Smyrna,'" in *Critical Essays on Ernest Hemingway's* In Our Time, ed. Michael S. Reynolds (Boston: G. K. Hall, 1983), 139.

43. Fenton, *The Apprenticeship of Ernest Hemingway*, 238; and E. R. Hagemann, "'Only Let the Story End as Soon as Possible': Time-and-History in Ernest Hemingway's *In Our Time*," in *New Critical Approaches to the Short Stories of Ernest Hemingway*, ed. Jackson J. Benson (Durham, NC: Duke University Press: 1990), 193.

44. George Cheatham, "The World War I Battle of Mons and Hemingway's *In Our Time* Chapter III," *Hemingway Review* 26, no. 2 (2007): 53–54.

45. Fenton, *The Apprenticeship of Ernest Hemingway*, 229–36.

46. Ibid., 233.

47. In *A Moveable Feast*, Hemingway says that "from the day I had found Sylvia Beach's library I had read all of Turgenev, what had been published in English of Gogol, the Constance Garnett translations of Tolstoi and the English translations of Chekov." Michael Reynolds states that Hemingway checked out *A Sportsman's Sketches* from Beach's shop three times. Hemingway, *A Moveable Feast*, 101; and Reynolds, *Hemingway: The Paris Years* (New York: W. W. Norton, 1999), 106.

48. Ernest Hemingway, "Refugees from Thrace," in *By-Line*, 60; and Carlos Baker, *Hemingway: A Life Story*, 99.

49. The *New York Times* printed two stories about the execution, but in *Hemingway's Laboratory: The Paris "in our time,"* Milton A. Cohen makes a convincing argument that Hemingway derived Chapter V from a story published in the Paris *Tribune*. Cohen, *Hemingway's Laboratory: The Paris "in our time"* (Tuscaloosa: University of Alabama Press, 2005), 149.

50. See Cohen, *Hemingway's Laboratory*, 148–49; and John O. Iatrides, "The United States and Greece in the Twentieth Century," in *Greece in the Twentieth Century*, ed. Theodore Couloumbis, Theodore Kariotis, and Fotini Bellou (New York: Frank Cass, 2004), 70–71.

51. Wendolyn E. Tetlow argues that this vignette is proof of Hemingway's familiarity with the Imagists. Tetlow, *Hemingway's* In Our Time*: Lyrical Dimensions* (Lewisburg, PA: Bucknell University Press, 1992), 29.

52. Ernest Hemingway to Ezra Pound, Paris, August 5, 1923, in Carlos Baker, ed., *Ernest Hemingway: Selected Letters, 1917–1961* (New York: Scribner, 1981), 91–92.

53. Ernest Hemingway, "A Way You'll Never Be," in *Winner Take Nothing* (New York: Scribner, 1970), 51.

54. This vignette employs what Gerry Brenner maintains was a technique Hemingway used frequently, calling it a "lexical riddle." These types of stories, Brenner continued, "pivot upon a lexical crux . . . unarticulated or ambiguous words." When the narrator says the men were "drunk," he means they were afraid. Gerry Brenner, "From 'Sepi Jingan' to 'The Mother of a Queen': Hemingway's Three Epistemologic Formulas for Short Fiction," in *New Critical Approaches to the Short Stories of Ernest Hemingway*, ed. Jackson J. Benson (Durham, NC: Duke University Press, 1990), 161.

55. Carlos Azevedo, "Oak Park as the Thing Left Out: Surface and Depth in 'Soldier's Home,'" in *Ernest Hemingway: The Oak Park Legacy*, ed. James Nagel (Tuscaloosa: University of Alabama Press, 1996), 102.

56. Joseph DeFalco writes, "'Home,' as implied in the title, becomes the ultimate irony for Krebs, for it stands as a symbol of the stultifying pressures which emasculate the individual spirit." DeFalco, *The Hero in Hemingway's Short Stories* (Pittsburgh: University of Pittsburgh Press, 1963), 138.

57. Ernest Hemingway, "Soldier's Home," manuscript, folder 708, Hemingway Collection, John F. Kennedy Library, Boston, 1–2.

58. Scott Donaldson, "'A Very Short Story' as Therapy," in *Hemingway's Neglected Short Fiction: New Perspectives*, ed. Susan F. Beegel (Tuscaloosa: University of Alabama Press, 1989), 105.

59. Agnes von Kurowsky to Ernest Hemingway, March 7, 1919, in Nagel, *Hemingway in Love and War*, 163.

60. Von Kurowsky to Hemingway, in Nagel, *Hemingway in Love and War*, 163.

61. See Ernest Hemingway, "Mr. and Mrs. Smith," manuscripts, folder 585, Hemingway Collection, John F. Kennedy Library, Boston; Reynolds, *Hemingway: The Paris Years*, 192; and Ernest Hemingway to Chard Powers Smith, Gstaad, January 21, 1927, in Carlos Baker, *Ernest Hemingway: Selected Letters, 1917–1961*, 242.

62. Kenneth G. Johnston, "Hemingway's 'Out of Season' and the Psychology of Errors," in *Critical Essays on Ernest Hemingway's* In Our Time, ed. Michael S. Reynolds (Boston: G. K. Hall, 1983), 228–29. While Johnston's Freudian argument is interesting, a doctor would be just as necessary in the case of a general illness as he would be for a birth or abortion.

63. Ernest Hemingway to F. Scott Fitzgerald, Schruns, circa December 24, 1925, in Carlos Baker, *Selected Letters 1917–1961*, 180.

64. Ibid., 180–81.

65. Hemingway, *A Moveable Feast*, 70–71.

66. See James Steinke, "'Out of Season' and Hemingway's Neglected Discovery: Ordinary Actuality," in *Hemingway's Neglected Short Fiction: New Perspectives*, ed. Susan F. Beegel (Tuscaloosa: University of Alabama Press, 1989), 63; Joseph Flora, *Ernest Hemingway: A Study of the Short Fiction* (Boston: G. K. Hall, 1989), 32; and Carlos Baker, *Hemingway: A Life Story*, 109.

67. Carlos Baker, *Hemingway: A Life Story*, 107, 109.

68. John Walford, *Great Themes in Art* (Upper Saddle River, NJ: Prentice Hall, 2002), 424; and Emily Stipes Watts, *Ernest Hemingway and the Arts* (Urbana: University of Illinois Press, 1971), 168. Also see Hemingway, "On Writing," in *The Nick Adams Stories* (New York: Scribner, 1972), 239–40.

69. Edmund Wilson, "Emergence of Ernest Hemingway," in *The Shores of Light: A Literary Chronicle of the 1920s and 1930s* (New York: Farrar, Straus, and Giroux, 1979), 121.

70. Hagemann, "'Only Let the Story End as Soon as Possible,'" 197.

71. Sheldon Norman Grebstein, *Hemingway's Craft* (Carbondale: Southern Illinois University Press, 1973), 2.

72. Cohen, *Hemingway's Laboratory*, 162.

73. Watts, *Hemingway and the Arts*, 137.

74. See Philip Young, *Ernest Hemingway: A Reconsideration* (University Park: Pennsylvania State University Press, 1966), 32, 41; Robert M. Slabey, "The Structure of *In Our Time*," in *Critical Essays on Ernest Hemingway's* In Our Time, ed. Michael S. Reynolds (Boston: G. K. Hall, 1983), 76–87; Clinton S. Burhans, "The Complex Unity of *In Our Time*," in *Critical Essays on Ernest Hemingway's* In Our Time, ed. Michael S. Reynolds (Boston: G. K. Hall, 1983), 94; and Joseph Flora, *Hemingway's Nick Adams* (Baton Rouge: Louisiana State University Press, 1982), 29–30.

75. Larry Grimes, for instance, posits that George may be the father, whereas G. Thomas Tanselle rejects the idea. See Grimes, *The Religious Design of Hemingway's Early Fiction* (Ann Arbor: UMI Research Press, 1985), 55–56; and Tanselle, "Hemingway's 'Indian Camp,'" in *Critical Essays on Ernest Hemingway's* In Our Time, ed. Michael S. Reynolds (Boston: G. K. Hall, 1983), 144–45.

76. Ernest Hemingway, "Indian Camp," manuscripts, folder 493, Hemingway Collection, John F. Kennedy Library, Boston, 3.

77. Hemingway, "Indian Camp," 6. The double parentheses indicate a word that was written in the space above a line.

78. Hemingway said that the story stems from his realization that his father, Clarence Hemingway, "was a coward." Joseph Flora, *Ernest Hemingway: A Study of the Short Fiction*, 18–19.

79. Sheridan Baker, *Ernest Hemingway: An Introduction and Interpretation* (New York: Holt, Rinehart and Winston, 1967), 28.

80. Carlos Baker, *Hemingway: A Life Story*, 132–33.

81. Ernest Hemingway, "The End of Something," manuscripts, folder 373, Hemingway Collection, John F. Kennedy Library, Boston, 2.

82. In an essay on "Cross-Country Snow," Olivia Carr Edenfield argues that Nick's freedom is threatened by feelings of "sexual entrapment" rather than a broader sense of responsibility. Edenfield, "Doomed Biologically: Sex and Entrapment in Ernest Hemingway's 'Cross-Country Snow,'" *Hemingway Review* 19, no. 1 (1999): 141–48.

83. Sherwood Anderson, "I Want to Know Why," in *The Triumph of the Egg* (New York: B. W. Huebsch, 1921), 5–20.

84. Joseph Flora notes that Bugs is a man who "believes in the ritual of food." Flora, *Hemingway's Nick Adams*, 93.

85. Young, *Hemingway: A Reconsideration*, 40.

86. Hemingway, "A Way You'll Never Be," 52.

87. Hemingway, *A Moveable Feast*, 72; and Carlos Baker, *Hemingway: A Life Story*, 131.

88. Kenneth G. Johnston, "Hemingway and Cézanne: Doing the Country," *American Literature* 56, no. 1 (1984): 34.

89. Sheridan Baker, "Hemingway's Two-Hearted River," in *The Short Stories of Ernest Hemingway: Critical Essays*, ed. Jackson J. Benson (Durham, NC: Duke University Press, 1975), 157.

90. See Tetlow, *Hemingway's* In Our Time, 14; and Wagner, *Hemingway and Faulkner*, 27–28.

91. William Adair, "Hemingway's 'Out of Season': The End of the Line," in *New Critical Approaches to the Short Stories of Ernest Hemingway*, ed. Jackson J. Benson (Durham, NC: Duke University Press, 1990), 343.

92. Carlos Baker, *Hemingway: A Life Story*, 107.

93. Hemingway, "Old Constan," in *By-Line*, 53–54.

94. Hemingway, "Refugees from Thrace," *By-Line*, 56.

95. In addition to the innuendo of "Mr. and Mrs. Elliot," Hemingway writes in a eulogistic tribute to Joseph Conrad that "it is agreed by most of the people I know that Conrad is a bad writer, just as it is agreed that T. S. Eliot is a good writer. If I knew that by grinding Mr. Eliot into a fine dry powder and sprinkling that powder over Mr. Conrad's grave Mr. Conrad would shortly appear, looking very annoyed at the forced return and commence writing I would leave for London early tomorrow morning with a sausage grinder." Ernest Hemingway, "Conrad, Optimist and Moralist," *Transatlantic Review* 2, no. 3 (1924): 341–42.

96. Ernest Hemingway to Gertrude Stein and Alice B. Toklas, Paris, August 15, 1924, in Carlos Baker, *Ernest Hemingway: Selected Letters, 1917–1961*, 122.

97. Ernest Hemingway, "Big Two-Hearted River: Part II," manuscripts, folder 274–2, Hemingway Collection, John F. Kennedy Library, Boston, 90.

98. Carlos Baker, *Hemingway: A Life Story*, 63.

99. Hemingway, "Big Two-Hearted River: Part II," 85.

100. Hemingway, "On Writing," 233–41.

101. Gertrude Stein, *The Autobiography of Alice B. Toklas* (New York: Vintage, 1990), 219.

102. Carol Sklenicka, *Raymond Carver: A Writer's Life* (New York: Scribner, 2009), 85.

Chapter 2

1. Michael Gorra, "Review of *Cathedral* by Raymond Carver," *Hudson Review* 37 (Spring 1984): 155.

2. Maryann Burk Carver, *What It Used to Be Like: A Portrait of My Marriage to Raymond Carver* (New York: St. Martin's Griffin, 2006), 10.

3. Sinda Gregory and Larry McCaffery, "An Interview with Raymond Carver," in *Conversations with Raymond Carver*, ed. Marshall Bruce Gentry and William L. Stull (Jackson: University Press of Mississippi, 1990), 110.

4. Adam Meyer, "Now You See Him, Now You Don't, Now You Do Again: The Evolution of Raymond Carver's Minimalism," *Critique* 30 (Summer 1989): 239.

5. In the note to *Beginners*, Stull and Carroll publish a letter in which Carver requests that Lish stop production of the book because the stories have been overedited. Lish did not acquiesce. See Raymond Carver, *Carver: Collected Stories*, ed. William L. Stull and Maureen P. Carroll (New York: Library of America, 2009), 990–98.

6. Carol Sklenicka, *Raymond Carver: A Writer's Life* (New York: Scribner, 2009), 398.

7. Carver, *Collected Stories*, 984.

8. In an interview with David Sexton, Carver described "Cathedral" as "different from anything I'd ever written," and that "all of the stories after that seemed to be fuller somehow and much more generous and maybe more affirmative." Sexton, "David Sexton Talks to Raymond Carver," in *Conversations with Raymond Carver*, 125.

9. Sklenicka, *Raymond Carver*, 69.

10. Jay McInerney, "Raymond Carver, Mentor," in *Remembering Ray: A Composite Biography of Raymond Carver* (Santa Barbara. CA: Capra, 1993), 123–24.

11. Maryann Burk Carver, *What It Used to Be Like*, 236.

12. See Raymond Carver, "Vitamins," *Esquire* 96 (October 1981): 130, 132, 134–39.

13. Carver's close friend Richard Ford said that "Ray had a passion and reverence for literature, and particularly for Chekhov." Sam Halpert, "Richard Ford," in . . . *when we talk about Raymond Carver* (Layton, UT: Gibbs Smith, 1991), 147.

14. Marc Oxoby, "The Voluminous Impact of Television in the Fiction of Raymond Carver," in *New Paths to Raymond Carver: Critical Essays on His Life, Fiction, and Poetry*, ed. Sandra Lee Kleppe and Robert Miltner (Columbia: University of South Carolina Press, 2008), 108. Oxoby cites Bruce Weber, "Raymond Carver: A Chronicler of Blue-Collar Despair," *New York Times Magazine* (June 24, 1984): 36–50.

15. Lewis Buzbee and Mona Simpson, "Raymond Carver," in *Conversations with Raymond Carver*, 44.

16. Douglas Unger opines that Carver may have even preferred writing poetry over prose: "I think writing poetry, more than fiction, was his first love. I don't believe that, after Ray was turned down for financial aid as a young poet that year at Iowa, that he ever gave up his youthful dream of being accepted by the world as a poet. Poetry, more than fiction, was an obsession for him. If he had a choice between writing a story or a poem—if writers really have that kind of choice—I think he'd favor the poem." Halpert, "Douglas Unger," in . . . *when we talk about Raymond Carver*, 70–71.

17. Michael Schumacher, "After the Fire, Into the Fire: An Interview with Raymond Carver," in *Conversations with Raymond Carver*, 215.

18. Sinda Gregory and Larry McCaffery, "An Interview with Raymond Carver," in *Conversations with Raymond Carver*, 111–12.

19. Raymond Carver, "On Writing," in *Call If You Need Me*, ed. William L. Stull (New York: Vintage Books, 2000), 89.

20. Robert Pope and Lisa McElhinny, "Raymond Carver Speaking," in *Conversations with Raymond Carver*, 17. Carver's comments about the influence of other authors appears in "Fires," in *Call If You Need Me*, 93.

21. The earlier versions of Carver's stories first appeared in a variety of journals and literary periodicals: "The Bridle," *New Yorker* 58 (July 19, 1982): 30–39; "Careful," *Paris Review* 25 (Summer 1983): 222–34; "Cathedral," *Atlantic Monthly* 248 (September 1981): 23–29; "Chef's House," *New Yorker* 57 (November 30, 1981): 42–43; "The Compartment," *Antioch Review* 41 (Spring 1983): 133–41; "Feathers," *Atlantic Monthly* 250 (September 1982): 62–69; "Fever," *North American Review* 268 (June 1983): 11–19; "Preservation," *Grand Street* 2 (Spring 1983): 7–16; "A Small, Good Thing," *Ploughshares* 8, nos. 1–2 (1982): 213–40; "The Train," *Antaeus* 49/50 (Spring/Summer 1983): 151–57; "Vitamins," *Esquire*; "Where I'm Calling From," *New Yorker* 58 (March 15, 1982): 41–48, 51.

22. Sklenicka, *Raymond Carver*, 499.

23. In "Fever," Carlyle's son, Keith, was originally named "Franklin." Franklin is the name of the other injured young man in "A Small, Good Thing." The character Spuds in "The Bridle" was originally named "Chef." In the original version of "Vitamins," the salesgirl Pam was named Sandy. Sandy is the protagonist in "Preservation."

24. Tom Jenks, "Shameless," in *Remembering Ray: A Composite Biography of Raymond Carver*, ed. William L. Stull and Maureen P. Carroll (Santa Barbara, CA: Capra Press, 1993), 142.

25. Quoted in Sklenicka, *Raymond Carver*, 371.

26. Sexton, "David Sexton Talks to Raymond Carver," in *Conversations with Raymond Carver*, 132.

27. Arthur F. Bethea, Arthur M. Saltzman, Mark A. R. Facknitz, Nelson Hathcock, and Peter Middleton discuss the narrative as if Robert's visit takes place in the narrator's present. See Bethea, *Technique and Sensibility in the Fiction of Raymond Carver* (New York: Routledge, 2001), 154–56; Mark A. R. Facknitz, "'The Calm,' 'A

Small Good Thing,' and 'Cathedral': Raymond Carver and the Rediscovery of Human Worth," *Studies in Short Fiction* 23 (Fall 1986): 287–96; Arthur M. Saltzman, *Understanding Raymond Carver* (Columbia: University of South Carolina Press, 1988), 151–54; Peter Middleton, "High Visibility: Images of Ethical Life in *The Tragic Muse* and Raymond Carver's 'Cathedral,'" *Rethinking History* 2, no. 3 (1998): 331–38; Nelson Hathcock, "'The Possibility of Resurrection': Re-Vision in Carver's 'Feathers' and 'Cathedral,'" *Studies in Short Fiction* 28 (Winter 1991): 31–39.

28. Cormac McCarthy, *No Country for Old Men* (New York: Vintage, 2006), 53.

29. Raymond Carver, "Cathedral," in *Cathedral* (New York: Vintage, 1989), 211. All subsequent references are from the same edition.

30. Facknitz, "'The Calm,'" 293.

31. This was a contentious issue for Carver. He said in an interview that he did not want to create a dynamic in his stories that positions himself and the reader on the inside and his character on the outside:

> **The Bloomsbury Review:** Some critics believe that if there's one thing uniting these writers and setting them apart from other postmoderns, it's their distaste for irony. Does that ring true to you?
>
> **Raymond Carver:** I think they mean that these writers, the so-called "minimalists," are not ironists in the sense that there are no secrets between the sophisticated writer and the writer's sophisticated audience. And I would agree with them there. I see irony as a sort of pact or compact between the writer and the reader in that they know more than the characters do. The characters are set up and then they're set down again in some sort of subtle pratfall or awakening. I don't feel any such complicity with the reader. I'm not talking down to my characters, or holding them up for ridicule, or slyly doing an end run around them.

In the context of "Cathedral," it is difficult to take Carver's statement at face value. But the story is remarkable in that it does not evoke a sense of animus toward the narrator. His blindness, in other words, is understandable. Raymond Carver and William L. Stull, "Matters of Life and Death," in *Conversations with Raymond Carver*, ed. Marshall Bruce Gentry and William L. Stull (Jackson: University Press of Mississippi, 1990), 185.

32. James Nagel, "Literary Impressionism and *In Our Time*," *Hemingway Review* 6, no. 2 (Spring 1987): 19.

33. H. Peter Stowell, *Literary Impressionism: James and Chekhov* (Athens: University of Georgia Press, 1980), 17.

34. Anton Chekhov, "The Grasshopper," in *Anton Chekhov's Short Stories*, ed. Ralph E. Matlaw, trans. Constance Garnett (New York: W. W. Norton, 1979), 89. All

subsequent references are to the same edition.

35. See chapter 3 of Kirk Nesset, *The Stories of Raymond Carver: A Critical Study* (Athens: Ohio University Press, 1995), 51–71.

36. See Sklenicka, *Raymond Carver*, 312.

37. The deleted line is in parentheses.

38. Halpert, "Geoffrey Wolff," in . . . *when we talk about Raymond Carver*, 111.

39. For details about Raymond Carver's journey, see Sklenicka, *Raymond Carver*, 384–86. Vance Carver's statement is on p. 410.

40. Saltzman writes at length about Myers's preoccupation with "inviolability" but does not take into account Myers's regret over traveling alone. See *Understanding Raymond Carver*, 131–34.

41. Carver ostensibly promulgates the faulty compositional history when he writes, "this story is expanded and revised from *What We Talk About When We Talk About Love*" at the bottom of the version of "A Small, Good Thing" published in *Ploughshares*. See Carver, "A Small, Good Thing," *Ploughshares*, 213.

42. See note 5, this book, this chapter. Raymond Carver, "A Small, Good Thing," *Beginners* in *Carver: Collected Stories*, ed. William L. Stull and Maureen P. Carroll (New York: Library of America, 2009), 804–30.

43. Carver, "A Small, Good Thing," *Ploughshares*, 238. This line is also included in the *Beginners* version.

44. Carver, "A Small, Good Thing," *Beginners* in *Carver: Collected Stories*, 806.

45. Halpert, "Maryann Burk Carver," in . . . *when we talk about Raymond Carver*, 91. Burk Carver says in her memoir that Raymond became resentful of her success and one day insisted that she had to choose between her job and her marriage. This led to what Burk Carver called a "prolonged sales slump." Maryann Burk Carver, *What It Used to Be Like*, 206.

46. Nesset, *The Stories of Raymond Carver: A Critical Study*, 64.

47. Halpert, "Douglas Unger," in . . . *when we talk about Raymond Carver*, 59.

48. Buzbee and Simpson, "Raymond Carver," 38. Photographs of Duffy's can be found in Bob Adleman and Tess Gallagher, *Carver Country: The World of Raymond Carver* (New York: Charles Scribner's Sons, 1990), 96, 99.

49. Nesset, *The Stories of Raymond Carver: A Critical Study*, 59.

50. Raymond Carver, "Where I'm Calling From," *New Yorker*, 45. The deleted lines are in parentheses.

51. John Cheever, "The Five-Forty-Eight," in *The Stories of John Cheever* (New York: Vintage, 2000), 238.

52. Cheever, "The Five-Forty-Eight," 239.

53. Ibid., 240.

54. Raymond Carver, "The Bridle," *New Yorker*, 35.

55. Ibid., 34.

Chapter 3

1. Jay McInerney, *The Good Life* (New York: Vintage, 2006), 165.

2. Günter Leypoldt, *Casual Silences: The Poetics of Minimal Realism from Raymond Carver and the New Yorker School to Bret Easton Ellis* (Trier: Wissenschaftlicher Verlag Trier, 2001), 218. Leypoldt prefers the term *minimal realism* to *Minimalism* but is basically describing the same mode.

3. Philip E. Simmons, *Deep Surfaces: Mass Culture and History in Postmodern American Fiction* (Athens: University of Georgia Press, 1997), 128–29. Simmons's observation about plain style is accurate, but his assertion about Minimalist writers adopting it as a "properly ironic" stance is speculative. Also noteworthy is Simmons's assertion that Minimalism does not begin until the "post-Vietnam" era in America (104).

4. David Kaufmann, "Yuppie Postmodernism," *Arizona Quarterly* 47, no. 2 (1991): 101.

5. Jay McInerney, "The Writers of Wrong," *Esquire* 112 (July, 1989): 114.

6. For McInerney's perspective on his relationship with Carver, see Jay McInerney, "Raymond Carver, Mentor," in *Remembering Ray: A Composite Biography of Raymond Carver*, edited by William L. Stull and Maureen Carroll (Santa Barbara, CA: Capra, 1993), 119–26.

7. Jay McInerney, *A Hedonist in the Cellar* (New York: Knopf, 2006), 114.

8. Zoltán Abádi Nagy, "The Narratorial Function in Minimalist Fiction," *Neohelicon* 27, no. 2 (2000): 241.

9. Jay McInerney, *How It Ended: New and Collected Stories* (New York: Knopf, 2009), x.

10. Joyce Wadler, "A Turn in the 'Bright Lights,'" *Washington Post*, December 12, 1984, F13.

11. Jay McInerney, "It's Six A.M. Do You Know Where You Are?" *Paris Review* 86 (Winter 1982): 181–88. This story also provides the title of the first chapter of *Bright Lights, Big City.*

12. Michael Schumacher, *Reasons to Believe: New Voices in American Fiction* (New York: St. Martin's Press, 1988), 96.

13. Peter Bricklebank, "Review of *Bright Lights, Big City* by Jay McInerney," *Library Journal* 109, no. 16 (1984): 1863; John Duka, "Notes on Fashion," *New York Times*, September 14, 1984, B9; and Michiko Kakutani, "Books of the Times," *New York Times*, October 30, 1984, C17.

14. Schumacher, *Reasons to Believe*, 89.

15. The protagonist receives a "framed needlepoint sampler" from his colleague Yasu Wade with a quotation from the song: "Facts all come with points of view / Facts don't do what I want them to." McInerney, *Bright Lights, Big City* (New York: Vintage, 1984), 23. All subsequent references are from this edition. Information on *Remain*

in Light can be found in "Remain in Light—1980," The Name of This Site Is Talking Heads, http://www.talking-heads.nl/index.php/discography/81-remain-in-light. Accessed February 15, 2010.

16. Schumacher, *Reasons to Believe,* 89.

17. Wadler, "A Turn in the 'Bright Lights,'" F13.

18. Monika Fludernik, "Second Person Fiction: Narrative You as Addressee and/or Protagonist," *AAA, Arbelten aus Anglistik und Amerikanistik* 18, no. 2 (1993): 218.

19. Kevin L. Ferguson, "Engaging the Eighties: Ethics, Objects, Periods" (PhD diss., City University of New York, 2007), 99. McInerney's third novel, *Story of My Life,* is a recontextualization of *The Catcher in the Rye.* The narrator-protagonist, Alison Poole, constantly berates people she believes are deceptive. Like Holden Caulfield, she narrates her tale from a medical facility.

20. Despite the claims of John W. Aldridge, the protagonist in *Bright Lights, Big City* never has sexual intercourse during the novel. Ferguson correctly states that the narrator "treats himself to lots of cocaine, nightclubs, and bootless one-night stands." Ferguson, *Engaging the Eighties,* 113.

21. Duka, "Notes on Fashion," B9.

22. "Review of *Bright Lights, Big City* by Jay McInerney," *Atlantic* 254, no. 6 (1984): 145.

23. Terence Moran, "Brief Review," *New Republic* 191, no. 22 (1984): 42.

24. Kakutani, "Books of the Times," C17.

25. David Remnick, "Jay McInerney's High Kicks in Tokyo," *Washington Post,* August 25, 1985, 5. In 1998, Remnick became editor of the *New Yorker* whose fact-checking department Remnick's review disparages. See http://www.newyorker.com/contributors/david-remnick. Accessed October 15, 2014.

26. Joseph Wood Krutch, "The End of Art," *The Nation* (November 16, 1927): 548.

27. Allen Tate, "Hard-Boiled," in *Critical Essays on Ernest Hemingway's* The Sun Also Rises, ed. James Nagel (New York: G. K. Hall, 1995), 43.

28. Sanford Pinsker, "Soft Lights, Academic Talk: A Conversation with Jay McInerney," *Literary Review* 30, no. 1 (1986): 108.

29. John W. Aldridge, *Talents and Technicians: Literary Chic and the New Assembly-Line Fiction* (New York: Scribner's, 1992), 8.

30. Gregor Wiebels-Balthaus, "The Self in Trouble: Young Adults in the Urban Consumer Society of the 1980s in Janowitz, Ellis, and McInerney" (PhD diss., Ruhr Universität Bochum, 2005), 248.

31. Pinsker, "Soft Lights, Academic Talk," 112.

32. See Carlos Baker, *Ernest Hemingway: A Life Story* (New York: Scribner, 1969), 31–37.

33. Quoted in Belén Boville, *The Cocaine War in Context: Drugs and Politics,* trans. Lorena Terando (New York: Algora, 2004), 49.

34. Wadler, "A Turn," F13.

35. Tom Feiling, *The Candy Machine: How Cocaine Took Over the World* (London: Penguin, 2009), 2.

36. Feiling, *The Candy Machine*, 222–23; Wadler, "A Turn," F13.

37. Ibid., 227–28.

38. Ibid., 39.

39. See chapter 7 of Feiling's *The Candy Machine.*

40. Bernard Elser, Hollace S. Mittleman, and Richard E. Mittleman, "Cocaine," *American Journal of Nursing* 84 (September 1984): 1092.

41. Elser, Mittleman, and Mittleman, "Cocaine," 1092, 1094.

42. Ferguson, *Engaging the Eighties*, 123.

43. Remnick, "Jay McInerney's High Kicks," 5.

44. Leypoldt, *Casual Silences*, 228.

45. *Catechism of the Catholic Church*, 2nd ed. (New York: Doubleday, 1997), 368.

46. J. I. Packer, *Concise Theology: A Guide to Historic Christian Beliefs* (Wheaton, IL: Tyndale House, 1993), 210.

47. Pinsker, "Soft Lights, Academic Talk," 114.

Chapter 4

1. Anne O'Malley, "An Interview with Susan Minot," *Poets and Writers Magazine* 15, no. 3 (1987): 13; Kelli Pryor, "The Story of Her Life," *New York* 22, no. 23 (1989): 54.

2. Dave Wiech, "Author Interviews: Back in Bed with Susan Minot," Powells.com. http://www.powells.com/authors/minot.html. Accessed May 20, 2009.

3. Scholarship on the short-story cycle has been fairly extensive. The best discussion of *Monkeys* as a cycle is James Nagel's "Susan Minot's *Monkeys* and the Cycle Paradigm," in *The Contemporary American Short-Story Cycle: The Ethnic Resonance of Genre* (Baton Rouge: Louisiana State University Press, 2001), 80–103.

4. Seven of the stories were published prior to the appearance of *Monkeys*; "Wildflowers" and "Party Blues" are the only original components of the book.

5. Pryor, "The Story of Her Life," 54.

6. Dinitia Smith, "The Minots: A Literary Clan Whose Stories Divide Them," *New York Times*, May 27, 2004, E5.

7. Sam Minot, *The Strange Poverty of the Rich* (Lincoln, NE: iUniverse, 2004), ix, 39. Sam's claim about first letters is only partly accurate: Caitlin for Carrie, Sophie for Susan, Delilah for Dinah, Gus for George, Sherman for Sam, and Chicky for Chris. Eliza's fictional counterpart is named Miranda, and Helen's is Rose.

8. "Review of *Monkeys* by Susan Minot," *Jim Kobak's Kirkus Reviews* 54 (March 1, 1986): 332.

9. Jonathan Yardley, "Children on Shaky Ground," *Washington Post*, April 23, 1986, B2.

10. Anne Tyler, "The Art of Omission," *New Republic* (June 23, 1986): 34, 36.

11. Walter Bede, "Pall in the Family," *Village Voice*, August 5, 1986, 46.

12. A. R. Gurney Jr., "Men, Women, and Children First," *New York Times Book Review*, April 27, 1986, 27; Michiko Kakutani, "It's Your Choice, Lilian: The Cad or the Cluck," Review of *Folly* by Susan Minot, *New York Times*, October 20, 1992, 17; Roxana Robinson, "Remains of the Day," Review of *Evening* by Susan Minot, *New York Times Book Review*, October 11, 1998, 12; Thomas Hinde, "Bursts of Lucidity," *Books and Bookmen* (September 1986): 37.

13. Nagel, "Susan Minot's *Monkeys*," 84–85.

14. Susan Minot, *Monkeys* (New York: E. P. Dutton, 1986), 1. All subsequent references are from the same edition.

15. "Team Awards," Official Website of Harvard University Athletics, http://www.gocrimson.com/sports/mice/history/teamawards. Accessed February 14, 2010. The website indicates that George Minot won the award for the 1949–50 season but was part of the graduating class of 1949.

16. Nagel, "Susan Minot's *Monkeys*," 87.

17. Deborah Solomon, "A Family History in Rewrite," *New York Times*, July 9, 2006, 32.

18. Smith, "The Minots," 5.

19. Tom Shales, "The Grand Old Man of TV Tots and Other Little Rascals," *Washington Post*, July 8, 1977, B9.

20. Nagel, "Susan Minot's *Monkeys*," 91.

21. Sam Minot, *The Strange Poverty*, 32–33.

22. "Boxed Island" is based on Burnt Island, off the coast of North Haven, Maine. Sam Minot talks about it frequently in his memoir. See, for example, Sam Minot, *The Strange Poverty*, 49.

23. James George Frazer, *The Golden Bough* (New York: Touchstone, 1996), 760, 762.

24. Nagel, "Susan Minot's *Monkeys*," 95.

25. Ludwig Bemelmans, *Madeline* (New York: Puffin Books, 1998); Bemelmans, *Madeline and the Gypsies* (New York: Puffin Books, 2000). I am indebted to James Nagel for identifying these titles. See Nagel, "Susan Minot's *Monkeys*," 94.

26. Susan Minot, "The Navigator," in *The Invisible Enemy: Alcoholism and the Modern Short Story*, ed. Miriam Dow and Jennifer Regan (St. Paul: Graywolf Press, 1989), 3–14.

27. This scene includes two important biographical parallels. In his memoir, Sam Minot explains that Helen Minot was referred to as "Carrie," a nickname her husband gave her as an allusion to the prohibitionist Carry Nation: "We, from alcoholic families, have a tendency to be drinkers. My mom didn't even drink; consequently, my dad nicknamed her 'Carrie' after the prohibitionist, Carry Nation. The results were that she adopted this name, dropping her former: Helen. Mom had expressed to me that both her parents were drinkers and she felt that if she drank alcohol that she would be an alcoholic as well. This was one galvanizing facts [*sic*] that I re-learned in rehab and

I wasn't bashful about letting my father know this." Sam describes many confrontations with his father, George, that involved alcohol. Sam Minot, *The Strange Poverty*, 36–37.

28. In Carver's "Vitamins," the protagonist returns home from a night of drinking and experiences a fittingly pathetic sequence of events: "I couldn't take any more tonight. 'Go back to sleep, honey. I'm looking for something,' I said. I knocked some stuff out of the medicine chest. Things rolled into the sink. 'Where's the aspirin?' I said. I knocked down some more things. I didn't care. Things kept falling" (109). Raymond Carver, "Vitamins," in *Cathedral* (New York: Vintage, 1989).

29. Nagel, "Susan Minot's *Monkeys*," 98.

30. Susan Minot, "Accident," *New Yorker* (November 7, 1983): 50–54.

31. See Nagel, "Susan Minot's *Monkeys*," 98.

32. Sam Minot, *The Strange Poverty*, 61.

33. George Minot's *The Blue Bowl* implies that Sam's anger toward his father was considerable. The Sam figure, Simon Curtis, is a painter and nomad. Early in the novel, he stalks his father, a cold and secretive alcoholic, while surreptitiously sleeping at the family home in Manchester-by-the-Sea, Massachusetts.

34. Solomon, "A Family History in Rewrite," 33.

35. Sam Minot, *The Strange Poverty*, 62.

36. Susan Minot, "The Silver Box," *Grand Street* 5 (Winter 1986): 26–33.

37. George Minot includes a version of the ash-scattering ceremony in *The Blue Bowl* (119).

Chapter 5

1. When asked how long it took her to write the novel, Cisneros often responded to interviewers that it took nine years (1993–2002). In an interview for an article that appeared in *The Oregonian*, however, she said, "I just found some tapes of my father talking from 1988, so the concept was around a lot longer, I guess." Jeff Baker, "Journey through the Heart," *The Oregonian*, October 5, 2003, E7.

2. Renee H. Shea, "Truth, Lies, and Memory: A Profile of Sandra Cisneros," *Poets and Writers* 30, no. 5 (2002): 35–36.

3. Gayle Elliott, "An Interview with Sandra Cisneros," *Missouri Review* 25, no. 1 (2002): 98.

4. Jeff Guinn, "Self-Possession," *St. Paul Pioneer-Press*, September 22, 2002, 10E.

5. Jeff Baker, "Journey through the Heart," E8.

6. For example, "Dirt" was published in 1996 in *Grand Street*. Several paragraphs were added to create the version that appears in *Caramelo*, most of which involve Zoila Reyes and Awful Grandmother. Other changes, such as the switch from "Vienna hot-dog stand" to "Jim's Original Hot Dogs," seem motivated by Cisneros's desire for historical and geographical accuracy. See "Dirt," *Grand Street* 57 (Summer 1996): 122–25; and "Dirt," in *Caramelo* (New York: Knopf, 2002), 294–98.

7. Sandra Cisneros, *Caramelo* (New York: Knopf, 2002), 56. All subsequent references are to the same edition.

8. Betsy Kline, "Cisneros Stirs Up a Spanish Treat," *Pittsburgh Post-Gazette*, October 27, 2002, F3.

9. Keir Graff, "Review of *Caramelo* by Sandra Cisneros," *Booklist* 98 (August 1, 2002): 1883; Adriana Lopez, "Sandra Cisneros's *Caramelo*: Caramel-Colored Prose," *Library Journal* 127, no. 15 (2002): 90.

10. Elizabeth Johnston, "Family Stories, Healthy Lies," *Toronto Star*, January 12, 2003, D14. Johnston apparently did not know that Cisneros had published parts of *Caramelo* as stand-alone stories before including them in the novel.

11. Ana Lopez, "Book World Raves: *Caramelo* or *Puro Cuento*," *Washington Post Book World*, December 1, 2002, 4.

12. Juanita Heredia, "Voyages South and North: The Politics of Transnational Gender Identity in *Caramelo* and *American Chica*," *Latino Studies* 5, no. 3 (2007): 348.

13. Gabriella Gutiérrez y Muhs, "Sandra Cisneros and Her Trade of the Free World," *Rocky Mountain Review of Language and Literature* 60, no. 2 (2006): 23–36.

14. Heather Alumbaugh, "Narrative Coyotes: Migration and Narrative Voice in Sandra Cisneros's *Caramelo*," *MELUS* 35, no. 1 (2010): 53–75; James Phelan, "Rhetoric, Politics, and Ethics in Sandra Cisneros's *Caramelo*," in *What Democracy Looks Like: New Critical Realism for a Post-Seattle World*, ed. Amy Schrager Lang and Cecelia Tichi (New Brunswick, NJ: Rutgers University Press, 2006), 114–22; and María José García Vizcaíno, "Voices, Discourse, and Identity in Chicano Narrative," *Journal of American Studies of Turkey* 23 (2006): 95–103.

15. See, for example, the notes on 9 and 123 of *Caramelo*.

16. Jessica Magnani, "Divided Loyalties: Latina Family Sagas and National Romances" (PhD diss., University of Florida, 2007), 146.

17. Robert Birnbaum, "Sandra Cisneros: Author of *Caramelo* Talks with Robert Birnbaum," *Identity Theory*. Web-based journal. http://www.identitytheory.com/people/birnbaum76.html. Accessed April 8, 2010.

18. Ed Morales, "Imaginary Homeland," *Críticas* 2, no. 5 (September/October, 2002): 29.

19. Margaria Fichtner, "Mouth of the Border," *Miami Herald*, November 17, 2002, 12M.

20. Birnbaum, "Sandra Cisneros"; Teresa K. Weaver, "Zen Informs Latina Novelist's Work," *Atlanta Constitution*, November 22, 2002, E7; Sandra Cisneros, "Do You Know Me?: I Wrote *The House on Mango Street*," *The Americas Review* 15, no. 1 (1987): 78. Cisneros's mention of *Dreamtigers* suggests that she was referring to a translation of Borges's *El Hacedor* (1960), or *The Maker*, completed by Mildred Boyer and Harold Morland. "Dreamtigers" is the name of a piece in the collection. Jorge Luis Borges, *Dreamtigers*, trans. Mildred Boyer and Harold Morland (New York: E. P. Dutton, 1970).

21. Eduardo Galeano, *The Book of Embraces*, trans. Cedric Belfrage (New York: Norton, 1992), 11.

22. Birnbaum, "Sandra Cisneros."

23. Cisneros is familiar with the form. In an interview with Robert Birnbaum, she talked about the work of Brazilian author Clarice Lispector. Birnbaum, "Sandra Cisneros."

24. Giovanni Pontiero, preface to *Selected Crônicas* by Clarice Lispector, trans. Giovanni Pontiero (New York: New Directions, 1992), vii.

25. Clarice Lispector, *Selected Crônicas*, trans. Giovanni Pontiero (New York: New Directions, 1992), 72.

26. Ray Suarez, "Conversation: Cisneros," transcript from *NewsHour with Jim Lehrer*, October 15, 2002. http://www.pbs.org/newshour/bb/entertainment-july-dec02-cisneros_10-15/. Accessed October 31, 2014.

27. Borges, "The Witness," in *Dreamtigers*, 39.

28. Shea, "Truth, Lies, and Memory," 33.

29. Cornelia Butler Flora and Jan L. Flora, "The Fotonovela as a Tool for Class and Cultural Domination," *Latin American Perspectives* 5, no. 1, Culture in the Age of Mass Media (Winter 1978): 135.

30. For in-depth discussions of telenovelas and Latino culture, see O. Hugo Benavides, *Drugs, Thugs, and Divas* (Austin: University of Texas Press, 2008); Vivian Barrera and Denise D. Bielby, "Places, Faces, and Other Familiar Things: The Cultural Experience of Telenovela Viewing among Latinos in the United States," *Journal of Popular Culture* 34, no. 4 (2001): 1–18; and Jorge González, "Understanding Telenovelas as a Cultural Front: A Complex Analysis of a Complex Reality," in *Telenovelas*, ed. Ilan Stavans (Santa Barbara, CA: Greenwood, 2010), 68–78.

31. González, "Understanding Telenovelas," 68–69.

32. Benavides, *Drugs, Thugs, and Divas*, 34.

33. Morales, "Imaginary Homeland," 32.

34. Annette Sandoval, *The Directory of Saints* (New York: Signet, 1997), 238.

35. Stefano Brufani, *Saint Anthony of Padua*, trans. Richard Pierce (Milan: Skira, 2008), 14.

36. Fritz Lanham, "Cisneros on Writing and Herself," *Texas: Houston Chronicle Magazine*, October 6, 2002, 8.

Chapter 6

1. Cormac McCarthy, Interview with Oprah Winfrey, "Oprah's Exclusive Interview with Cormac McCarthy Video," Oprah's Book Club, added July 8, 2008, http://www.oprah.com/oprahsbookclub/Oprahs-Exclusive-Interview-with-Cormac-McCarthy-Video, accessed August 3, 2010. *The Road* is dedicated to John Francis McCarthy, who was eight years old when the book was published in 2006.

2. In her analysis of the stylistic difference between *Blood Meridian* and *The Road*,

Ashley Kunsa maintains that "in *Blood Meridian* 'War is god' . . . , linguistically and metaphysically. The novel 'sings hymns of violence' (Shaviro 145) in prose often allusive and baroque to the breaking point, prose frequently likened to that of William Faulkner. The style of *The Road*, on the contrary, is pared down, elemental, a triumph over the dead echoes of the abyss and, alternately, over relentless ironic gesturing." Kunsa's description of McCarthy's prose works equally well as a description of Minimalistic style. Kunsa, "'Maps of the World in Its Becoming': Post-Apocalyptic Naming in Cormac McCarthy's *The Road*," *Journal of Modern Literature* 33, no. 1 (2009): 58. Kunsa cited Steven Shaviro, "'The Very Life of the Darkness': A Reading of *Blood Meridian*," in *Perspectives on* Blood Meridian, ed. Edwin T. Arnold and Dianne C. Luce (Jackson: University Press of Mississippi, 1999), 145–58.

3. Cormac McCarthy, *The Road* (New York: Vintage, 2006), 26. All subsequent references are to the same edition.

4. For a detailed examination of the geography of *The Road*, see Wesley G. Morgan, "The Route and Roots of *The Road*," *Cormac McCarthy Journal* 6 (Autumn 2008): 39–47.

5. Laura Philpot Benedict, "'The Road': A Post-Apocalyptic Masterpiece: Cormac McCarthy's Father-Son Road Trip by Turns Grim and Tender," *Grand Rapids Press*, October 22, 2006, J8.

6. Cliff Froehlich, "Bleak Landscape, Spare Language Frame Survival Story," *St. Louis Post-Dispatch*, October 8, 2006, F9.

7. Kenneth Lincoln, *Cormac McCarthy: American Canticles* (New York: Palgrave Macmillan, 2009), 164. The italics are Lincoln's emphasis.

8. Mark Schechner, "McCarthy's Latest Travels His Bleakest Terrain Yet," *Buffalo News*, October 8, 2006, G5.

9. Cormac McCarthy and Oprah Winfrey, http://www.oprah.com/oprahsbookclub/Oprahs-Exclusive-Interview-with-Cormac-McCarthy-Video. Accessed August 3, 2010.

10. See Cormac McCarthy, "The Road—1st Draft," manuscripts, box 87, folder 6, leaves 74–80, 87, 141–153, Cormac McCarthy Papers, The Witliff Collections, Southwestern Writers Collection, Alkek Library, Texas State University–San Marcos, San Marcos, Texas. McCarthy's early drafts are not paginated; leaf numbers are assigned according to the order the pages were in as of May 12–13, 2010.

11. The man's lack of faith in God, coupled with his conclusion that Nature is indifferent, echoes the sentiment expressed in Stephen Crane's "96" from the collection *War Is Kind*:

> A man said to the universe:
> "Sir, I exist!"
> "However," replied the universe,
> "The fact has not created in me
> A sense of obligation."

Crane, "96," *The Portable Stephen Crane*, ed. Joseph Katz (New York: Penguin, 1977), 548.

12. Cormac McCarthy, "The Road—1st Draft," leaf 141. Words and phrases McCarthy writes in the space above a completed sentence have been placed in double parentheses.

13. McCarthy, "The Road—1st Draft," leaf 141. McCarthy moved the term "soundless" to the position marked with an asterisk.

14. McCarthy, "The Road—1st Draft," leaves 141–44, 146 49.

15. Cormac McCarthy, "Road—Old 2nd Draft," manuscripts, box 87, folder 7, p. 85, Cormac McCarthy Papers, The Witliff Collections, Southwestern Writers Collection, Alkek Library, Texas State University-San Marcos, San Marcos, Texas.

16. In *Understanding Cormac McCarthy*, Steven Frye posits that "the overall style is minimalist and reminiscent of Ernest Hemingway, and McCarthy orchestrates an homage to his predecessor in a number of vivid allusions. As the third-person narrator recounts the father's memory of the boy's birth, the mother's pain and the father's response are rendered in detail: 'Her cries meant nothing to him' (59). This is a line taken almost verbatim from Hemingway's 'Indian Camp,' as Nick Adams's father performs a cesarean section on an Indian woman while his son watches." Frye's comment is insightful, but he is incorrect in his assertion that McCarthy has quoted Hemingway "almost verbatim." Dr. Adams tells Nick that "her screams are not important. I don't hear them because they are not important" (16). The implications are similar, however, as both men are able to unemotionally focus on the task at hand because they are doctors. Frye, *Understanding Cormac McCarthy* (Columbia: University of South Carolina Press, 2009), 171–72; and Ernest Hemingway, "Indian Camp," in *In Our Time* (New York: Scribner, 1930), 16.

17. McCarthy, "The Road—1st Draft," leaf 5.

18. Cormac McCarthy, "Old Road Notes," manuscripts, box 87, folder 3, leaf 36, Cormac McCarthy Papers, The Witliff Collections, Southwestern Writers Collection, Alkek Library, Texas State University–San Marcos, San Marcos, Texas.

19. McCarthy, "The Road—1st Draft," leaf 54.

20. Steven H. Miles, *The Hippocratic Oath and the Ethics of Medicine* (Oxford: Oxford University Press, 2004), xiv. Miles examines this part of the oath from a number of perspectives. He considers whether it is a vow against euthanasia, assisting in executions, or murder. Given the historical context of the oath, he concludes that it is a promise not to kill or assist in plots to take another person's life (66–80).

21. Richard B. Woodward, "Cormac McCarthy's Venomous Fiction," *New York Times Magazine* (April 19, 1992), 30.

22. McCarthy, "The Road—1st Draft," leaf 51.

23. Johannes de Silentio [Søren Kierkegaard], "Fear and Trembling, Dialectical Lyric," in *The Essential Kierkegaard*, ed. Howard V. Hong and Edna H. Hong (Princeton, NJ: Princeton University Press, 2000), 101.

24. Genesis 19:1–10.

25. Tim Blackmore, "Life of War, Death of the Rest: The Shining Path of Cormac McCarthy's Thermonuclear America," *Bulletin of Science and Technology Society* 29, no. 19 (2009): 18.

26. The massive amounts of ash and snow described in *The Road* could have been caused by either a comet-asteroid strike or "nuclear winter." For a thorough explanation of "dust theory," see John S. Lewis, *Rain of Iron and Ice: The Very Real Threat of Comet and Asteroid Bombardment* (New York: Perseus, 1997), 91–99.

27. McCarthy, "Old Road Notes," leaf 13.

28. Ibid., leaf 14.

29. While it is debatable whether Sylder kills Rattner in self-defense, the narrator describes how the latter begins to run away after the initial attack. Instead of letting him go, Sylder catches him and chokes him to death. McCarthy adumbrates the murder in an earlier scene in which Sylder nearly kills a coworker before being stopped by the appearance of his boss.

30. Whether the war has anything to do with Nick's journey into the wilderness is a point of contention. For an excellent synopsis of the debate, see George Monteiro, "By the Book: 'Big Two-Hearted River' and Izaak Walton," in *Ernest Hemingway: The Oak Park Legacy*, ed. James Nagel (Tuscaloosa: University of Alabama Press, 1996), 145–61.

31. Ernest Hemingway, "Big Two-Hearted River: Part I," in *In Our Time* (New York: Scribner, 1925), 133.

32. Thomas H. Schaub, "Secular Scripture and Cormac McCarthy's *The Road*," *Renascence* 61, no. 3 (2009): 156.

33. Hemingway, "River: Part I," 138.

34. Hemingway, "Indian Camp," 19.

35. McCarthy, "Old Road Notes," leaf 24.

36. "By the Numbers: New England: September 21, 2008, Marks the 70th Anniversary of the Great Hurricane of 1938," *Yankee* 72, no. 5 (2008): 34. An Associated Press article printed on September 22, 1938, details the breadth of the destruction, reporting damage from Vermont, Massachusetts, and Rhode Island. See "Storm Batters All New England; Providence Hit by Tidal Wave," *New York Times*, September 22, 1938, 1, 18.

37. Hemingway, "Indian Camp," 18.

38. Luke 23:39–43.

39. Allen Josephs, "What's at the End of *The Road*?" *South Atlantic Review* 74 (Summer 2009): 29–30.

Conclusion

1. Richard B. Woodward, "Cormac McCarthy's Venomous Fiction," *New York Times Magazine* (April 19, 1992), 30.

2. Ann-Marie Karlsson, "The Hyperrealistic Short Story: A Postmodern Twilight Zone," in *Criticism in the Twilight Zone: Postmodern Perspectives on Literature and*

Politics, ed. Danuta Zadworna-Fjellstad and Lennart Björk (Stockholm: Almqvist & Wiksell International, 1990), 147.

3. Cormac McCarthy, *The Road* (New York: Vintage, 2006), 21.

4. Raymond Carver, "Cathedral," in *Cathedral* (New York: Vintage, 1989), 209.

5. Carver, "Cathedral," 227.

6. Raymond Carver and William L. Stull, "Matters of Life and Death," in *Conversations with Raymond Carver*, ed. Marshall Bruce Gentry and William L. Stull (Jackson: University Press of Mississippi, 1990), 185.

7. Stephen Crane, *Maggie: A Girl of the Streets, The Portable Stephen Crane*, ed. Joseph Katz (New York: Viking, 1977), 74.

8. Ernest Hemingway, "Indian Camp," in *In Our Time* (New York: Scribner, 1930), 19.

9. Ernest Hemingway, "Chapter VI," in *In Our Time* (New York: Scribner, 1930), 63.

10. Hemingway, "Indian Camp," manuscripts, folder 493, Hemingway Collection, John F. Kennedy Library, Boston, 5–6.

11. Susan Minot, *Monkeys* (New York: Vintage, 1986), 158.

12. McInerney, *Bright Lights, Big City* (New York: Vintage, 1984), 43.

13. Wyndham Lewis, "The Dumb Ox: A Study of Ernest Hemingway, 'Life and Letters,'" in *Hemingway: The Critical Heritage*, ed. Jeffrey Meyers (Boston: Routledge and Kegan Paul, 1982), 187.

14. For a concise summary of Hemingway's involvement in *The Spanish Earth*, see Carlos Baker, *Hemingway: A Life Story* (New York: Macmillan, 1969), 307–12.

15. Quoted in Philip E. Simmons, *Deep Surfaces: Mass Culture and History in Postmodern American Fiction* (Athens: University of Georgia Press, 1997), 125.

16. Mark Helprin, "Introduction: The Canon under Siege," in *The Best American Short Stories 1988* (Boston: Houghton Mifflin, 1988), xxiv.

17. Robert Rebein, *Hicks, Tribes, and Dirty Realists: American Fiction after Postmodernism* (Lexington: University of Kentucky Press, 2009), 42.

18. Sandra Cisneros, *Caramelo* (New York: Knopf, 2002), 18.

19. Ernest Hemingway, "Big Two-Hearted River: Part I," in *In Our Time* (New York: Scribner, 1930), 139.

20. McCarthy, *The Road*, 88.

21. Rebein, *Hicks, Tribes, and Dirty Realists*, 38–39.

22. John W. Aldridge, *Talents and Technicians: Literary Chic and the New Assembly-Line Fiction* (New York: Scribner's, 1992), 48–49.

23. See Ernest Hemingway, *Death in the Afternoon* (New York: Scribner, 1932), 192.

24. Arthur Miller, Gore Vidal, Richard Watts, John Beaufort, Martin Dworkin, David W. Thompson, and Phillip Gelb, "'Death of a Salesman': A Symposium," *Tulane Drama Review* 2, no. 3 (1958): 67.

25. Simmons, *Deep Surfaces*, 124.

26. Sheldon Norman Grebstein, *Hemingway's Craft* (Carbondale: Southern Illinois University Press, 1973), 26.

Bibliography

Abádi Nagy, Zoltán. "Minimalism vs. Postmodernism In Contemporary Fiction." *Neohelicon* 28, no. 1 (2001): 129–44.

———. "The Narratorial Function in Minimalist Fiction." *Neohelicon* 27, no. 2 (2000): 237–48.

Adair, William. "Hemingway's 'Out of Season': The End of the Line." In *New Critical Approaches to the Short Stories of Ernest Hemingway*, edited by Jackson J. Benson, 341–46. Durham, NC: Duke University Press, 1990.

Adleman, Bob, and Tess Gallagher. *Carver Country: The World of Raymond Carver.* New York: Charles Scribner's Sons, 1990.

Aldridge, John W. *Talents and Technicians: Literary Chic and the New Assembly-Line Fiction.* New York: Scribner's, 1992.

Alumbaugh, Heather. "Narrative Coyotes: Migration and Narrative Voice in Sandra Cisneros's *Caramelo*." *MELUS* 35, no. 1 (2010): 53–75.

Anderson, Sherwood. "I Want to Know Why." In *The Triumph of the Egg*, 5–20. New York: B. W. Huebsch, 1921.

Azevedo, Carlos. "Oak Park as the Thing Left Out: Surface and Depth in 'Soldier's Home.'" In *Ernest Hemingway: The Oak Park Legacy*, edited by James Nagel, 96–107. Tuscaloosa: University of Alabama Press, 1996.

Baker, Carlos. *Ernest Hemingway: A Life Story.* New York: Macmillan, 1988.

———. *Hemingway: The Writer as Artist.* Princeton, NJ: Princeton University Press, 1972.

Baker, Carlos, ed. *Ernest Hemingway: Selected Letters, 1917–1961.* New York: Scribner, 1981.

Baker, Sheridan. *Ernest Hemingway: An Introduction and Interpretation.* New York: Holt, Rinehart and Winston, 1967.

———. "Hemingway's Two-Hearted River." In *The Short Stories of Ernest Hemingway: Critical Essays*, edited by Jackson J. Benson, 150–59. Durham, NC: Duke University Press, 1975.

Banks, Russell. "Raymond Carver: Our Stephen Crane." *The Atlantic* 268, no. 2 (1991): 99–103.

Barrera, Vivian, and Denise D. Bielby. "Places, Faces, and Other Familiar Things: The Cultural Experience of Telenovela Viewing among Latinos in the United States." *Journal of Popular Culture* 34, no. 4 (2001): 1–18.

Barth, John, "A Few Words about Minimalism." *New York Times Book Review*, December 28, 1986, 1–2, 25.

Bashō, Matsuo. *The Sound of Water.* Trans. Sam Hamill. Boston: Shambhala, 2000.

Battcock, Gregory, ed. *Minimal Art: A Critical Anthology*. New York: E. P. Dutton, 1968.

Bede, Walter. "Pall in the Family." *Village Voice*, August 5, 1986, 46–47.

Bellamy, Joe David. "A Symposium on Contemporary American Fiction: Joe David Bellamy." Part 1 of 2. *Michigan Quarterly Review* 26, no. 4 (1987): 695–96.

Bemelmans, Ludwig. *Madeline*. New York: Puffin Books, 1998.

———. *Madeline and the Gypsies*. New York: Puffin Books, 2000.

Benavides, O. Hugo. *Drugs, Thugs, and Divas*. Austin: University of Texas Press, 2008.

Benedict, Laura Philpot. "'The Road': A Post-Apocalyptic Masterpiece: Cormac McCarthy's Father-Son Road Trip by Turns Grim and Tender." *Grand Rapids Press*, October 22, 2006, J8.

Bethea, Arthur F. *Technique and Sensibility in the Fiction of Raymond Carver*. New York: Routledge, 2001.

Birkerts, Sven. *American Energies: Essays on Fiction*. New York: William Morrow, 1992.

Birnbaum, Robert. "Sandra Cisneros: Author of *Caramelo* Talks with Robert Birnbaum." *Identity Theory*. Web-based journal. http://www.identitytheory.com/people/birnbaum76.html. Accessed April 8, 2010.

Blackmore, Tim. "Life of War, Death of the Rest: The Shining Path of Cormac McCarthy's Thermonuclear America." *Bulletin of Science and Technology Society* 29, no. 19 (2009): 18–36.

Borges, Jorge Luis. *Dreamtigers*. Trans. Mildred Boyer and Harold Morland. New York: E. P. Dutton, 1970.

Boville, Belén. *The Cocaine War in Context: Drugs and Politics*. Trans. Lorena Terando. New York: Algora, 2004.

Boyle, T. Coraghessan. "A Symposium on Contemporary American Fiction: T. Coraghessan Boyle." Part 1 of 2. *Michigan Quarterly Review* 26, no. 4 (1987): 707, 709.

Brenner, Gerry. "From 'Sepi Jingan' to 'The Mother of a Queen': Hemingway's Three Epistemologic Formulas for Short Fiction." In *New Critical Approaches to the Short Stories of Ernest Hemingway*, edited by Jackson J. Benson, 156–71. Durham, NC: Duke University Press, 1990.

Bricklebank, Peter. "Review of *Bright Lights, Big City* by Jay McInerney." *Library Journal* 109, no. 16 (1984): 1863.

Bruccoli, Matthew J. *Ernest Hemingway's Apprenticeship: Oak Park, 1916–1917*. Washington, DC: Microcard Editions, 1971.

Brufani, Stefano. *Saint Anthony of Padua*. Trans. Richard Pierce. Milan: Skira, 2008

Buford, Bill. "Dirty Realism: New Writing from America." *Granta* 8 (1983): 4–5.

Burhans, Clinton S. "The Complex Unity of *In Our Time*." In *Critical Essays on Ernest Hemingway's* In Our Time, edited by Michael S. Reynolds, 88–102. Boston: G. K. Hall, 1983.

Buzbee, Lewis, and Mona Simpson. "Raymond Carver." In *Conversations with Raymond Carver*, edited by Marshall Bruce Gentry and William L. Stull, 31–52. Jackson: University Press of Mississippi, 1990.

"By the Numbers: New England: September 21, 2008, Marks the 70th Anniversary of the Great Hurricane of 1938." *Yankee* 72, no. 5 (2008): 34.

Campbell, Ewing. *Raymond Carver: A Study of the Short Fiction*. New York: Twayne, 1992.

Carver, Maryann Burk. *What It Used to Be Like: A Portrait of My Marriage to Raymond Carver*. New York: St. Martin's Griffin, 2006.

Carver, Raymond. "The Bridle." *New Yorker* 58 (July, 1982): 30–39.

———. "Careful." *Paris Review* 25 (Summer 1983): 222–34.

———. *Carver: Collected Stories*. Edited by William L. Stull and Maureen P. Carroll. New York: Library of America, 2009.

———. *Cathedral*. New York: Vintage Contemporaries, 1989.

———. "Cathedral." *Atlantic Monthly* 248 (September 1981): 23–29.

———. "Chef's House" *New Yorker* 57 (November 30, 1981): 42–43.

———. "The Compartment." *Antioch Review* 41 (Spring 1983): 133–41.

———. "Errand." In *Elephant and Other Stories*, 111–24. London: Vintage, 2003.

———. "Feathers." *Atlantic Monthly* 250 (September 1982): 62–69.

———. "Fever." *North American Review* 268 (June 1983): 11–19.

———. "On Writing." In *Call If You Need Me*, edited by William L. Stull, 87–92. New York: Vintage Books, 2000.

———. "Preservation." *Grand Street* 2 (Spring 1983): 7–16.

———. "A Small, Good Thing." *Ploughshares* 8, nos. 1–2 (1982): 213–40.

———. "A Symposium on Contemporary American Fiction: Raymond Carver." Part 1 of 2. *Michigan Quarterly Review* 26, no. 4 (1987): 710–11.

———. "The Train." *Antaeus* 49/50 (Spring/Summer 1983): 151–57.

———. "Vitamins." *Esquire* 96 (October 1981): 130, 132, 134–39.

———. "Where I'm Calling From." *New Yorker* 58 (March 15, 1982): 41–48, 51.

Carver, Raymond, and William L. Stull. "Matters of Life and Death." In *Conversations with Raymond Carver*, edited by Marshall Bruce Gentry and William L. Stull, 177–91. Jackson. University Press of Mississippi, 1990.

Catechism of the Catholic Church. 2nd ed. New York: Doubleday, 1997.

Cheatham, George. "The World War I Battle of Mons and Hemingway's *In Our Time* Chapter III." *Hemingway Review* 26, no. 2 (2007): 44–57.

Cheever, John. "The Five-Forty-Eight." In *The Stories of John Cheever*, 236–47. New York: Vintage, 2000.

Chekhov, Anton. "The Grasshopper." In *Anton Chekhov's Short Stories*, edited by Ralph E. Matlaw, 69–90. Trans. Constance Garnett. New York: W. W. Norton, 1979.

Cisneros, Sandra. *Caramelo*. New York: Knopf, 2002.

———. "Do You Know Me? I Wrote *The House on Mango Street*." *The Americas Review* 15, no. 1 (1987): 77–79.

———. "Dirt." *Grand Street* 57 (Summer 1996): 122–25.

———. *The House on Mango Street*. New York: Vintage, 1991.

Clark, Robert C. "Keeping the Reader in the House: American Minimalism, Literary Impressionism, and Raymond Carver's Cathedral." *Journal of Modern Literature* 36, no. 1 (2012): 104–18.

Cohen, Milton A. *Hemingway's Laboratory: The Paris "in our time."* Tuscaloosa: University of Alabama Press, 2005.

Comley, Nancy R., and Robert Scholes. *Hemingway's Genders: Rereading the Hemingway Text*. New Haven, CT: Yale University Press, 1994.

Cox, Ida. "Cherry Picking Blues." In *Complete Recorded Works, 1923–1938: Volume 2, 1924–1925*. Compact disc. Document Records, 1995.

Crane, Stephen. *Maggie: A Girl of the Streets. The Portable Stephen Crane*. Edited by Joseph Katz, 3–74. New York: Viking, 1977.

———. "96." *The Portable Stephen Crane*. Edited by Joseph Katz, 548. New York: Penguin, 1977.

Curnutt, Kirk. *Wise Economies: Brevity and Storytelling in American Short Stories*. Moscow: University of Idaho Press, 1997.

De Chasca, Edmund S. *John Gould Fletcher and Imagism*. Columbia: University of Missouri Press, 1978.

DeFalco, Joseph. *The Hero in Hemingway's Short Stories*. Pittsburgh: University of Pittsburgh Press, 1963.

Donaldson, Scott. *By Force of Will: The Life and Art of Ernest Hemingway*. Lincoln, NE: iUniverse, 2001.

———. "'A Very Short Story' as Therapy." In *Hemingway's Neglected Short Fiction: New Perspectives*, edited by Susan F. Beegel, 99–105. Tuscaloosa: University of Alabama Press, 1989.

Duka, John. "Notes on Fashion." *New York Times*, September 14, 1984: B9.

Edenfield, Olivia Carr. "Doomed Biologically: Sex and Entrapment in Ernest Hemingway's 'Cross-Country Snow.'" *Hemingway Review* 19, no. 1 (1999): 141–48.

Elliott, Gayle. "An Interview with Sandra Cisneros." *Missouri Review* 25, no. 1 (2002): 98.

Elser, Bernard, Hollace S. Mittleman, and Richard E. Mittleman. "Cocaine." *American Journal of Nursing* 84 (September 1984): 1092–95.

Facknitz, Mark A. R. "'The Calm,' 'A Small, Good Thing,' and 'Cathedral': Raymond Carver and the Rediscovery of Human Worth." *Studies in Short Fiction* 23 (Fall 1986): 287–96.

Feiling, Tom. *The Candy Machine: How Cocaine Took Over the World*. London: Penguin, 2009.

Fenton, Charles A. *The Apprenticeship of Ernest Hemingway: The Early Years*. New York: Viking, 1960.

Ferguson, Kevin L. "Engaging the Eighties: Ethics, Objects, Periods." PhD diss., City University of New York, 2007.

Fichtner, Margaria. "Mouth of the Border." *The Miami Herald*, November 17, 2002: 1M, 12M.

Flora, Cornelia Butler, and Jan L. Flora. "The Fotonovela as a Tool for Class and Cultural Domination." *Latin American Perspectives* 5, no. 1, Culture in the Age of Mass Media (1978): 134–50.

Flora, Joseph. *Ernest Hemingway: A Study of the Short Fiction*. Boston: G. K. Hall, 1989.

———. *Hemingway's Nick Adams*. Baton Rouge: Louisiana State University Press, 1982.

Fludernik, Monika. "Second Person Fiction: Narrative You as Addressee and/or Protagonist." *AAA, Arbelten aus Anglistik und Amerikanistik* 18, no. 2 (1993): 217–47.

Ford, Richard. "A Symposium on Contemporary American Fiction: Richard Ford." Part 1 of 2. *Michigan Quarterly Review* 26, no. 4 (1987): 730–31.

Frazer, James George. *The Golden Bough*. New York: Touchstone, 1996.

Froehlich, Cliff. "Bleak Landscape, Spare Language Frame Survival Story." *St. Louis Post-Dispatch*, October 8, 2006: F9.

Frye, Steven. *Understanding Cormac McCarthy*. Columbia: University of South Carolina Press, 2009.

Galeano, Eduardo. *The Book of Embraces*. Translated by Cedric Belfrage. New York: Norton, 1992.

García Vizcaíno, María José. "Voices, Discourse, and Identity in Chicano Narrative." *Journal of American Studies of Turkey* 23 (2006): 95–103.

Garland, Hamlin. *Crumbling Idols: Twelve Essays on Art Dealing Chiefly with Literature Painting and the Drama*. Edited by Jane Johnson. Cambridge, MA: Belknap Press of Harvard University Press, 1960.

González, Jorge. "Understanding Telenovelas as a Cultural Front: A Complex Analysis of a Complex Reality." In *Telenovelas*, edited by Ilan Stavans, 68–78. Santa Barbara, CA: Greenwood, 2010.

Gorra, Michael. "Review of *Cathedral* by Raymond Carver." *Hudson Review* 37 (Spring 1984): 155–58.

Graff, Keir. "Review of *Caramelo* by Sandra Cisneros." *Booklist* 98 (August 1, 2002): 1883.

Grebstein, Sheldon Norman. *Hemingway's Craft*. Carbondale: Southern Illinois University Press, 1973.

Gregory, Sinda, and Larry McCaffery. "An Interview with Raymond Carver." In *Raymond Carver: A Study of the Short Fiction*, by Ewing Campbell, 98–114. New York: Twayne, 1993.

Grimes, Larry. *The Religious Design of Hemingway's Early Fiction*. Ann Arbor: UMI Research Press, 1985.

Guinn, Jeff. "Self-Possession." *St. Paul Pioneer-Press*, September 22, 2002, 10E.

Gurney, A. R., Jr. "Men, Women, and Children First." *New York Times Book Review*, April 27, 1986, 1, 27.

Gutiérrez y Muhs, Gabriella. "Sandra Cisneros and Her Trade of the Free World." *Rocky Mountain Review of Language and Literature* 60, no. 2 (2006): 23–36.

Hagemann, E. R. "'Only Let the Story End as Soon as Possible': Time-and-History in Ernest Hemingway's *In Our Time*." In *New Critical Approaches to the Short Stories of Ernest Hemingway*, edited by Jackson J. Benson, 192–99. Durham, NC: Duke University Press, 1990.

Hakutani, Yoshinobu. "Ezra Pound, Yone Noguchi, and Imagism." *Modern Philology* 90, no. 1 (1992): 46–69.

———. *Haiku and Modernist Poetics*. New York: Palgrave Macmillan, 2009.

Hallett, Cynthia Whitney. "Minimalism and the Short Story." *Studies in Short Fiction* 33, no. 4 (1996): 487–95.

———. *Minimalism and the Short Story—Raymond Carver, Amy Hempel, and Mary Robison*. Lewiston, NY: Edwin Mellen Press, 1999.

Halpert, Sam. *. . . when we talk about Raymond Carver*. Layton, UT: Gibbs Smith, 1991.

Harmer, J. B. *Victory in Limbo: Imagism, 1908–1917*. New York: St. Martin's Press, 1975.

Hasbany, Richard. "The Shock of Vision: An Imagist Reading of *In Our Time*." In *Ernest Hemingway: Five Decades of Criticism*, edited by Linda W. Wagner, 224–40. East Lansing: Michigan State University Press, 1974.

Hathcock, Nelson. "'The Possibility of Resurrection': Re-Vision in Carver's 'Feathers' and 'Cathedral.'" *Studies in Short Fiction* 28 (Winter 1991): 31–39.

Helprin, Mark. "Introduction: The Canon under Siege." In *The Best American Short Stories 1988*, xi–xxxi. Boston: Houghton Mifflin, 1988.

Hemingway, Ernest. "Big Two-Hearted River: Part II." Manuscripts. Folder 274-2. Hemingway Collection, John F. Kennedy Library, Boston.

———. *By-Line: Ernest Hemingway*. Edited by William White. New York: Scribner, 1967.

———. "Conrad, Optimist and Moralist." *Transatlantic Review* 2, no. 3 (1924): 341–42.

———. "Crossroads—An Anthology: Pauline Snow." Reprinted in Peter Griffin, *Along with Youth*, 124. New York: Oxford University Press, 1985.

———. *Death in the Afternoon*. New York: Scribner, 1932.

———. "The End of Something." Manuscripts. Folder 373. Hemingway Collection, John F. Kennedy Library, Boston.

———. *Ernest Hemingway: 88 Poems*. Edited by Nicholas Gerogiannis. New York: Harcourt Brace, 1979.

———. *Ernest Hemingway: Selected Letters, 1917–1961.* Edited by Carlos Baker. New York: Scribner, 1981.

———. "IN OUR TIME." *Little Review* 9 (Spring 1923): 3–5.

———. *In Our Time.* New York: Scribner, 1930.

———. "Indian Camp." Manuscripts. Folder 493. Hemingway Collection, John F. Kennedy Library, Boston.

———. "Judgment of Manitou." *Tabula* 22 (February 1916): 9–10.

———. "Love." Manuscripts. Folder 633. Hemingway Collection, John F. Kennedy Library, Boston.

———. *A Moveable Feast.* New York: Scribner, 2009.

———. "Mr. and Mrs. Smith." Manuscripts. Folder 585. Hemingway Collection, John F. Kennedy Library, Boston.

———. "On Writing." In *The Nick Adams Stories*, 233–41. New York: Scribner, 1972.

———. "Soldier's Home." Manuscript. Folder 708. Hemingway Collection, John F. Kennedy Library, Boston.

———. *The Sun Also Rises.* New York: Scribner, 1926.

———. *Winner Take Nothing.* New York: Scribner, 1970.

Hemingway, Ernest, and George Plimpton. "The Art of Fiction XXI: Ernest Hemingway." *Paris Review* 18 (Spring 1958): 60–89.

Hemingway, Ernest, and Fred Wilcoxen. "Athletic Verse: The Tackle." *Tabula* 23 (March 1917): 39.

Heredia, Juanita. "Voyages South and North: The Politics of Transnational Gender Identity in *Caramelo* and *American Chica.*" *Latino Studies* 5, no. 3 (2007): 340–57.

Herzinger, Kim A. "Introduction: On the New Fiction." *Mississippi Review* 40–41 (Winter 1985): 7–22.

Hinde, Thomas. "Bursts of Lucidity." *Books and Bookmen* (September 1986): 37.

Hoagland, Edward. "A Symposium on Contemporary American Fiction: Edward Hoagland." Part 1 of 2. *Michigan Quarterly Review* 26, no. 4 (1987): 745.

Hulme, T. E. *Selected Writings.* Edited by Patrick McGuinness. New York: Routledge, 2003.

Ianonne, Carol. "The Fiction We Deserve." *Commentary* 83, no. 6 (1987): 60–63.

Iatrides, John O. "The United States and Greece in the Twentieth Century." In *Greece in the Twentieth Century*, edited by Theodore Couloumbis, Theodore Kariotis, and Fotini Bellou, 69–110. New York: Frank Cass, 2004.

Jenks, Tom. "Shameless." In *Remembering Ray: A Composite Biography of Raymond Carver*, edited by William L. Stull and Maureen P. Carroll, 141–43. Santa Barbara, CA: Capra Press, 1993.

Johnston, Elizabeth. "Family Stories, Healthy Lies." *Toronto Star*, January 12, 2003: D14.

Johnston, Kenneth G. "Hemingway and Cézanne: Doing the Country." *American Literature* 56, no. 1 (1984): 28–37.

———. "Hemingway's 'Out of Season' and the Psychology of Errors." In *Critical Essays on Ernest Hemingway's* In Our Time, edited by Michael S. Reynolds, 227–34. Boston: G. K. Hall, 1983.

Jones, Peter, ed. Introduction. *Imagist Poetry.* New York: Penguin, 2001.

Josephs, Allen. "What's at the End of *The Road*?" *South Atlantic Review* 74, no. 3 (2009): 20–30.

Kakutani, Michiko. "Books of the Times." *New York Times,* October 30, 1984: C17.

———. "It's Your Choice, Lilian: The Cad or the Cluck." Review of *Folly* by Susan Minot. *New York Times,* October 20, 1992: 17

Karl, Frederick R. *American Fictions, 1940–1980.* New York: Harper and Row, 1985.

Karlsson, Ann-Marie. "The Hyperrealistic Short Story: A Postmodern Twilight Zone." In *Criticism in the Twilight Zone: Postmodern Perspectives on Literature and Politics,* edited by Danuta Zadworna-Fjellstad and Lennart Björk, 144–53. Stockholm: Almqvist and Wiksell International, 1990.

Kaufmann, David. "Yuppie Postmodernism." *Arizona Quarterly* 47 (Summer 1991): 93–116.

Kenner, Hugh. *The Pound Era.* Berkeley: University of California Press, 1971.

Kirschke, James J. *Henry James and Impressionism.* New York: Whitston, 1981.

Kline, Betsy. "Cisneros Stirs Up a Spanish Treat." *Pittsburgh Post-Gazette,* October 27, 2002: F3.

Koch, Stephen, moderator. "Throwing Dirt on the Grave of Minimalism." *Columbia: A Magazine of Poetry and Prose* 14 (1989): 42–61.

Kronegger, Maria Elizabeth. *Literary Impressionism.* New Haven, CT: College and University Press, 1973.

Krutch, Joseph Wood. "The End of Art." *The Nation* (November 16, 1927): 548.

Kunsa, Ashley. "'Maps of the World in Its Becoming': Post-Apocalyptic Naming in Cormac McCarthy's *The Road.*" *Journal of Modern Literature* 33 (Fall 2009): 57–74.

Lanham, Fritz. "Cisneros on Writing and Herself." *Texas: Houston Chronicle Magazine,* October 6, 2002, 8–12, 14–15.

Leiter, Louis H. "Neural Projections in Hemingway's 'On the Quai at Smyrna.'" In *Critical Essays on Ernest Hemingway's* In Our Time, edited by Michael S. Reynolds, 138–40. Boston: G. K. Hall, 1983.

Levin, Harry. "Observations on the Style of Ernest Hemingway." In *Hemingway and His Critics,* edited by Carlos Baker, 93–115. New York: Hill and Wang, 1961.

Lewis, John S. *Rain of Iron and Ice: The Very Real Threat of Comet and Asteroid Bombardment.* New York: Perseus, 1997.

Lewis, Wyndham. "The Dumb Ox: A Study of Ernest Hemingway, 'Life and Letters.'" In *Hemingway: The Critical Heritage,* edited by Jeffrey Meyers, 186–209. Boston: Routledge and Kegan Paul, 1982.

Leypoldt, Günter. *Casual Silences: The Poetics of Minimal Realism from Raymond Carver and the New Yorker School to Bret Easton Ellis.* Trier: Wissenschaftlicher Verlag Trier, 2001.

Lincoln, Kenneth. *Cormac McCarthy: American Canticles*. New York: Palgrave Macmillan, 2009.

Lispector, Clarice. *Selected Crônicas*. Translated by Giovanni Pontiero. New York: New Directions, 1992.

Lopez, Adriana. "Sandra Cisneros's *Caramelo*: Caramel-Colored Prose." *Library Journal* 127, no. 15 (2002): 90.

Lopez, Ana. "Book World Raves: *Caramelo* or *Puro Cuento*." *Washington Post Book World*, December 1, 2002, 4.

Magnani, Jessica. "Divided Loyalties: Latina Family Sagas and National Romances." PhD diss., University of Florida, 2007.

Mandelbaum, David G. *The Plains Cree: An Ethnographic, Historical, and Comparative Study*. Regina, SK: Canadian Plains Research Center, 1979.

Marut, David. "Out of the Wastebasket: Hemingway's High School Stories." In *Ernest Hemingway: The Oak Park Legacy*, edited by James Nagel, 81–95. Tuscaloosa: University of Alabama Press, 1996.

McCarthy, Cormac. Interview with Oprah Winfrey. "Oprah's Exclusive Interview with Cormac McCarthy Video," Oprah's Book Club, added July 8, 2008. http://www.oprah.com/oprahsbookclub/Oprahs-Exclusive-Interview-with-Cormac-McCarthy-Video. Accessed August 3, 2010.

———. *No Country for Old Men*. New York: Vintage, 2006.

———. "Old Road Notes." Manuscripts. Box 87, folder 3. Cormac McCarthy Papers. The Witliff Collections, Southwestern Writers Collection, Alkek Library, Texas State University–San Marcos, San Marcos, Texas.

———. *The Road*. New York: Vintage, 2006.

———. "The Road—1st Draft." Manuscripts. Box 87, folder 6. Cormac McCarthy Papers. The Witliff Collections, Southwestern Writers Collection, Alkek Library, Texas State University–San Marcos, San Marcos, Texas.

———. "Road—Old 2nd Draft." Manuscripts. Box 87, folder 7. Cormac McCarthy Papers. The Witliff Collections, Southwestern Writers Collection, Alkek Library, Texas State University–San Marcos, San Marcos, Texas.

McDermott, James Dishon. *Austere Style in Twentieth-Century Literature: Literary Minimalism*. Lewiston, NY: Edwin Mellen Press, 2006.

McInerney, Jay. *Bright Lights, Big City*. New York: Vintage, 1984.

———. *The Good Life*. New York: Vintage, 2007.

———. *A Hedonist in the Cellar*. New York: Knopf, 2006.

———. *How It Ended: New and Collected Stories*. New York: Alfred A. Knopf, 2009.

———. "It's Six A.M. Do You Know Where You Are?" *Paris Review* 86 (Winter 1982): 181–88.

———. "Raymond Carver, Mentor." In *Remembering Ray: A Composite Biography of Raymond Carver*, edited by William L. Stull and Maureen Carroll, 119–26. Santa Barbara, CA: Capra, 1993.

———. "The Writers of Wrong." *Esquire* (July 1989): 104–11, 114.

McSweeney, Kerry. *The Realist Short Story of the Powerful Glimpse: Chekhov to Carver.* Columbia: University of South Carolina Press, 2007.

Meyer, Adam. "Now You See Him, Now You Don't, Now You Do Again: The Evolution of Raymond Carver's Minimalism." *Critique* 30 (Summer 1989): 239–51.

Middleton, Peter. "High Visibility: Images of Ethical Life in *The Tragic Muse* and Raymond Carver's 'Cathedral.'" *Rethinking History* 2, no. 3 (1998): 331–38.

Miles, Steven H. *The Hippocratic Oath and the Ethics of Medicine.* Oxford: Oxford University Press, 2004.

Miller, Arthur, Gore Vidal, Richard Watts, John Beaufort, Martin Dworkin, David W. Thompson, and Phillip Gelb. "'Death of a Salesman': A Symposium." *Tulane Drama Review* 2, no. 3 (1958): 63–69.

Minot, George. *The Blue Bowl.* New York: Knopf, 2004.

Minot, Sam. *The Strange Poverty of the Rich.* Lincoln, NE: iUniverse, 2004.

Minot, Susan. "Accident." *New Yorker* (November 7, 1983): 50–54.

———. *Monkeys.* New York: E. P. Dutton, 1986.

———. "The Navigator." In *The Invisible Enemy: Alcoholism and the Modern Short Story,* edited by Miriam Dow and Jennifer Regan, 3–14. St. Paul: Graywolf Press, 1989.

———. "The Silver Box." *Grand Street* 5 (Winter 1986): 26–33.

Morales, Ed. "Imaginary Homeland." *Críticas* 2, no. 5 (September/October 2002): 29–32.

Moran, Terence. "Brief Review." *New Republic* 191, no. 22 (1984): 41–42.

Morgan, Wesley G. "The Route and Roots of *The Road.*" *Cormac McCarthy Journal* 6 (Autumn 2008): 39–47.

Monteiro, George. "By the Book: 'Big Two-Hearted River' and Izaak Walton." In *Ernest Hemingway: The Oak Park Legacy,* edited by James Nagel, 145–61. Tuscaloosa: University of Alabama Press, 1996.

Montgomery, Constance Cappel. *Hemingway in Michigan.* New York: Fleet, 1966.

Nagel, James. *Anthology of the American Short Story.* Boston: Houghton Mifflin, 2008.

———. *The Contemporary American Short-Story Cycle: The Ethnic Resonance of Genre.* Baton Rouge: Louisiana State University Press, 2001.

———. *Hemingway in Love and War: The Lost Diary of Agnes Von Kurowsky.* New York: Hyperion, 1995.

———. "Literary Impressionism and *In Our Time.*" *Hemingway Review* 6, no. 2 (1987): 17–26.

———. *The Portable American Realism Reader,* edited by James Nagel and Tom Quirk. New York: Penguin, 1987, xx–xxxii.

Nesset, Kirk. *The Stories of Raymond Carver: A Critical Study.* Athens: Ohio University Press, 1995.

Noguchi, Yone. *The Pilgrimage.* 2 Vols. Kamakura: Valley Press, 1909.

———. *The Spirit of Japanese Poetry.* New York: E. P. Dutton, 1914.

O'Malley, Anne. "An Interview with Susan Minot." *Poets and Writers Magazine* 15, no. 3 (1987): 11–15.

Oxoby, Marc. "The Voluminous Impact of Television in the Fiction of Raymond Carver." In *New Paths to Raymond Carver: Critical Essays on His Life, Fiction, and Poetry*, edited by Sandra Lee Kleppe and Robert Miltner, 104–14. Columbia: University of South Carolina Press, 2008.

Packer, J. I. *Concise Theology: A Guide to Historic Christian Beliefs*. Wheaton, IL: Tyndale House, 1993.

Phelan, James. "Rhetoric, Politics, and Ethics in Sandra Cisneros's *Caramelo*." In *What Democracy Looks Like: New Critical Realism for a Post-Seattle World*, edited by Amy Schrager Lang and Cecelia Tichi, 114–22. New Brunswick, NJ: Rutgers University Press, 2006.

Pinsker, Sanford. "Soft Lights, Academic Talk: A Conversation with Jay McInerney." *Literary Review* 30, no. 1 (1986): 107–14.

Pizer, Donald. *Realism and Naturalism in Nineteenth-Century American Literature*. Carbondale: Southern Illinois University Press, 1984.

Poe, Edgar Allan. "The Philosophy of Composition." In *Poe: Poetry, Tales, and Selected Essays*. New York: Library of America, 1996, 1373–85.

Pontiero, Giovanni. Preface to *Selected Crônicas* by Clarice Lispector. Translated by Giovanni Pontiero. New York: New Directions, 1992, vii–x.

Pope, Robert, and Lisa McElhinny. "Raymond Carver Speaking." In *Conversations with Raymond Carver*, edited by Marshall Bruce Gentry and William L. Stull, 11–23. Jackson: University Press of Mississippi, 1990.

Pound, Ezra. *The ABC of Reading*. New York: New Directions: 1987.

———. *Cathay*. London: Elkins Matthew, 1915.

———. "Fan-Piece for Her Imperial Lord." In *Des Imagistes*, 45. New York: Albert and Charles Boni, 1914.

———. "Imagisme." In *Ezra Pound: Early Writings, Poems, and Prose*, 209–10. New York: Penguin, 2005.

———. "Liu Ch'e." In *Des Imagistes*, 44. New York: Albert and Charles Boni, 1914.

Pryor, Kelli. "The Story of Her Life." *New York* 22, no. 23 (1989): 52–55.

Rebein, Robert. *Hicks, Tribes, and Dirty Realists: American Fiction after Postmodernism*. Lexington: University of Kentucky Press, 2009.

"Remain in Light—1980." The Name of This Site Is Talking Heads. http://www.talking-heads.nl/index.php/discography/81-remain-in light. Accessed February 15, 2010.

Remnick, David. "Jay McInerney's High Kicks in Tokyo." *Washington Post*, August 25, 1985, 5.

"Review of *Bright Lights, Big City* by Jay McInerney." *Atlantic* 254, no. 6 (1984): 145.

"Review of *Monkeys* by Susan Minot." *Jim Kobak's Kirkus Reviews* 54 (March 1, 1986): 332.

Reynolds, Michael. *Hemingway: The Paris Years*. New York: W. W. Norton, 1999.

———. *The Young Hemingway.* New York: W. W. Norton, 1986.

Robinson, Roxana. "Remains of the Day." Review of *Evening* by Susan Minot. *New York Times Book Review,* October 11, 1998, 12.

Saltzman, Arthur M. *Understanding Raymond Carver.* Columbia: University of South Carolina Press, 1988.

Sandoval, Annette. *The Directory of Saints.* New York: Signet, 1997.

Schaub, Thomas H. "Secular Scripture and Cormac McCarthy's *The Road.*" *Renascence* 61, no. 3 (2009): 153–68.

Schechner, Mark. "McCarthy's Latest Travels His Bleakest Terrain Yet." *Buffalo News,* October 8, 2006: G5.

Schumacher, Michael. "After the Fire, Into the Fire: An Interview with Raymond Carver." In *Conversations with Raymond Carver,* edited by Marshall Bruce Gentry and William L. Stull, 214–37. Jackson: University Press of Mississippi, 1990.

———. *Reasons to Believe: New Voices in American Fiction.* New York: St. Martin's Press, 1988.

Sexton, David. "David Sexton Talks to Raymond Carver." In *Conversations with Raymond Carver,* edited by Marshall Bruce Gentry and William L. Stull, 120–32. Jackson: University Press of Mississippi, 1990.

Shales, Tom. "The Grand Old Man of TV Tots and Other Little Rascals." *Washington Post,* July 8, 1977, B9.

Shea, Renee H. "Truth, Lies, and Memory: A Profile of Sandra Cisneros." *Poets and Writers* 30, no. 5 (2002): 35–36.

Silentio, Johannes de [Søren Kierkegaard]. "Fear and Trembling, Dialectical Lyric." In *The Essential Kierkegaard,* edited by Howard V. Hong and Edna H. Hong, 93–101. Princeton, NJ: Princeton University Press, 2000.

Simmons, Philip E. *Deep Surfaces: Mass Culture and History in Postmodern American Fiction.* Athens: University of Georgia Press, 1997.

Sklenicka, Carol. *Raymond Carver: A Writer's Life.* New York: Scribner, 2009.

Slabey, Robert M. "The Structure of *In Our Time.*" In *Critical Essays on Ernest Hemingway's* In Our Time, edited by Michael S. Reynolds, 76–87. Boston: G. K. Hall, 1983.

Smith, Dinitia. "The Minots, A Literary Clan Whose Stories Divide Them." *New York Times,* May 27, 2004: E1, E5.

Sodowsky, Roland. "The Minimalist Short Story: Its Definition, Writers, and (Small) Heyday." *Studies in Short Fiction* 33, no. 4 (1996): 529–40.

Solomon, Deborah. "A Family History in Rewrite." *New York Times,* July 9, 2006: 30–35.

Spencer, Jim. "Raymond Carver: No Shortcuts to a Good Story." In *Conversations with Raymond Carver,* edited by Marshall Bruce Gentry and William L. Stull. Jackson: University Press of Mississippi, 1990, 24–27.

Stein, Gertrude. *The Autobiography of Alice B. Toklas.* New York: Vintage, 1990.

Steinke, James. "'Out of Season' and Hemingway's Neglected Discovery: Ordinary

Actuality." In *Hemingway's Neglected Short Fiction: New Perspectives*, edited by Susan F. Beegel, 61–73. Tuscaloosa: University of Alabama Press, 1989.

Stoneback, H. R. *Reading Hemingway's* The Sun Also Rises: *Glossary and Commentary*. Kent, OH: Kent State University Press, 2007.

"Storm Batters All New England; Providence Hit by Tidal Wave." *New York Times*, September 22, 1938: 1, 18.

Stowell, H. Peter. *Literary Impressionism: James and Chekhov*. Athens: University of Georgia Press, 1980.

Stronks, James B. "A Realist Experiments with Impressionism: Hamlin Garland's 'Chicago Studies.'" *American Literature* 36, no. 1 (1964): 38–52.

Suarez, Ray. "Conversation: Cisneros." Transcript from *NewsHour with Jim Lehrer*. October 15, 2002. http://www.pbs.org/newshour/conversation/july-dec02/cisneros_10-15.html. Accessed April 9, 2010.

Svoboda, Frederic J. "Who Was That Black Man? A Note on Eugene Bullard and *The Sun Also Rises*." *Hemingway Review* 17, no. 2 (1998): 105–10.

Tanselle, G. Thomas. "Hemingway's 'Indian Camp.'" In *Critical Essays on Ernest Hemingway's* In Our Time, edited by Michael S. Reynolds, 144–45. Boston: G. K. Hall, 1983.

Tate, Allen. "Hard-Boiled." In *Critical Essays on Ernest Hemingway's* The Sun Also Rises, edited by James Nagel, 42–43. New York: G. K. Hall, 1995.

"Team Awards." Official Website of Harvard University Athletics. http://www.gocrimson.com/sports/mice/history/teamawards. Accessed February 14, 2010.

Tetlow, Wendolyn E. *Hemingway's* In Our Time: *Lyrical Dimensions*. Lewisburg, PA: Bucknell University Press, 1992.

Thomas, George Francis. *Legends of the Land of Lakes; or, History, Traditions, and Mysteries, Gleaned from Years of Experience among the Pioneers, Voyageurs, and Indians*. Chicago: G. F. Thomas, 1884.

Tyler, Anne. "The Art of Omission." *New Republic* (June 23, 1986): 34, 36.

Updike, John. "A Symposium on Contemporary American Fiction: John Updike." Part 2 of 2. *Michigan Quarterly Review* 27, no. 1 (1988): 126.

Wadler, Joyce. "A Turn in the 'Bright Lights.'" *Washington Post*, December 12, 1984, F1, F13.

Wagner, Linda Welshimer. *Hemingway and Faulkner: inventors/masters*. Metuchen, NJ: Scarecrow, 1975.

Walford, John. *Great Themes in Art*. Upper Saddle River, NJ: Prentice Hall, 2002.

Watts, Emily Stipes. *Ernest Hemingway and the Arts*. Urbana: University of Illinois Press, 1971.

Weaver, Teresa K. "Zen Informs Latina Novelist's Work." *Atlanta Constitution*, November 22, 2002, E1, E7.

Weber, Bruce. "Raymond Carver: A Chronicler of Blue-Collar Despair." *New York Times Magazine* (June 24, 1984): 36–50.

Wiebels-Balthaus, Gregor. "The Self in Trouble: Young Adults in the Urban Consumer Society of the 1980s in Janowitz, Ellis, and McInerney." PhD diss., Ruhr Universität Bochum, 2005.

Wiech, Dave. "Author Interviews: Back in Bed with Susan Minot." Powells.com. http://www.powells.com/authors/minot.html. Accessed May 20, 2009.

Wilson, Edmund. *The Shores of Light: A Literary Chronicle of the 1920s and 1930s.* New York: Farrar, Straus, and Giroux, 1979.

Woodward, Richard B. "Cormac McCarthy's Venomous Fiction." *New York Times Magazine* (April 19, 1992): 28–31.

Young, Philip. *Ernest Hemingway: A Reconsideration.* University Park: Pennsylvania State University Press, 1966.

Index